Chicken Pies, page 169

THE Chicken Collection

Food & Wine BOOKS

American Express Publishing Corporation
New York

FOOD & WINE MAGAZINE
Editor in Chief: Dana Cowin
Food Editor: Tina Ujlaki

FOOD & WINE BOOKS
Editor in Chief: Judith Hill
Managing Editor: Terri Mauro
Copy Editor: Barbara A. Mateer
Wine Editor: Steve Miller
Editorial Consultants: Katherine G. Ness and Judith Sutton
Art Director: Nina Scerbo
Editorial/Art Assistant: Evette Manners
Production Manager: Yvette Williams-Braxton

Vice President, Books and Information Services: John Stoops
Marketing Director: Mary V. Cooney
Marketing/Promotion Manager: Roni Stein
Operations Manager: Doreen Camardi
Business Manager: Joanne Ragazzo

PHOTOGRAPHY
COVER PHOTO: **Mary Ellen Bartley** (Clay-Pot Chicken with Olives, page 161)
BACK COVER PHOTOS: **Mary Ellen Bartley**
Top row, left to right: Chicken and Sausage Stew with Parsley and Lemon, page 279; Mediterranean Chicken and Ratatouille Salad, page 65.
Middle row, left to right: Baked Acorn Squash Stuffed with Curried Chicken, page 287; Spicy Stuffed Chicken Breasts, page 141.
Bottom row, left to right: Grilled Deviled Chicken, page 189; Chicken with Piquant Sauce, page 299.
Food Stylist: Brett Kurzweil
Prop Stylist: Christine McCabe

Mary Ellen Bartley: 2, 6, 8, 10, 16, 22, 28, 36, 46, 52, 58, 62, 64, 72, 78, 92, 94, 100, 108, 114, 126, 134, 138, 140, 150, 160, 170, 176, 182, 188, 192, 212, 224, 226, 230, 242, 248, 256, 258, 266, 280, 284, 286, 292, 298, 306; **Thom DeSanto:** 220, 274; **Dennis Gelante:** 178; **Rita Mass,** 84, 88; **Maria Robledo:** 12, 166, 236; **Lisa Charles Watson:** 38, 116, 196, 198; **Elizabeth Watt:** 206.

AMERICAN EXPRESS PUBLISHING CORPORATION
©1997 American Express Publishing Corporation

LIBRARY OF CONGRESS CATALOGING-IN-PUBLICATION DATA
The chicken collection.
p.   cm.
Includes biographical references and index.
ISBN 0-916103-39-0
1. Cookery (Chicken)   I. Food & wine (New York, N.Y.)
TX750.5.C45C433   1997
641.6'65—dc21   97-26074
CIP

Published by American Express Publishing Corporation
1120 Avenue of the Americas, New York, New York 10036
Manufactured in the United States of America

CONTENTS

Chicken and Sausage Stew with Parsley and Lemon, page 279

INTRODUCTION

Roast or bake, grill or broil, stew or braise, sauté, fry, or stir-fry—honestly, you can do anything with chicken. And over the years at FOOD & WINE, we've used all these methods to good effect. We have also featured chicken in pasta and rice dishes, soups and salads, curries and casseroles, and more.

The FOOD & WINE test kitchen and our star-studded cast of contributors to the magazine have approached each technique in a multitude of interesting ways. In our roasting chapter alone, we have fourteen recipes, from three top chefs and nine well-known food writers, representing at least twelve different takes on the best way to roast a chicken. You're the beneficiary of possibilities galore, and one is sure to become your own personal favorite.

From elegantly simple to authentically ethnic to excitingly innovative, our best chicken recipes from the last decade are gathered here in one convenient book. We hope you'll consult it as often as we expect to do ourselves.

Editor in Chief
FOOD & WINE Magazine

Editor in Chief
FOOD & WINE Books

Peach-Glazed Chicken Thighs, page 151

WINE AND CHICKEN

Chicken is pure joy for the wine lover. Like an artist's blank canvas, chicken can be prepared in an almost infinite range of styles, perfect for an equally vast array of wines. But flexible as chicken is, on the spectrum of food weight and intensity its swath is skewed toward the lighter end. Wines also fall along a spectrum, from light-bodied whites to fuller whites, rosés, and light reds to powerfully tannic, monster red wines.

As you might expect, it is the wines at the lighter end—the whites, rosés, and easier reds—that partner best with most chicken dishes. These make up the bulk of my recommendations, though you will find the occasional sturdy red for some particularly robust recipe. What you won't find are the dry, muscular red wines such as cabernet sauvignon or barolo. Their tannic bite will swamp just about any chicken dish.

I have used two guiding principles in selecting wines; they can be summed up simply as "contrast" and "match." Take, for example, chicken in a cream sauce. When we look for its key elements we find that it is low in acid and full-bodied with intense cream and butter flavors. We can match all that quite spectacularly by pairing it with a rich and buttery California chardonnay. On the other hand, we may also opt for contrast by serving a crisp white wine with minerally flavors. The acidity cuts through the voluptuousness of the sauce and refreshes the palate.

In both cases, however, it is important to match the flavor intensities. A delicate wine, whether contrasting or matching, will be steamrolled by a hearty dish, just as a powerful wine will obliterate a more subtle preparation. As you read through these recipes and their accompanying wine suggestions, you will see these principles in action.

For each recipe, I have selected a wine that will make a combination that's more interesting than either the food or drink would be on its own. But does this mean that there is only one perfect wine for each dish? Not at all. Today's wine world is so vast, with so many delicious choices from so many more places than ever before, that you always have other options.

Read the descriptions carefully. They contain important clues to help you in your selection of alternatives. For example, while I may suggest a white Burgundy because a rich, full-bodied white wine with broad, ripe fruit and crisp acidity is called for, many other wines fit that description and will work wonderfully too.

STEVE MILLER

chapter *1*

HORS D'OEUVRES &
FIRST COURSES

Rosemary Chicken Lollipops with Spicy Tomato Dipping Sauce, page 17

SPICED-HONEY DRUMETTES WITH POPPY AND SESAME SEEDS

The drumette—the section closest to the body—is the meatiest part of the chicken wing. Here, drumettes are coated with honey and seeds for a spicy, sticky treat. They can also be served as a main dish; figure on about six per person.

WINE RECOMMENDATION
A fresh, spring-flower-scented sparkling Vouvray from France's Loire Valley is a knockout with these aromatic hors d'oeuvres. The wine's taut acidity plays counterpoint to the sweetness of the honey.

MAKES ABOUT 24 DRUMETTES

  1 tablespoon dry mustard

  1 teaspoon ground ginger

 ¼ teaspoon ground allspice

  1 teaspoon salt

  1 teaspoon fresh-ground black pepper

 ⅓ cup poppy seeds

 ⅓ cup sesame seeds

 ⅓ cup honey

  2 pounds chicken drumettes, or drumettes from 4 pounds whole chicken wings (see "Cutting Drumettes," page 15)

1. Heat the oven to 400°. Line a baking sheet with aluminum foil and set a rack on top of it.

2. In a large bowl, combine the mustard, ginger, allspice, salt, pepper, poppy seeds, sesame seeds, and honey; stir well. Toss the chicken drumettes in this mixture until they are thoroughly coated.

3. Put the drumettes on the rack on the baking sheet and bake for 20 minutes. Turn the drumettes and bake them for 20 minutes longer.

4. Preheat the broiler. Broil the drumettes 4 to 5 inches from the heat, watching carefully and turning them once, until nicely browned, 1 to 2 minutes per side.

—BOB CHAMBERS

FRIED CHICKEN DRUMETTES WITH LEMONGRASS

The woody herb known as lemongrass turns up twice here, in the marinade for the chicken wings and in the dipping sauce. Together with soy sauce, cilantro, and ginger, it gives these hors d'oeuvres a distinctly Asian accent.

WINE RECOMMENDATION
Pungent lemongrass calls for the crisp mineral and citrus flavors of riesling. The heat from the ginger and pepper narrows the search to Germany, where many wines have the sweetness and low alcohol to put out the fire. Try a succulent auslese riesling from the Mosel-Saar-Ruwer.

MAKES ABOUT 24 DRUMETTES

2 pounds chicken drumettes, or drumettes from 4 pounds whole chicken wings (see "Cutting Drumettes," opposite page)

1 tablespoon soy sauce

1½ teaspoons salt

2 stalks lemongrass,* bottom third only, finely minced

2 tablespoons dry sherry

1 tablespoon flour

1 tablespoon cornstarch

2 teaspoons fresh-ground black pepper

1 teaspoon dried red-pepper flakes

¼ cup minced cilantro

2 cups peanut oil

Lemongrass Dipping Sauce, opposite page

*Available at Asian markets and many supermarkets

1. In a medium bowl, combine the chicken drumettes with the soy sauce and salt and toss to coat. Let the drumettes marinate at room temperature for 1 hour, tossing them occasionally.

2. Put the lemongrass and sherry in a small heatproof bowl. Set the bowl in a steamer basket or on a rack in a saucepan over boiling water. Cover and steam for 15 minutes.

3. Combine the flour, cornstarch, black pepper, red-pepper flakes, and cilantro in a small bowl. Mix well and add to the chicken drumettes along with the lemongrass mixture. Toss well to coat the drumettes.

4. In a large frying pan or wok, heat the oil over moderate heat to 375°. Fry the drumettes in batches, without crowding, until golden brown, 5 to 7 minutes. Drain on paper towels and serve hot, with the dipping sauce on the side.

—BRUCE COST

CUTTING DRUMETTES

If your supermarket doesn't carry the chicken-wing sections called drumettes, buy whole chicken wings instead. Cut through the upper joint of each chicken wing to separate the larger top section (the drumette) from the lower portion and tip. Save the unused wing portions in the freezer and use them for making stock—or make a batch of Vietnamese Stuffed Chicken Wings, page 20.

LEMONGRASS DIPPING SAUCE

MAKES ABOUT 1/3 CUP

- 1   tablespoon peanut oil
- 1   stalk lemongrass,* bottom third only, finely minced
- 1½   teaspoons minced fresh ginger
- 2   tablespoons soy sauce
- 2   tablespoons rice vinegar
- 1   tablespoon Asian sesame oil
- 1   teaspoon Asian chili oil*
- ½   teaspoon sugar

*Available at Asian markets and many supermarkets

In a small saucepan, heat the peanut oil over moderate heat. Add the lemongrass and ginger and cook until fragrant, about 30 seconds. Remove the pan from the heat and add the soy sauce, vinegar, sesame oil, chili oil, and sugar. Stir to dissolve the sugar. Pour the dipping sauce into a small bowl and let stand at room temperature for 1 hour.

ROSEMARY CHICKEN LOLLIPOPS WITH SPICY TOMATO DIPPING SAUCE

Essentially drumettes with all the meat pulled to one end, chicken lollipops are nice for cocktail parties because they're easy to eat with your fingers. Of course, you could also make this recipe without turning the drumettes into lollipops.

 WINE RECOMMENDATION
The tomato sauce suggests a red wine, but the jalapeños, which accentuate both alcohol and tannins, make for a tough match. A Barbera d'Asti, with its low tannin and moderate alcohol, is a good choice.

MAKES ABOUT 24 LOLLIPOPS

2 pounds chicken drumettes, or drumettes from 4 pounds whole chicken wings (see "Cutting Drumettes," page 15)

½ cup olive oil

1 tablespoon dried rosemary, crumbled

½ teaspoon salt

¼ teaspoon fresh-ground black pepper

Spicy Tomato Dipping Sauce, right

1. Using a sharp knife, cut through the tendons at the base of the narrower end of each drumette. With the knife, gently scrape the meat from the bone, pushing it toward the large end. Pull the loosened meat around the top of the bone to form a lollipop shape.

2. Heat the oven to 400°. In a medium bowl, combine the oil, rosemary, salt, and pepper. Add the lollipops, a few at a time, and toss to coat.

3. Put the lollipops in a roasting pan or large baking dish. Bake until golden and slightly crisp, about 20 minutes. Serve with the dipping sauce on the side.

—JOHN ROBERT MASSIE

SPICY TOMATO DIPPING SAUCE

MAKES ABOUT 2½ CUPS

3½ cups canned tomatoes (one 28-ounce can), drained

2 jalapeño peppers, minced

1 small clove garlic, minced

2 large shallots, minced

1 teaspoon salt

¼ teaspoon fresh-ground black pepper

2 fresh tomatoes, peeled, seeded, and diced

In a blender or food processor, puree the canned tomatoes, jalapeños, garlic, shallots, salt, and pepper until smooth. Pour the puree into a bowl and stir in the diced tomatoes.

BUFFALO CHICKEN WINGS WITH CELERY AND BLUE-CHEESE DIPPING SAUCE

A happy-hour staple, Buffalo wings are spicy little mouthfuls that have been fried and then tossed with hot-pepper sauce. The creamy blue-cheese dipping sauce is cool by comparison, but even it has a bit of cayenne for good measure.

WINE RECOMMENDATION
The hot-pepper sauce, vinegar, and other strong, tangy flavors here will overpower almost any wine. Happily, a rich, malty craft-beer will fill the bill perfectly.

MAKES ABOUT 24 PIECES

 1 tablespoon finely chopped onion
 ½ teaspoon minced garlic
 2 tablespoons minced fresh parsley
 ½ cup mayonnaise
 ¼ cup sour cream
 ½ cup crumbled blue cheese
 1½ teaspoons lemon juice
 1½ teaspoons white-wine vinegar
 ⅛ teaspoon salt
 ⅛ teaspoon fresh-ground black pepper
   Pinch cayenne
 4 tablespoons butter
 2 tablespoons hot-pepper sauce, or to taste
 2 pounds chicken wings (about 12)
   About 1½ quarts cooking oil or lard
 2 ribs celery, cut into sticks

1. In a medium bowl, whisk together the onion, garlic, parsley, mayonnaise, sour cream, blue cheese, lemon juice, vinegar, salt, black pepper, and cayenne. Cover the dipping sauce and refrigerate until 30 minutes before serving.

2. In a large frying pan, melt the butter and add the hot-pepper sauce. Mix well and set the pan aside.

3. Cut the chicken wings into three pieces at the joints. Discard the tips or reserve them for stock. Pat the remaining pieces dry with paper towels.

4. In a deep fryer or a deep heavy frying pan, heat the oil to 375°. Fry the chicken pieces in batches until browned and crisp, about 10 minutes. Drain on paper towels.

5. Reheat the hot-sauce mixture in the frying pan. Add the chicken pieces and toss to coat thoroughly. Remove the frying pan from the heat, cover, and let stand for 5 minutes.

6. Serve the chicken wings with the celery sticks and the dipping sauce.

—JANICE OKUN

CHICKEN WINGS WITH GARLIC SAUCE

You can find *pollo al ajillo* on just about every restaurant menu in Spain. This slightly more sophisticated version of the dish makes an elegant hors d'oeuvre.

WINE RECOMMENDATION

Look no farther than Spain itself to find a perfect wine match for this native Spanish dish. A traditional white Rioja, with its intriguing nutty flavors and acidity, is what you want; search for wines such as Marques de Murietta's Castello Y'Gay.

MAKES ABOUT 24 PIECES

- 2 pounds chicken wings (about 12)
- ⅓ cup olive oil
- 15 large cloves garlic
- 1½ tablespoons brandy
- ¾ teaspoon flour
- ⅓ cup dry white wine
- ⅓ cup Chicken Stock, page 61, or canned low-sodium chicken broth
  Salt
- 1½ tablespoons minced fresh parsley
  Pinch saffron
- 5 peppercorns, cracked

1. Cut the chicken wings into three pieces at the joints. Discard the tips or reserve them for stock. Pat the remaining pieces dry with paper towels.

2. In a large frying pan, heat the oil over moderately high heat until it begins to smoke. Add the chicken and garlic and cook, stirring until golden, about 10 minutes.

Remove the garlic cloves as they color and put them in a mortar or small bowl.

3. Add the brandy to the pan and carefully ignite it with a match. As soon as the flames subside, sprinkle the flour into the pan. Stir in the wine and stock and season with salt. Cover and simmer for 10 minutes.

4. Meanwhile, mash the garlic cloves. Add the parsley, saffron, and peppercorns; mash to a paste.

5. Stir the parsley mixture into the pan. Cook, covered, for 10 minutes longer.

—PENELOPE CASAS

MAKE IT AHEAD

The chicken wings can be made several hours in advance. Reheat in the sauce over low heat before serving.

VIETNAMESE STUFFED CHICKEN WINGS

Many recipes use the meaty drumette portion of the chicken wing, but this one uses the other end—the bonier half that includes the tip. What to do with the unused drumettes? Make Spiced-Honey Drumettes with Poppy and Sesame Seeds, page 13, or Fried Chicken Drumettes with Lemongrass, page 14.

WINE RECOMMENDATION
The sweet and the savory are often juxtaposed in Asian cooking; here, the vinegar and lime juice in the dipping sauce are balanced by sugar and offset by zesty crushed hot pepper. A traditional German spätlese riesling, with its low alcohol and similar tension between acidity and sweetness, will make a superb partner.

MAKES ABOUT 24 PIECES

  4   pounds chicken wings (about 24)

  2   pounds boneless, skinless chicken breasts (about 6), cut into thin slices

  4   teaspoons cornstarch

  1   teaspoon baking powder

  1/2 teaspoon sugar

  1/2 teaspoon black pepper

  2   tablespoons Asian fish sauce (nam pla or nuoc mam)*

      About 1 1/2 quarts cooking oil

  1/2 pound mushrooms, minced

  2   large scallions including green tops, cut into thin slices

      Nuoc Cham Dipping Sauce, opposite page

      *Available at Asian markets and many supermarkets

1. Cut through the upper joint of each chicken wing to separate the drumette (the large top section) from the lower portion and tip. Reserve the drumettes for another use. Pat the remaining pieces dry with paper towels.

2. With a small sharp knife, scrape around the exposed joint of each wing to loosen the meat. With your hand, work the meat down the double bone toward the wing tip, squeezing and pushing to separate the skin and meat from the bones. Snap the double bones off at the joint, leaving the meat attached to the wing tip.

3. In a medium bowl, combine the chicken-breast slices, cornstarch, baking powder, sugar, black pepper, fish sauce, and 1 tablespoon of the oil. Mix well. Cover and freeze until very firm, about 15 minutes.

4. In a food processor, puree the chicken-breast mixture until it is very smooth and stiff, about 1 minute. Return the mixture to the medium bowl and stir in the mushrooms and scallions.

5. With oiled hands, hold a boned chicken wing in one hand and push the mushroom stuffing into the pocket with the other hand,

packing it in firmly and stuffing the wing generously. Repeat, using all the stuffing and chicken wings.

6. Heat the oven to 200°. Put six of the stuffed wings into a large saucepan and add oil to cover. Set the pan over high heat and cook, stirring occasionally, until the wings are golden brown and crisp, about 20 minutes. Remove the wings with tongs and drain on paper towels. Keep warm in the oven on a baking sheet.

7. Remove the pan from the heat for 3 to 4 minutes to cool slightly. Over moderate heat, add six more stuffed chicken wings to the oil, and cook until golden brown and crisp, about 15 minutes. Remove the wings with tongs, drain on paper towels, and put on the baking sheet with the other wings. Repeat with the remaining wings. Serve the wings with the dipping sauce on the side.

—MARCIA KIESEL

MAKE IT AHEAD

You can prepare the dipping sauce up to three days in advance. Store it in a covered jar in the refrigerator and bring to room temperature before serving.

NUOC CHAM DIPPING SAUCE

MAKES ABOUT 2 1/2 CUPS

2 teaspoons dried red-pepper flakes

2 tablespoons white vinegar

1 cup Asian fish sauce (nam pla or nuoc mam)*

1/2 cup lime juice

1 carrot, finely shredded, rinsed, and squeezed dry

4 small cloves garlic, minced

1 cup sugar

3 cups warm water

*Available at Asian markets and many supermarkets

1. In a small dish, soak the red-pepper flakes in the vinegar for 2 minutes.

2. In a small bowl, combine the fish sauce, lime juice, carrot, garlic, and sugar. Add the water and the vinegar mixture and stir until the sugar dissolves.

CHICKEN ROLLS WITH SPINACH-AND-FETA STUFFING

You can serve these rolls hot as a first course, but we prefer them chilled, with each roll sliced into lovely little spinach-filled hors d'oeuvres.

WINE RECOMMENDATION
Goat and sheep cheeses, with their distinctive tang, seem made for the herbal, lemony flavors of sauvignon blanc. Try one from the Sancerre commune of Chavignol.

MAKES 32 PIECES

- 1/3 pound spinach, stems removed and leaves washed
- 1 1/2 tablespoons butter
- 1/2 clove garlic, minced
- 1/2 teaspoon dried rosemary, crumbled
- 1/4 cup feta cheese (about 1 1/2 ounces)
- 1 1/2 tablespoons fresh bread crumbs
- 1 egg yolk
- 1/4 teaspoon fresh-ground black pepper
- 4 boneless, skinless chicken breasts (about 1 1/2 pounds)

1. In a large pot of boiling, salted water, cook the spinach just until it wilts, about 1 minute. Drain and rinse under cold water. Drain again and squeeze a handful of the spinach at a time to remove as much water as possible. Chop the spinach; you should have about 1 cup.

2. In a small frying pan, melt the butter over low heat. Add the garlic and rosemary and cook just until fragrant, about 1 minute. Don't allow the garlic to color.

3. Combine the spinach and feta in a medium bowl. Pour the butter mixture over the spinach and feta and mix until thoroughly blended. Stir in the bread crumbs, egg yolk, and pepper.

4. Using a meat pounder, mallet, or rolling pin, flatten the chicken breasts into 5- or 6-inch squares or ovals about 1/4 inch thick. Put about 1/4 cup of the filling down the center of each breast. Roll the breasts up tightly to enclose the filling and wrap each one in plastic.

5. In a steamer basket set over a saucepan of boiling water, steam the chicken rolls, still in their plastic wrap, for 15 minutes. Remove the rolls from the steamer and let cool. Refrigerate for at least 1 hour.

6. When the chicken rolls are thoroughly chilled, unwrap them. Trim off the ends of each roll and slice into rounds.

CHICKEN HAZELNUT QUENELLES

Quenelles—poached dumplings—make a light, elegant appetizer. Hazelnuts add a subtle sweetness to the chicken mixture, and the tomato cream sauce provides a counterpoint of flavor and color.

 WINE RECOMMENDATION Hazelnuts immediately call to mind the great white Burgundies of Meursault, the intoxicating aromas of which are often said to be reminiscent of the nuts. A good Meursault will beautifully complement the creamy intensity of this dish.

SERVES 4

- 3 tablespoons hazelnuts
- ½ pound boneless, skinless chicken breasts (2 small), cut into ½-inch pieces
- 1 teaspoon dried sage, crumbled
  Salt and white pepper
- 1 egg white
- 1¾ cups plus 2 tablespoons heavy cream
- 4 white peppercorns
- 2 sprigs parsley
- ½ bay leaf
- 1½ cups Chicken Stock, page 61, or canned low-sodium chicken broth
- ½ cup dry white wine
- ¼ cup chopped onion
- ¼ cup chopped carrot
- 2 tablespoons tomato paste

1. Pulse the hazelnuts in a food processor until ground. Remove the hazelnuts.

Refrigerate the processor bowl and blade along with the chicken for about 10 minutes.

2. Put the chicken, ¾ teaspoon of the sage, ¾ teaspoon salt, and ¼ teaspoon pepper in the chilled processor container and process for about 1 minute. Add the egg white and the hazelnuts and process for 30 seconds. With the machine running, add 1 cup plus 2 tablespoons of the cream in a slow, steady stream. Transfer the mixture to a glass or stainless-steel bowl and refrigerate.

3. Tie the peppercorns, parsley, bay leaf, and the remaining ¼ teaspoon sage in cheesecloth, or put them in a tea ball. Put this bouquet garni and the stock, wine, onion, and carrot in a small saucepan. Bring to a boil, reduce the heat, and simmer for 30 minutes. Remove the bouquet garni. Put the sauce through a food mill or push it through a sieve with a wooden spoon. Transfer the sauce to a small saucepan.

4. In a small bowl, slowly add the remaining ¾ cup cream to the tomato paste, whisking constantly until smooth. Add the mixture to the sauce and bring to a boil over moderate heat. Cook until the sauce is reduced to about ¾ cup. Remove the pan from the heat and season the sauce with salt and pepper.

5. Bring 2 inches of salted water to a simmer in a shallow frying pan. Using two soup spoons dipped in hot water, form the quenelles: Scoop up a heaping spoonful and then use the other spoon to shape a neat oval. Gently slide the ovals into the simmering water. Cook until just firm, 6 to 8 minutes. Remove the quenelles with a slotted spoon, drain on paper towels, and put on a platter. Cover and put in a warm spot while you cook the remaining quenelles. Reheat the sauce and spoon it onto four plates. Top with the quenelles and serve.

CORN CRÊPE CAKE WITH CHICKEN CHILE FILLING

For a variation on the usual filled-and-rolled crêpes, we layer a stack of crêpes with the filling and then cut the cake into wedges for serving.

WINE RECOMMENDATION A top-quality, not-too-dry California sparkling wine is a fine partner for this complex and flavorful dish. Its high acidity will stand up to the tomato, while the touch of sweetness will balance the jalapeño's heat.

SERVES 4

- ½ cup fresh (cut from 1 ear) or frozen corn kernels
- 2 large eggs
- ½ cup milk
- ½ cup water
- ½ cup flour
- ¼ cup yellow cornmeal
- 4 tablespoons cooking oil, plus more for frying
- 2 teaspoons sugar
- 1 teaspoon ground cumin
- ½ teaspoon salt
- ⅛ teaspoon fresh-ground black pepper
- ½ medium onion, chopped
- 1 clove garlic, minced
- 2 plum tomatoes, peeled, seeded, and chopped
- 2 tablespoons chopped cilantro
- 1½ cups diced cooked chicken (see box, opposite)
- 3 scallions including green tops, cut into thin slices
- 1 jalapeño pepper, seeds and ribs removed, cut into slivers
- ¼ cup grated Parmesan cheese
- 2 ounces aged Monterey Jack cheese, shredded (about ½ cup)
- 2 tablespoons sour cream, plus more for serving

1. In a blender or food processor, puree the corn with the eggs, milk, and water until smooth. Add the flour, cornmeal, 2 tablespoons of the oil, the sugar, cumin, salt, and pepper and blend well. Cover the batter and refrigerate for about 1 hour.

2. Heat a 6- to 7-inch crêpe pan over moderate heat. Brush with a little oil. Pour about 3 tablespoons of the crêpe batter into the center of the pan and swirl to cover the bottom evenly. Cook until the bottom of the crêpe is lightly browned, about 1 minute. Turn the crêpe and cook until it is dry and spotted with brown on the other side, about 10 seconds. Repeat with the remaining batter, stacking the finished crêpes between paper towels. Reserve six crêpes for making the cake; wrap the rest well and freeze for another use (see "Leftover Crêpes," opposite).

3. Heat the oven to 400°. Oil a baking sheet. In a medium frying pan, heat the remaining 2 tablespoons oil over moderate heat. Add the onion and garlic and cook, stirring occasionally, until the onion is translucent, about 3 minutes. Add the tomatoes and cilantro and cook, stirring occasionally, until the sauce thickens, about 10 minutes. Remove the pan from the heat and stir in the chicken, scallions, and jalapeño.

4. In a small bowl, combine the Parmesan and the Monterey Jack. Put one crêpe on the oiled baking sheet and spread about one fifth of the chicken mixture over it in an even layer. Sprinkle with 2 tablespoons of the cheese mixture. Place another crêpe on top and press lightly. Repeat with the remaining filling, 8 more tablespoons of the cheese, and the remaining crêpes, finishing with a crêpe. Spread the 2 tablespoons sour cream over the top of the cake and sprinkle with the remaining cheese.

5. Bake the crêpe cake until the cheese melts and the filling is heated through, 10 to 15 minutes. Let rest for 5 minutes. Use a large spatula to transfer the cake to a serving platter. Cut it into wedges and serve a bowl of sour cream on the side.

—JEANNETTE FERRARY AND LOUISE FISZER

VARIATION

In place of the Monterey Jack cheese, use an additional quarter cup of grated Parmesan.

COOKED CHICKEN

A Good Roast Chicken, page 117, is a fine source of leftover cooked chicken meat to be diced for the filling here. If you don't have any cooked chicken on hand, you can bake, poach, or steam two boneless, skinless chicken breasts; let cool before dicing. You may not need all of the chicken.

LEFTOVER CRÊPES

You're liable to have several crêpes left over after making this recipe, even allowing for a "practice" one or two. Store them in the freezer until you're ready to use them, then try one of these serving ideas:
• Fill the crêpes with grated cheese. Bake to melt; top with sour cream.
• Make a crêpe "burrito" filled with refried beans. Serve with salsa.
• Fill the crêpes with sautéed vegetables, and melt cheese over the top.

CHICKEN-AND-BROCCOLI TARTS

Assemble these picturesque tarts and then glaze them all at once while the glaze is still hot. To cut the tarts without disturbing the design, use a long, heavy, sharp knife and, instead of sawing back and forth, simply apply pressure along the back of the blade.

 WINE RECOMMENDATION
A rich, full-bodied sauvignon blanc from New Zealand, full of ripe fruit and penetrating acidity, makes a nice match for the buttery pastry with its touch of mayonnaise and broccoli accent.

MAKES TWO 5-BY-10-INCH TARTS

Butter-Pastry Dough, page 31

1 egg yolk

1 teaspoon water

2 boneless, skinless chicken breasts (about ⅔ pound in all)

½ red bell pepper

16 ¼-inch-wide strips green bell pepper

6 broccoli florets, each about 2 inches long

20 carrot slices

½ cup mayonnaise

1 tablespoon minced fresh parsley

½ teaspoon dried basil

½ teaspoon dried oregano

1 teaspoon cornstarch

6 tablespoons Chicken Stock, page 61, or canned low-sodium chicken broth, at room temperature, fat skimmed off

1. Heat the oven to 400°. On a lightly floured surface, roll half of the chilled dough into an 11-inch square about ⅛ inch thick or slightly thicker. Work quickly so that the dough does not soften.

2. Using a paring knife, cut two 5-by-10-inch rectangles of dough. Then cut eight ¼-inch-wide strips, four that are 9½ inches long, and four that are 5 inches long. Using a lightly floured spatula, transfer the two rectangles to an ungreased baking sheet.

3. In a small cup, beat the egg yolk with the water. Brush the outer edge of one pastry rectangle with this egg glaze. Then edge the rectangle with four corresponding strips of pastry, laying the strips flat so that a ⅛-inch-deep rim is formed around the rectangle. Brush the top of the rim with glaze. Repeat this procedure to make and glaze the second tart shell.

4. Prick the bottoms of the tart shells all over with a fork. Bake the shells until they are golden brown and crisp, 12 to 15 minutes. Cool the shells on the baking sheets for about 5 minutes. Then, using a spatula, carefully transfer the shells to a wire rack and cool completely.

5. Prepare the toppings for the tarts: Steam, poach, or bake the chicken breasts,

cool slightly, and then put the chicken in the refrigerator to chill. Roast the red bell pepper over a gas flame or grill or broil it, turning with tongs until charred all over, about 10 minutes. When the pepper is cool enough to handle, pull off the skin and remove the stem, seeds, and ribs. Cut the pepper into 36 small diamond shapes. Steam or boil the green bell-pepper strips, broccoli florets, and carrot slices separately.

6. Halve the broccoli florets lengthwise. Cut each of the chicken breasts into nine slices.

7. In a medium bowl, combine the mayonnaise, parsley, basil, and oregano. Using a small spoon, carefully spread one quarter of the herb mayonnaise over the bottom of each tart shell.

8. With a short side of a tart shell toward you, make two crosswise rows of five carrot rounds each to divide the tart into thirds. Make a border of two green-bell-pepper strips on both sides of each carrot row.

9. Place two broccoli florets in each third of the tart, stem-end toward you. Put three slices of chicken in each third of the tart, alternating with the broccoli florets. Place a red-bell-pepper diamond in the middle of each piece of chicken. Repeat from step 8 to decorate the second tart.

10. In a small saucepan, combine the cornstarch and stock. Bring to a boil over moderate heat, stirring constantly. Carefully

spoon the hot cornstarch mixture over the tarts. Let the glaze cool to room temperature and then chill the tarts, uncovered, for 1 hour. If you need to hold them longer, cover them loosely with plastic wrap or aluminum foil. To serve, cut each tart into thirds for a first course or into ninths for hors d'oeuvres.

—JIM FOBEL

MAKE IT AHEAD

The pastry can be made and the tart shells baked up to a day in advance. Keep them at room temperature, loosely covered with aluminum foil.

BUTTER-PASTRY DOUGH

**MAKES ENOUGH FOR TWO
5-BY-10-INCH TART SHELLS**

1½ cups flour

¼ teaspoon salt

¼ pound unsalted butter, cut into thin
   slices, well chilled

3 tablespoons vegetable shortening

5 tablespoons cold water

1. Combine the flour and salt in a large bowl. Using a pastry blender or two knives, quickly work the butter into the flour until the mixture resembles coarse meal. Cut in the shortening in the same way. Do not allow the mixture to get warm, or it will not make a flaky pastry. Refrigerate it briefly if necessary.

2. Sprinkle half of the cold water over the flour mixture and stir rapidly with a fork. Sprinkle the remaining water over the dough and continue mixing rapidly with the fork only until blended.

3. Divide the dough in half. Shape each half into a disk, wrap tightly, and refrigerate for at least 2 hours.

CHICKEN PANCAKES WITH PEAR SALSA

Tiny chicken-and-potato pancakes served with a sweet-hot-and-sour sauce taste adventuresome and comforting at the same time. We've given instructions for cooking the chicken, but you can certainly cut up leftover chicken instead; you'll need about one-and-three-quarter cups.

WINE RECOMMENDATION
The vinegar and hot peppers in the salsa are hard to match with wine, but a light and delicate Moscato d'Asti, from Italy's Piedmont region, would be an inspired choice. The wine's tangy sweetness, light spritz, and seductive aromas of musk, flowers, and orange peel are impossible to resist.

SERVES 4

1 pound chicken thighs
¾ teaspoon salt
  Fresh-ground black pepper
4 ounces baking potato (about ½ medium)
½ small onion, grated
1 tablespoon flour
  Dash hot-pepper sauce
2 small eggs, lightly beaten
1 tablespoon butter
1 tablespoon cooking oil
  Pear Salsa, opposite page

1. Heat the oven to 375°. Season the chicken thighs with ¼ teaspoon salt and ¼ teaspoon pepper. Put the thighs skin-side up in a baking dish just large enough to hold them. Bake until just done, about 35 minutes. Turn off the oven and leave the chicken in the oven for another 45 minutes without opening the door.

2. Remove and discard the chicken skin and bones. Chop the chicken.

3. Peel and grate the potato and squeeze out as much liquid as possible. In a medium bowl, combine the potato, onion, flour, hot sauce, the remaining ½ teaspoon salt, and ⅛ teaspoon pepper. Mix well. Add the chicken and eggs and mix well.

4. In a large nonstick frying pan, heat the butter with the oil over moderate heat until hot but not smoking. Drop rounded tablespoons of the batter into the frying pan, allowing room for the pancakes to spread. Increase the heat to moderately high and cook until the pancakes are golden on the bottom and set, about 4 minutes. Turn over, flatten slightly with a spatula, and cook until golden on the bottom, about 2 minutes. Serve the pancakes with the salsa on the side.

—LEE BAILEY

MAKE IT AHEAD

• Cook the chicken thighs a day ahead and store the chopped meat, covered, in the refrigerator. Bring to room temperature before continuing with the recipe.

• The salsa can be prepared in advance. Keep it at room temperature for up to three hours, or cover and refrigerate overnight.

SALSA VARIATIONS

• In the summer, substitute a peach for the pear.

• If you like your salsa hot, add more jalapeño pepper.

PEAR SALSA

MAKES ABOUT 1 1/2 CUPS

1 plum tomato

1 firm pear, such as Bosc, peeled, cored, and cut into 1/4-inch dice

1 1/2 teaspoons lemon juice

3 large scallions including green tops, chopped

1 1/2 teaspoons seeded, minced jalapeño pepper

3 tablespoons olive oil

1 tablespoon sherry vinegar

1/2 teaspoon honey

1. Blanch the tomato in a small saucepan of boiling water for 15 seconds. Cool in cold water. Slip off the skin, cut the tomato in half, and scoop out the seeds. Cut the tomato into 1/4-inch strips.

2. In a medium bowl, toss the pear with the lemon juice. Stir in the tomato, scallions, and jalapeño.

3. In a small bowl, whisk together the oil, vinegar, and honey. Drizzle this over the pear mixture and toss to coat.

4. Serve the salsa using a slotted spoon, allowing most of the juices to drain off.

CHICKEN-AND-SPINACH CAKES WITH SHIITAKE-MUSHROOM SAUCE

These bread-crumb-coated cakes are deep-fried for about six minutes and then baked for another ten, so they emerge golden brown and deliciously crisp. If you can't find shiitakes for the sauce, substitute any other wild mushroom, or even regular white mushrooms.

WINE RECOMMENDATION

Mushrooms and pinot noir go together like Romeo and Juliet—but not just any pinot noir. Try a silky-textured red Burgundy from Nuits-St-Georges to highlight the sensual, earthy flavors of the shiitakes and the sweetness of the caramelized shallots.

SERVES 4

2½ tablespoons cooking oil

8 shallots, cut into thin slices

1 pound spinach, stems removed and leaves washed

⅔ pound boneless, skinless chicken breasts (about 2), cut into ½-inch cubes

3 slices bacon, chopped

6 tablespoons heavy cream

¾ cup fresh bread crumbs

Salt and fresh-ground black pepper

⅛ teaspoon cayenne

1½ teaspoons butter

1 pound shiitake mushrooms, stems removed and caps cut into thin slices

¼ teaspoon dried thyme

½ cup Chicken Stock, page 61, or canned low-sodium chicken broth

1. In a large saucepan, heat 1 tablespoon of the oil over moderate heat. Add the shallots and cook, stirring occasionally, until just golden, 8 to 10 minutes.

2. In a large pot of boiling, salted water, cook the spinach just until it wilts, about 1 minute. Drain and rinse under cold water. Drain again and squeeze a handful of the spinach at a time to remove as much water as possible. Chop the spinach; you should have about ¾ cup.

3. Put the chicken in a food processor and pulse until minced. Transfer the chicken to a medium bowl. Add the bacon, spinach, 3 tablespoons of the cream, 3 tablespoons of the bread crumbs, ¼ cup of the cooked shallots, ⅛ teaspoon salt, ½ teaspoon black pepper, and the cayenne. Mix well. Form the mixture into eight round cakes.

4. Heat the oven to 400°. In a shallow bowl, mix the remaining bread crumbs with ¼ teaspoon black pepper. Coat the cakes with the seasoned bread crumbs.

5. In a large frying pan, heat 1 tablespoon of the oil over moderately high heat.

Add the cakes and cook, turning once, until browned on both sides, about 3 minutes per side. Transfer the cakes to a baking sheet and bake until firm, 10 to 12 minutes.

6. Meanwhile, reheat the remaining shallots in the saucepan over high heat. Stir in the butter, mushrooms, thyme, and the remaining 1½ teaspoons oil. Cover and cook, stirring frequently, until the mushrooms soften and begin to brown, 4 to 5 minutes.

7. Stir the broth and the remaining 3 tablespoons cream into the mushroom mixture and bring to a boil. Cook until the sauce has thickened slightly, about 10 minutes. Season with salt and pepper.

8. To serve, put two chicken cakes on each of four plates. Top with the mushroom sauce.

—BOB CHAMBERS

FROZEN SPINACH

If you like, you can use frozen spinach in place of the fresh spinach here. You'll need half of a ten-ounce package. Thaw the frozen spinach slightly until you can cut the block in half, and then wrap the unused half well and return it to the freezer for future use. Let the half you'll be using in the recipe thaw completely, and then squeeze it dry. It doesn't need to be cooked; just add it to the recipe in step 3.

chapter 2

SOUPS

Grandpa's Hearty Chicken Noodle Soup, page 47

DOUBLE-CHICKEN SOUP

A whole chicken is cooked in chicken stock, giving both the bird and the broth extra flavor. When the chicken is done, the meat is sliced and placed in soup bowls, to be covered with the steaming broth. You won't find a more chicken-y chicken soup.

WINE RECOMMENDATION
This rich, flavorful soup calls for an equally rich, full-bodied chardonnay. Seek out a lightly oaked Napa or Sonoma chardonnay for its buttery fruit and sumptuous texture.

SERVES 4

- 1 chicken (3 to 3½ pounds)
- 5 carrots, quartered lengthwise
- 4 leeks, white and light-green parts only, quartered lengthwise and washed well
- 4 ribs celery, cut into 2-inch pieces
- 3 parsnips, peeled and quartered lengthwise
- 2 bay leaves, crumbled
  Salt
- ½ teaspoon peppercorns
- 2 quarts Chicken Stock, page 61, or canned low-sodium chicken broth
- 1 quart water
  Fresh-ground black pepper

1. Put the chicken, carrots, leeks, celery, parsnips, bay leaves, 1 teaspoon salt, and the peppercorns in a large pot. Add the stock and water and bring to a boil over moderately low heat. Reduce the heat and simmer, uncovered, skimming occasionally, until the chicken is cooked through, about 1 hour.

2. Remove the chicken and vegetables, cover loosely with foil, and set aside in a warm spot. Strain the broth.

3. Return the broth to the pot and bring to a boil over high heat. Boil until reduced to 6 cups, 30 to 40 minutes. Season with salt and fresh-ground pepper.

4. Carve the chicken. Put slices of both white and dark meat in each of four soup bowls, along with the carrots, leeks, celery, and parsnips. Ladle the broth over all.

—MOLLY O'NEILL

CALDO POLLO

It's chicken soup, pure and simple. The clean, clear broth, which gets its refreshing taste from a scattering of mint leaves, is delicious on its own as a first course, or make it without the mint leaves and use it as a stock in other dishes. The recipe makes about five cups.

WINE RECOMMENDATION
To highlight the soup's simple virtues, serve it with a good Prosecco, the sparkling white from Italy's Veneto region. The wine's lively, slightly herbal flavors won't upstage the subtlety of the soup.

SERVES 4

1 chicken (3 to 3½ pounds), cut into 8 pieces

½ medium onion, quartered

1 rib celery, chopped

1 clove garlic, crushed

10 fresh mint leaves

1 teaspoon salt

½ teaspoon cracked black pepper

6 cups water

1. Put the chicken, onion, celery, garlic, mint, salt, pepper, and water in a large pot and bring to a boil. Reduce the heat and simmer until the stock is very flavorful, 1 to 1½ hours.

2. Remove the chicken and reserve for another use. Strain the stock and press the vegetables firmly to get as much liquid as possible. Skim the fat from the surface.

—CHATA DUBOSE

ANOTHER USE

There's no end of uses for the cooked chicken that's left over after making this soup. Many of the recipes in this book—including Mediterranean Chicken and Ratatouille Salad, page 65, and Corn Crêpe Cake with Chicken Chile Filling, page 26—call for cooked chicken. It's also great to have on hand for sandwiches. You can store cooked chicken in the refrigerator for up to two days, and in the freezer for as long as two months.

FENNEL-SCENTED CHICKEN SOUP WITH SPINACH

Here's a great way to get your vegetables. Fennel, leek, scallions, and lots of spinach make this a particularly healthful bowl of chicken soup. Since the chicken is skinless breast meat, the soup is low in fat, too.

 WINE RECOMMENDATION
With its thyme, fennel, bay leaf, and garlic, this soup is deeply rooted in Mediterranean tradition. Try an earthy, full-bodied white from the sunny south of France to keep up the theme. A white grenache-based Châteauneuf-du-Pape or Corbières blanc should do nicely.

SERVES 4

1½ teaspoons olive oil

3¼ cups chopped fennel with tops (about 2 bulbs)

1   leek, white and light-green parts only, split lengthwise, chopped, and washed well

2   cloves garlic, unpeeled

1   sprig fresh thyme, or ⅛ teaspoon dried thyme

1   bay leaf

3   peppercorns

    Salt

1½ cups Chicken Stock, page 61, or canned low-sodium chicken broth

1½ cups water

¾   cup diced red potatoes

⅔   pound boneless, skinless chicken breasts (about 2), cut into ½-inch dice

¼   cup chopped scallions, including green tops

2   cups firmly packed shredded spinach

1. In a large pot, heat the oil over low heat. Add 3 cups of the fennel, the leek, garlic, thyme, bay leaf, and peppercorns. Sprinkle with salt, stir well, cover, and cook, stirring occasionally, until the fennel is softened but not browned, about 10 minutes. Add the stock and water, bring to a simmer, and continue simmering, partially covered, for 45 minutes.

2. Strain the stock and press the vegetables firmly to get as much liquid as possible. Return the broth to the pan and bring to a boil. Add the potatoes and cook until just tender, about 10 minutes. Add the chicken, scallions, and the remaining ¼ cup fennel and simmer until the chicken is cooked through, about 5 minutes.

3. Bring the soup to a boil, stir in the spinach, and cook until it is just wilted, about 1 minute. Season with salt.

UDON WITH CHICKEN AND LEEKS IN GINGER BROTH

A bowl of noodles in broth is a typical workday lunch in Japan, and this ginger-infused version is especially invigorating. The udon cook longer than most noodles—about twenty-five minutes, whether fresh or dried.

WINE RECOMMENDATION
A mature Champagne, with its subtle mélange of nutty, herbal, and mushroomy flavors, makes a superb partner here. The fizz provides a lovely counterpoint to the dense noodles as well.

SERVES 4

¾ cup Chicken Stock, page 61, or canned low-sodium chicken broth

4 tablespoons sake or dry white wine

4 tablespoons shoyu (Japanese soy sauce)*

2 bone-in chicken breasts (about 1 pound in all), skin removed

Dashi, opposite page

2 tablespoons plus 1 teaspoon sugar

1½ tablespoons minced fresh ginger

1 leek, white and light-green parts only, chopped and washed well

1 pound fresh udon or ¾ pound dried*

2 scallions including green tops, minced

Marinated Fresh Ginger, opposite page

Shichimi togarashi, or 1 small dried red chile pepper, minced, plus 2 tablespoons toasted sesame seeds

*Available at Asian markets

1. In a large saucepan, bring the stock, 1 tablespoon of the sake, and 1 tablespoon of the shoyu to a simmer over high heat. Add the chicken; reduce the heat to moderately low. Cover and simmer, turning the chicken occasionally, until cooked through, about 25 minutes. Let the chicken cool slightly in the broth, and then remove it and shred the meat. Discard the bones.

2. Add enough Dashi to the broth to make 5 cups. Stir in the sugar and the remaining 3 tablespoons each of sake and shoyu and bring to a boil over high heat. Reduce the heat, cover, and simmer for 4 minutes. Remove from the heat and stir in the ginger.

3. Put 1 cup of the broth in a small saucepan; bring to a boil over high heat. Add the leek, reduce the heat, and simmer until just tender, about 10 minutes. Using a slotted spoon, transfer the leek to a bowl. Add the 1 cup broth to the rest of the broth.

4. Bring a large pot of salted water to a boil over high heat. Add the fresh udon, if using, and simmer until soft, about 25 minutes. Drain well. Alternatively, if using dried udon, add the noodles to the boiling water

and, when the water returns to a boil, add ¾ cup cold water and bring to a boil again. Repeat three more times, for a total of about 12 minutes cooking time. Remove the pot from the heat, cover, and set aside until the noodles are soft, about 15 minutes; drain.

5. Add the noodles to the broth and heat through. Using tongs, put the noodles in four soup bowls. Top with the chicken and leek; add the broth. Sprinkle with the scallions and the marinated ginger. Serve the *shichimi togarashi* alongside.

—LINDA BURUM

MARINATED FRESH GINGER

MAKES ⅓ CUP

1 2-inch piece fresh ginger, peeled
⅓ cup rice-wine vinegar
1 tablespoon sugar
1 teaspoon soy sauce

Cut the ginger on the diagonal into thin slices, and then cut the slices into very thin strips. In a small bowl, combine the vinegar, sugar, and soy sauce, stirring until the sugar is dissolved. Add the ginger and marinate for several hours or overnight.

DASHI

Dashi is a flavorful broth used in many Japanese dishes.

MAKES ABOUT 5 CUPS

2 pieces dried kelp,* each 6 inches by 2 inches
5 cups water
½ cup loosely packed bonito flakes* (about ¼ ounce)

*Available at Asian markets

1. Put the kelp and water in a medium saucepan and bring to a simmer over low heat. Immediately remove the saucepan from the heat and test the kelp with a fork. If it isn't tender, let it steep in the broth for up to 15 minutes.

2. Remove and discard the kelp. Add the bonito flakes to the broth and simmer for 5 minutes. Strain the Dashi through a fine strainer.

CHICKEN BROTH WITH FREGULA

In Sardinia, chicken is most often used for making a clear broth (*brodo di pollo*). Here, the broth is paired with another Sardinian staple, the tiny saffron-flavored balls of pasta called *fregula*.

WINE RECOMMENDATION
Regional dishes often pair best with wines from the same area; over the centuries, the two evolve into almost inseparable partners. The wine of choice here is a vermentino, an aromatic, robust white made from Sardinia's most widely planted grape.

SERVES 4

- 1 chicken (3 to 3½ pounds), cut into 8 pieces
- 1 tomato, seeded and chopped
- 1 onion, unpeeled, halved
- 1 carrot, halved
- 1 rib celery with leaves, halved
- 1 small bulb fennel with top
- ⅓ cup chopped flat-leaf parsley, plus about 20 stems
- 1 bay leaf
- ¼ teaspoon peppercorns
- Salt
- Fregula, opposite page
- ¼ cup grated Pecorino Romano cheese

1. Put the chicken, tomato, onion, carrot, celery, fennel, parsley stems, bay leaf, and peppercorns in a large pot. Add enough water to cover by several inches. Partially cover and bring to a boil. Lower the heat and simmer gently, occasionally skimming the foam from the surface, for 3 to 4 hours; do not boil. Let cool.

2. Skim the fat off the stock. Strain the stock and press the meat and vegetables firmly to get as much liquid as possible. Return the stock to the pot, bring to a boil, and boil until reduced to 6½ cups, about 30 minutes. For a stronger stock, boil for another 10 minutes. Season with salt.

3. Add the Fregula and simmer until just done, about 5 minutes. Ladle the soup into bowls and sprinkle with the chopped parsley and the cheese.

—JULIA DELLA CROCE

MAKE IT AHEAD

The broth and the Fregula can be made up to four days ahead of time, but don't combine them until ready to serve. Then, skim the fat from the broth, reheat it, add the Fregula, and let simmer for five minutes.

FREGULA

MAKES ABOUT ²/₃ CUP

Large pinch saffron

⅛ teaspoon salt

1½ tablespoons boiling water

½ cup fine semolina flour,* more if needed

*Available at Italian markets and specialty-food stores

1. In a small bowl, combine the saffron and the salt. Add the boiling water. Steep until the saffron has dissolved, about 10 minutes.

2. To form the fregula, spread about ¼ cup of the flour in a wide, shallow bowl. Using one hand, sprinkle some of the warm saffron water over the flour and rub the mixture to form crumbs. Using your dry hand, add more semolina. Keep sprinkling water and flour until you have used the ½ cup flour and formed firm, uneven crumbs. Add a little more plain water if the dough seems too dry or more flour if it seems too moist.

3. Spread the fregula on a kitchen towel to dry for about 30 minutes.

GRANDPA'S HEARTY CHICKEN NOODLE SOUP

The secret to this traditional soup is long, slow simmering. It's easiest as a two-day affair: On the first day you make the stock; on the second, you make the soup. If you want to make the soup all in one go, skim the fat from the hot stock before proceeding.

WINE RECOMMENDATION
To make this traditional chicken soup truly shine, serve it with a white Burgundy. St-Romain in particular has a distinctive mushroomy character that goes nicely here.

SERVES 4

1   chicken (3 to 3½ pounds)
1   onion, halved
3   carrots, halved
2   ribs celery with leaves, halved
1   rutabaga or 2 turnips (about ¾ pound in all), peeled and halved
½   cup firmly packed dill sprigs
1   cup fine egg noodles (1½ ounces)
2   tablespoons minced fresh parsley
    Salt and fresh-ground black pepper

1. In a large pot, combine the chicken, onion, carrots, celery, rutabaga, and dill. Add enough water to just cover the chicken and vegetables. Bring to a boil over high heat. Immediately reduce the heat to a bare simmer and cook, partially covered, skimming occasionally, until the chicken is cooked through, about 1 hour.

2. Remove the chicken and let cool slightly. Test the vegetables for doneness; the rutabaga may need to simmer for another 10 minutes. When the vegetables are tender, remove two carrot halves, two celery halves, and one rutabaga half and let cool. Continue to simmer the remaining vegetables, partially covered. Cut the cooled vegetables into ½-inch pieces. Separate the chicken meat from the skin and bones, reserving all three. Cut the meat into 1-inch strips. Wrap the chicken and vegetables and refrigerate.

3. Return the chicken bones and skin to the pot and continue to simmer, partially covered, for at least 2 hours more. For a very full-bodied soup, simmer the stock for a total of 4 hours.

4. Strain the stock and press the bones and vegetables firmly to get as much liquid as possible. Let the stock cool, and then cover and refrigerate overnight.

5. The next day, in a medium saucepan of boiling, salted water, cook the egg noodles until just done, about 6 minutes. Drain, rinse the noodles with cold water, and set them aside. ➤

6. Scrape the fat from the stock. In a large pot, bring the stock to a simmer over moderately high heat. Add the noodles along with the cooked chicken and vegetables. Simmer until heated through, about 15 minutes. Stir in the parsley and season with salt and pepper.

—Susan Shapiro Jaslove

VARIATIONS

Noodles and chicken soup are a classic combination, but there's plenty of room for substitution. Instead of the noodles, try adding rice, orzo, matzo balls, kreplach (noodle dumplings filled with meat or cheese), or meat or cheese tortellini.

MAKE IT AHEAD

If you like, you can make the stock and freeze it, and then prepare the soup at a later date.

SMOKY ONION AND CHICKEN SOUP WITH PINTO BEANS

Protein-packed pinto beans turn this earthy chicken soup into a meal-in-a-bowl. The smoky taste comes from the chunk of ham that flavors the broth.

WINE RECOMMENDATION
Sherry often performs well with soups where most table wines fail. A dry amontillado will be a hit here; its complex nutty taste makes a fine foil for the earthy, smoky, savory soup.

SERVES 4

1 tablespoon butter

1 large Spanish onion (about 1 pound), chopped

2 small cloves garlic, unpeeled

3 peppercorns

1 small bay leaf

1½ cups Chicken Stock, page 61, or canned low-sodium chicken broth

1 cup water

¼ pound smoked ham, in one piece

½ cup dry white wine

1¼ cups carrots cut into matchstick strips

1 cup shredded green cabbage

⅔ pound boneless, skinless chicken breasts (about 2), cut into ½-inch dice

½ cup scallions including green tops cut into matchstick strips

¾ cup drained and rinsed canned pinto beans

Salt

1. In a large pot, melt the butter over moderate heat. Add the onion, garlic, peppercorns, and bay leaf and cook, stirring occasionally, until the onions are golden, 10 to 15 minutes.

2. Add the stock, water, and ham and bring to a boil. Reduce the heat and simmer, partially covered, for 45 minutes.

3. Add the wine and bring back to a boil. Reduce the heat to low and simmer for 3 minutes. Strain the stock and press the vegetables and ham firmly to get as much liquid as possible.

4. Return the stock to the pot and bring to a boil. Add the carrots and cabbage and cook until the carrots are just tender, about 10 minutes.

5. Add the chicken and scallions and cook until the chicken is cooked through, about 5 minutes. Add the beans and cook until heated through, about 1 minute. Season with salt.

CHICKEN AND TWO-POTATO SOUP

The Swiss chard in this hearty Sunday-night soup is particularly potent and remains distinctive even after it has been simmered with the other vegetables.

 WINE RECOMMENDATION A full-bodied pinot gris will be able to handle the many flavors here. Try one of the superb examples now coming out of Oregon.

SERVES 4

1   chicken (3 to 3½ pounds)

5   large ribs celery with leaves, chopped

1   pound Swiss chard, torn into bite-size pieces

2½ tablespoons butter

½   cup chopped scallions including green tops

1   large baking potato (about ¾ pound), peeled and cut into ½-inch dice

½   head Boston lettuce, torn into bite-size pieces

1   small sweet potato (about ½ pound), peeled and cut into ½-inch dice

½   teaspoon ground coriander

2   teaspoons salt

¼   teaspoon fresh-ground black pepper

    Pinch cayenne

1. Stuff the cavity of the chicken with 2 cups of the celery and put the chicken in a large pot along with the remaining celery. Add enough water to cover. Bring to a boil over high heat. Reduce the heat and simmer, partially covered, until the chicken is cooked through, 1 to 1½ hours. Let the chicken cool in the broth.

2. Remove the chicken meat from the bones and chop. Discard the skin and return the bones and the celery from inside the chicken to the broth. Bring to a simmer and cook until reduced to 5 cups, about 45 minutes. Strain the broth and press the bones and celery firmly to get as much liquid as possible. Skim the fat from the surface.

3. Strip the leaves from the chard and set them aside. Chop the chard stems into ½-inch pieces. Melt the butter in the pot over low heat. Add the scallions and cook until softened but not browned, about 5 minutes. Add about ½ cup of the broth, the potato, and the chopped chard stems. Cover and cook until the potato is almost tender, about 8 minutes.

4. Add the chard leaves and the lettuce to the pot with the sweet potato, coriander, salt, black pepper, and cayenne. Cover and cook, stirring once, until the sweet potato is almost tender, about 8 minutes.

5. Add the remaining stock and the chicken to the pot. Simmer until the vegetables are tender and the chicken is heated through, about 5 minutes.

—LEE BAILEY

CHICKEN SOUP WITH SAUSAGE, RICE, AND YELLOW SQUASH

The combination of chicken, sausage, and rice makes this a hearty soup, fine for supper with a green salad and some crusty bread. Though you can make the soup with any type of rice, it's best with basmati or another aromatic rice.

WINE RECOMMENDATION
The soup's strong garlicky aroma and delicate summer squash call for a relatively neutral, but crisp, foil. A light Italian white such as Gavi, with its unique steeliness and hints of lime, would make a good choice. If you prefer red, a fruity Valpolicella would work equally well.

SERVES 4

1½ teaspoons olive oil

2½ cups chopped celery, plus ½ cup sliced

1 large leek, white and light-green parts only, enough cut into matchstick strips to make ¼ cup, the rest finely chopped, all washed well

1 clove garlic, unpeeled, lightly crushed

2 cups Chicken Stock, page 61, or canned low-sodium chicken broth

1 cup water

1 small bay leaf

¼ teaspoon dried thyme

3 peppercorns

2 ounces garlic sausage, such as kielbasa, cut into ½-inch dice

½ pound boneless, skinless chicken breasts (2 small), cut into ½-inch dice

1¾ cups yellow summer squash, cut into ½-inch dice

¾ cup cooked rice

1. In a large pot, heat the oil over moderate heat. Add the chopped celery and the chopped leek, cover, and cook until translucent, about 5 minutes.

2. Add the garlic, stock, water, bay leaf, thyme, and peppercorns. Bring to a boil. Reduce the heat and simmer, partially covered, skimming occasionally, for 45 minutes.

3. Strain the stock and press the vegetables firmly to get as much liquid as possible. Return the stock to the pot and bring to a boil. Add the sausage and cook for 2 minutes.

4. Add the chicken, the sliced celery, the matchstick strips of leek, and the squash and cook until the chicken is cooked through, about 5 minutes. Add the rice. Cook until heated through, about 1 minute.

MUSHROOM AND CHICKEN SOUP WITH BACON AND LEEKS

Mushrooms that are slightly past their prime, with opened caps and exposed dark gills, are a good choice for this recipe. They will contribute a fuller flavor to the soup than would perfect, plump, firm specimens.

WINE RECOMMENDATION
Here's a soup whose mushroomy richness and savory bacon accent long for the perfumed sensuality of a red Burgundy. For earthiness and rusticity, try a premier cru Mercurey; for a bit more elegance, a villages-level Gevrey-Chambertin.

SERVES 4

- 1 tablespoon butter
- 2 onions, unpeeled, chopped
- 1 clove garlic, unpeeled, chopped
- 1/3 pound plum tomatoes, 1 diced, the rest quartered
- 2/3 pound mushrooms, chopped
- 1 1/2 cups Chicken Stock, page 61, or canned low-sodium chicken broth
- 1 1/2 cups water
- 3 peppercorns
- 1 small bay leaf
- 3 slices bacon
- 1/2 pound boneless, skinless chicken breasts (2 small), cut into 1/2-inch dice
- 2 leeks, white and light-green parts only, sliced and washed well
- 1/2 cup diced celery
- 3/4 cup cooked rice

1. In a large pot, melt the butter over moderate heat. Add the onions and cook, stirring occasionally, until translucent, about 5 minutes. Add the garlic, the quartered tomatoes, the mushrooms, stock, water, peppercorns, and bay leaf. Bring to a boil, reduce the heat, and simmer, partially covered, skimming occasionally, for 45 minutes.

2. Meanwhile, cook the bacon in a large frying pan over moderately high heat until crisp, about 10 minutes. Drain on paper towels and then crumble.

3. Strain the stock and press the vegetables firmly to get as much liquid as possible.

4. Return the stock to the pan and bring to a boil. Add the chicken, leeks, and celery and bring back to a boil. Reduce the heat and simmer until the chicken is cooked through, about 5 minutes.

5. Stir in the rice and the diced tomato and cook for another minute. Stir in the crumbled bacon.

CHICKEN CONGEE

Congee can be a thin, watery rice gruel or a thick, comforting rice porridge, depending on whether the rice is cooked until it becomes a smooth paste or only until soft. This hearty version is essentially an uncomplicated dish, greatly enlivened by the variety of condiments that are served with it.

WINE RECOMMENDATION

A rosé Champagne, with its vivid acidity and festive bubbles, is just the thing to accent the soup and negotiate the flavor minefield of the condiments.

SERVES 4

2 slices fresh ginger, plus ¼ cup slivered fresh ginger

6 cups water, plus boiling water if needed

1¼ pounds chicken legs and breasts

1 cup Thai or jasmine rice*

Salt

2 teaspoons peanut oil

8 cloves garlic, minced

Light soy sauce

Chinese chili paste*

Chinese hot chili oil (*la yu*)*

3 tablespoons dried shrimp*

3 tablespoons Chinese preserved vegetables,* chopped fine

¼ cup cilantro leaves

3 shallots, chopped fine

¼ cup roasted peanuts, chopped (see box, opposite page)

*Available at Asian markets and specialty-food stores

1. In a large pot, combine the ginger slices and the 6 cups water and bring to a boil over high heat. Add the chicken and reduce the heat to moderate. Simmer until the chicken is cooked through, 30 to 40 minutes.

2. Remove the chicken from the broth and allow it to cool slightly. Remove the meat from the bones and discard the skin and bones. Shred the meat. Skim the fat from the surface of the broth. Discard the ginger slices.

3. Bring the broth to a boil over high heat. Add the rice and ¼ teaspoon salt and return to a boil, stirring. Reduce the heat and simmer, covered, until the rice is tender, about 15 minutes. Stir in the shredded chicken and heat through, about 2 minutes. The congee should be fairly liquid. If the rice has absorbed all of the broth, add boiling water, ½ cup at a time, until the desired consistency is reached. Season the congee with salt.

4. Meanwhile, in a small frying pan, heat the peanut oil over moderate heat. Reduce the heat to moderately low, add the garlic, and cook until golden brown, about 1 minute.

5. Put the garlic, the slivered ginger, the soy sauce, chili paste, chili oil, shrimp, preserved vegetables, cilantro, shallots, and peanuts in separate small bowls. Ladle the congee into four soup bowls. Serve the condiments alongside.

—JEFFREY ALFORD AND NAOMI DUGUID

MAKE IT AHEAD

Prepare the broth and the chicken, through step 2, up to one day in advance; refrigerate separately. Bring the chicken to room temperature before proceeding with the recipe.

ROASTED PEANUTS

Though you can use store-bought roasted peanuts for this recipe, we recommend roasting raw peanuts yourself. The process is easy, and the flavor is significantly better. Just put the quarter-cup of shelled, skinned peanuts in a small heavy frying pan and roast over moderately high heat, stirring constantly, until browned, about five minutes.

JULIA CHILD'S CREAM OF CHICKEN SOUP PRINTANIÈRE

The unbelievably velvety texture of this soup comes from the rice and onion puree; the sour cream is added for flavor and enrichment alone. To make a low-fat version, cook the onions for the soup base in a little stock instead of butter and omit the sour cream altogether.

WINE RECOMMENDATION
For this thick but not particularly rich soup, a soft, fruity, low-tannin red such as pinot noir will be a lovely accompaniment—especially one of the many fine examples from the Russian River Valley or Carneros, both in California.

SERVES 4

- 1 cup onion cut into thin slices
- 1 cup carrots cut into thin slices
- 1 cup leeks cut into thin slices, white part only, washed well
- 1 cup celery hearts cut into thin slices
- ⅔ pound boneless, skinless chicken breasts (about 2)
- 3 cups Chicken Stock, page 61, or canned low-sodium chicken broth
- ½ cup dry vermouth
  Salt and fresh-ground black pepper
  Rice and Onion Soup Base, opposite page
- ½ cup sour cream or crème fraîche
- 1 tablespoon chopped fresh parsley

1. Put the onion, carrots, leeks, celery hearts, chicken, stock, and vermouth in a large pot and bring to a simmer. Cook, skimming occasionally, until the chicken is just slightly springy to the touch, about 4 minutes.

2. Remove the chicken and cut lengthwise into matchsticks. Continue to cook the vegetables until tender, about 5 minutes. Season with salt and pepper and remove from the heat. Return the chicken to the pot and let steep for 5 minutes or longer.

3. Return the pot to the heat, add the soup base, and bring just to a simmer. Season with salt and pepper. Ladle into bowls, top each serving with a dollop of sour cream, and sprinkle with parsley.

—JULIA CHILD

RICE AND ONION SOUP BASE

MAKES 5 CUPS

2 tablespoons butter

2 cups onions cut into thin slices

½ cup rice

5 cups Chicken Stock, page 61, or canned low-sodium chicken broth, more if needed

Salt and fresh-ground black pepper

1. Melt the butter in a large heavy saucepan over moderately low heat. Add the onions; cook, stirring frequently, until very tender, 7 to 8 minutes.

2. Add the rice and 4 cups of the stock, stir, and bring to a simmer. Cook until the rice is very tender, about 20 minutes.

3. Puree the mixture in a blender until very smooth, adding a little more stock if needed. Return the soup base to the pan, add the remaining 1 cup stock, and season with salt and pepper.

CHICKEN BOUILLABAISSE

Originally, bouillabaisse was a humble dish made by fishermen from whatever fish were cheap or difficult to sell. When the fishing was poor and they didn't bring back much of anything, so the story goes, they coped by using a chicken from the backyard.

WINE RECOMMENDATION
A powerful, earthy rosé from Bandol is this Provençal classic's traditional partner. Don't be surprised if the wine is more yellow than pink; the mourvèdre grape is so tannic and rich that just a little skin contact provides all the flavor Bandol needs, but not much in the way of color.

SERVES 4

- 2 quarts water
- 1 large chicken (about 5 pounds), cut into 8 pieces
- 1 bottle (750 ml) dry white wine
- 2 cups Chicken Stock, page 61, or canned low-sodium chicken broth
- 1 cup Madeira
- 6 small white onions, cut in half
- 1 clove garlic
- 3 parsley sprigs
- 2 bay leaves
- ¼ teaspoon ground saffron, or ½ teaspoon turmeric
- 12 green olives, pitted
- 6 large tomatoes, peeled and quartered
- 12 thick slices French bread

1. In a large pot, bring the water to a boil. Add the chicken and return to a boil. Lower the heat and cook for 10 minutes. Remove the chicken, let cool, and then discard the skin.

2. Add the wine, stock, Madeira, onions, garlic, parsley, bay leaves, and saffron to the pot and bring to a simmer over moderately high heat. Reduce the heat and continue simmering for 15 minutes.

3. Add the chicken pieces and simmer for 45 minutes. Then add the olives and tomatoes and cook until heated through, about 2 to 3 minutes.

4. Meanwhile, heat the oven to 350°. Trim the crusts from the bread. Put the bread on a baking sheet and toast in the oven until well dried, about 8 minutes.

5. Spread the bread slices in a single layer in a large shallow serving dish. Pour the bouillabaisse over the slices and serve immediately.

—MONIQUE GUILLAUME

Kentucky Chicken, Mushroom, and Rice Chowder

Rice takes the place of potatoes in this super-smooth chowder. The sautéed mushrooms add depth, and the cream brings all the ingredients together into a satisfying main dish.

WINE RECOMMENDATION Navarra, just across Spain's river Ebro from its more famous cousin, Rioja, is renowned for its vibrant, dry rosés. Try one with this creamy chowder; the mushrooms and red peppers want a rosé's red-fruit flavors, and the cream and rice need its crispness as a counterpoint.

SERVES 4

2 pounds chicken parts

1 onion, unpeeled, cut in half

1 carrot, cut into thick slices

1 rib celery, chopped

1 parsnip, cut into thick slices

2 parsley sprigs, plus 1 tablespoon chopped fresh parsley

5 peppercorns

4 cups Chicken Stock, opposite page, or canned low-sodium chicken broth

1½ cups water

¼ pound mushrooms, sliced (about 1½ cups)

1 tablespoon lemon juice

1½ tablespoons butter, plus 1 teaspoon at room temperature

1 small clove garlic, minced

2 leeks, white and light-green parts only, split lengthwise, cut into thin slices, and washed well

3 tablespoons chopped red bell pepper

⅓ cup rice

½ teaspoon all-purpose flour

⅔ cup heavy cream, at room temperature

Pinch grated nutmeg

Salt and fresh-ground black pepper

1. Put the chicken in a large pot. Add the onion, carrot, celery, parsnip, parsley sprigs, peppercorns, stock, and water. Bring to a boil over high heat. Reduce the heat, cover, and simmer until the stock is very flavorful, about 1 hour. Remove the chicken and let cool slightly. Remove the meat from the bones, reserving the skin and the bones. Shred enough of the meat to make ⅔ cup; reserve the remainder of the chicken for another use.

2. Return the chicken skin and bones to the pot and cook over moderate heat until the stock has reduced to 4 cups, about 10 minutes. Strain the stock and press the bones and vegetables firmly to get as much liquid as possible.

3. Meanwhile, toss the mushrooms with 2 teaspoons of the lemon juice and let sit for 10 minutes.

4. In a large saucepan, melt the 1½ tablespoons butter over moderately high heat. Add the mushrooms and cook, stirring frequently, until lightly browned, about 5 minutes. Reduce the heat to moderately low and stir in the garlic, leeks, and bell pepper. Cook, stirring occasionally, until the vegetables are slightly softened, about 5 minutes. Stir in the stock and rice and bring to a boil. Reduce the heat to low, cover, and cook until the rice is tender, about 20 minutes.

5. In a small bowl, blend the flour with the remaining 1 teaspoon butter.

6. Transfer ¼ cup of the chowder to a blender, add the cream, and puree. Return the puree to the chowder and whisk in the flour mixture. Bring the chowder to a boil over moderate heat. Reduce the heat to low and simmer gently for 10 minutes. Stir in the ⅔ cup shredded chicken, the nutmeg, and the remaining 1 teaspoon lemon juice. Season with salt and pepper and simmer for 3 minutes. Ladle the chowder into bowls and sprinkle with the parsley.

—PHILLIP STEPHEN SCHULZ

CHICKEN STOCK

MAKES ABOUT 3 QUARTS

 7 pounds chicken carcasses, backs, wings, and/or necks, plus gizzards (optional)
 4 onions, quartered
 4 carrots, quartered
 4 ribs celery, quartered
15 parsley stems
 2 bay leaves
10 peppercorns
 4 quarts water

1. Put all the ingredients in a large pot and bring to a boil. Skim the foam from the surface. Reduce the heat and simmer, partially covered, skimming occasionally, for 2 hours.

2. Strain the stock and press the bones and vegetables firmly to get as much liquid as possible. If using immediately, skim the fat from the surface. If not, refrigerate for up to a week or freeze. Scrape off the fat before using the stock.

chapter 3

SALADS

Mediterranean Chicken and Ratatouille Salad, page 65

MEDITERRANEAN CHICKEN AND RATATOUILLE SALAD

Chicken joins traditional ratatouille ingredients—eggplant, onion, bell peppers, squash, garlic, and tomatoes—to make a full-flavored main-dish salad.

WINE RECOMMENDATION
A bright Beaujolais offers charming contrast to the caramel flavor of roasted eggplant. Look for a Beaujolais-Villages; the step up in quality is worth the difference in price.

SERVES 4

1	small eggplant (about 1 pound)
1	teaspoon salt
5	tablespoons olive oil
1	onion, chopped
1	red bell pepper, cut into 1-by-½-inch strips
1	yellow bell pepper, cut into 1-by-½-inch strips
2	small zucchini, quartered lengthwise and sliced 1 inch thick
2	small yellow summer squash, quartered lengthwise and sliced 1 inch thick
1	clove garlic, minced
½	teaspoon fresh thyme leaves, or ¼ teaspoon dried thyme
¼	pound plum tomatoes (about 2), cut in half lengthwise and sliced 1 inch thick
½	teaspoon fresh-ground black pepper
3	cups diced cooked chicken
½	cup basil leaves cut into thin slices, plus extra leaves for serving
2½	tablespoons lemon juice

1. Cut the eggplant in half lengthwise, lay flat on a work surface, and cut each half lengthwise into eight slices. Cut the slices crosswise every 1 inch and put them in a colander. Toss with ½ teaspoon of the salt and let the eggplant drain for at least 1 hour.

2. Heat the oven to 450°. Pat the eggplant pieces dry with paper towels. Put them on a baking sheet and toss with 2 tablespoons of the oil. Spread the eggplant pieces in a single layer and roast until well browned, 40 to 45 minutes. Let cool slightly.

3. Meanwhile, heat 1 tablespoon of the oil in a heavy saucepan over moderately high heat. Add the onion and cook, stirring frequently, until beginning to brown, about 5 minutes. Add the bell peppers, zucchini, and summer squash. Cook, stirring frequently, until barely tender, 12 to 15 minutes. Stir in the garlic and cook for 1 minute. Add the thyme, tomatoes, and ¼ teaspoon of the pepper.

4. Put the tomato mixture in a bowl and let cool slightly. Stir in the eggplant, chicken, the sliced basil, the lemon juice, and the remaining 2 tablespoons oil, ½ teaspoon salt, and ¼ teaspoon pepper. Top with the basil leaves.

—BOB CHAMBERS

WARM CHICKEN SALAD WITH WALNUT-OIL DRESSING

Fanned-out slices of warm chicken breast crown a mound of shredded lettuces for an exuberant summertime salad. The walnut oil in the dressing and the pine nuts on top provide a subtle sweetness.

WINE RECOMMENDATION
Riesling, with its tangy fruitiness, is right at home with vinegar-dressed salads. Here, go for a kabinett riesling from the Erdener Treppchen Vineyard, whose wines have a distinctive flavor of walnuts.

SERVES 4

- 4 boneless, skinless chicken breasts (about 1⅓ pounds)
  Salt and fresh-ground black pepper
- 3 tablespoons cooking oil
- 2 teaspoons chopped fresh tarragon or dill
- 2 teaspoons chopped fresh parsley
- ¼ cup scallion tops cut into thin slices
- 1 tablespoon plus 1 teaspoon red-wine vinegar
- 2 tablespoons pine nuts
- ½ pound mixed salad greens, such as Bibb, romaine, red leaf lettuce, and watercress, shredded (about 2 quarts)
- 2 tomatoes, diced
  Walnut-Oil Dressing, opposite page

1. Sprinkle the chicken breasts with salt and pepper. Heat the oil in a large frying pan over moderately high heat. Cook the chicken until lightly browned and just done, about 1½ minutes on each side. Remove from the pan and set aside to rest.

2. Add the tarragon, parsley, scallions, vinegar, and pine nuts to the pan and reduce the heat. Cook, stirring, for 1 minute. Remove from the heat.

3. In a large bowl, toss the greens and tomatoes with the Walnut-Oil Dressing. Put the salad on four plates. Cut the chicken breasts lengthwise into thick slices, keeping them together to retain the shape of the breast. Fan out a breast on top of each salad. Pour the pine-nut mixture over the chicken.

WALNUT-OIL DRESSING

MAKES ABOUT ¹/₂ CUP

- 1 teaspoon minced garlic
- 2 tablespoons Dijon mustard
- 2 tablespoons plus 2 teaspoons
  red-wine vinegar
- ¹/₂ teaspoon salt
- ¹/₄ teaspoon white pepper
- ¹/₄ cup walnut oil

In a medium bowl, whisk together
the garlic, mustard, vinegar, salt, and
pepper. Add the oil slowly, whisking.

FRESH HERBS

To store fresh herbs, wrap them in a
paper towel, put them in a plastic bag,
close it loosely, and put it in the refrigerator. The bag will hold in moisture,
and the paper towel will absorb any
excess. Herbs wrapped this way should
stay fresh for four to five days.

MA LA CHICKEN

Chicken and scallions rest on a bed of aromatic vegetables in this Chinese version of chicken salad. The Szechuan peppercorns are just hot enough to make your tongue tingle—pass them separately so everyone can add them to taste.

WINE RECOMMENDATION
The spicy heat calls for a bit of sweetness in a wine. Look for a spätlese riesling from the Pfalz in Germany for greater richness and riper fruit than an equivalent wine from the Mosel-Saar-Ruwer.

SERVES 4

- 1 chicken (3 to 3½ pounds)
- 1 large cucumber
- ¼ cup Szechuan peppercorns*
- 3 ribs celery, cut into 3-inch matchstick strips
- ½ carrot, cut into 3-inch matchstick strips
- ¼ teaspoon salt
- 2½ tablespoons soy sauce
- 1 tablespoon Asian sesame oil
- 1½ teaspoons Asian chili oil*
- ½ teaspoon vinegar
- ½ teaspoon sugar
- ⅛ teaspoon white pepper
- 4 scallions, green tops only, cut into 3-inch matchstick strips
- 1 tablespoon minced garlic

*Available at Asian markets and specialty-food stores

1. Put the chicken in a pot just large enough to hold it and add water to cover by 1 inch. Bring to a boil over high heat. Reduce the heat and simmer until the chicken is cooked through, about 1 hour. Drain and let cool slightly. Remove the chicken meat from the bones and shred it; discard the skin and bones. Put the meat on a plate and cover to keep warm.

2. Meanwhile, peel the cucumber and cut it lengthwise in half. Remove the seeds and cut the cucumber into 3-inch matchstick strips. Drain on paper towels.

3. In a small heavy frying pan, toast the peppercorns over high heat until they begin to smoke. Grind the pepper in a mortar with a pestle or in a spice grinder or blender.

4. Combine the celery, carrot, and cucumber in a bowl. Toss with the salt and mound in a serving dish. Put the chicken on top of the vegetables.

5. In a small bowl, whisk together the soy sauce, sesame oil, chili oil, vinegar, sugar, and white pepper. Pour over the chicken.

6. Sprinkle the salad with the scallion tops. Pass the ground peppercorns and the minced garlic separately.

CHINESE CHICKEN SALAD WITH CARROTS AND STAR ANISE

Use only the sweetest carrots for this light salad—that usually means the thinnest ones you can find. The dark brown pods called star anise are available in many supermarkets, as well as in Asian markets or specialty-food stores.

 WINE RECOMMENDATION
A crisp Italian white such as a Soave Classico, with its delicate almond flavors, should strike just the right note. The word *classico* on the label is important. It means you are getting a wine from the higher-quality hillside vineyards.

SERVES 4

¼ cup plus 2 tablespoons light soy sauce

1 tablespoon plus 1 teaspoon sugar

¾ teaspoon Asian sesame oil

4 star anise, broken

1 3-inch piece fresh ginger, peeled and cut into thin slices

1 pound boneless, skinless chicken breasts (about 3)

2 cups water

4 small carrots, cut into thin diagonal slices

2 tablespoons rice-wine vinegar

3 tablespoons peanut oil

2 scallions, green tops only, cut into thin diagonal slices

1. In a medium bowl, combine the soy sauce, the sugar, ¼ teaspoon of the sesame oil, the star anise, and the ginger. Add the chicken, turning to coat with the marinade. Cover and refrigerate for at least 2 hours, or overnight.

2. Put the chicken and the marinade in a medium saucepan. Add the water and bring to a boil over high heat. Reduce the heat, turn the chicken over, and simmer for 3 minutes. Remove from the heat and let cool.

3. Remove the chicken from the poaching liquid and cut into thin slices. Boil the poaching liquid over high heat until reduced to ½ cup, about 5 minutes. Strain into a small bowl and cool to room temperature.

4. Meanwhile, cook the carrots in a small saucepan of boiling, salted water until tender, about 2 minutes. Drain and let cool.

5. Whisk the vinegar into the reduced poaching liquid. Gradually whisk in the peanut oil and the remaining ½ teaspoon sesame oil.

6. Arrange the chicken and carrots on four salad plates. Spoon the dressing over the salads and let stand for about 5 minutes. Sprinkle the scallions on top.

—DAVID ROSENGARTEN

69

AVOCADOS STUFFED WITH CHICKEN AND ARTICHOKE HEARTS

Loaded with chicken and served on a bed of lettuce, a stuffed avocado makes a fine summer supper. Hass avocados have a dark, almost black, skin with a pebbly texture. To make sure they're ripe, press them gently; they should be fairly soft.

WINE RECOMMENDATION

Artichokes have a devilish way of making wines seem sweet, but a bone-dry Vernaccia di San Gimignano, with its clean, herbal flavors, will give this dish the summery partner it needs. The wine's crispness also cuts the richness of the avocados.

SERVES 4

- 2 tablespoons lemon juice

  Salt and fresh-ground black pepper

- 1/4 cup plus 2 tablespoons olive oil, preferably extra-virgin

- 2 pounds boneless, skinless chicken breasts (about 6), cooked and cut into bite-size pieces

- 8 artichoke hearts canned in brine, quartered

- 2 tablespoons capers

- 4 avocados, preferably Hass

  Lettuce leaves, for serving

  Lemon wedges, for serving

1. In a large bowl, whisk together the lemon juice, 2 teaspoons salt, and 1 teaspoon pepper. Add the oil slowly, whisking. Add the chicken, the artichoke hearts, and the capers.

2. Cut each avocado lengthwise in half and remove the pit. Gently run a paring knife between the skin and the flesh, keeping the skin intact. Without piercing the skin, cut the flesh lengthwise into 1/2-inch slices and then slice crosswise to make 1/2-inch cubes. Using a spoon, scoop out the cubed avocado and add it to the chicken mixture. Toss gently to mix. Season with salt and pepper.

3. Spoon the chicken mixture into the avocado shells, heaping it generously. Put the lettuce leaves on four salad plates and place two stuffed avocado halves on each. Serve with the lemon wedges.

—MOLLY O'NEILL

ARTICHOKE SALAD WITH CHICKEN AND AGED MONTEREY JACK

Also known as dry Jack, aged Monterey Jack is firmer, richer, sharper, and more yellow in color than its familiar, creamy-white, unaged counterpart. If you can't find it, good-quality Parmesan is a fine substitute in this first-course salad.

WINE RECOMMENDATION
Look to Italy, specifically the north-eastern regions of Friuli and Alto Adige, for the right wine for this dish: a pinot bianco. The best of these dry, floral wines are true treasures that are often overlooked in favor of pinot grigio.

SERVES 4

- 2 tablespoons lemon juice
- 4 large artichokes
- 2 cups Chicken Stock, page 61, or canned low-sodium chicken broth
- 2 cups water
- ⅔ pound boneless, skinless chicken breasts (about 2)
- ¼ teaspoon salt
  Fresh-ground black pepper
- 3 tablespoons olive oil
- ¼ cup coarse-grated aged Monterey Jack or Parmesan cheese
- 2 tablespoons minced fresh parsley

1. Put 1 tablespoon of the lemon juice in a small bowl. Break off all the large outer leaves from the artichokes and save 20 leaves. Cut off the stem and the cone of tender leaves from each artichoke and scrape the chokes from the artichoke bottoms. Cut the artichoke bottoms into matchstick strips and toss with the lemon juice.

2. Bring a large saucepan of water to a boil. Add the artichoke bottoms with their lemon juice and the artichoke leaves. Cook until barely tender, about 1 minute. Drain, rinse with cold water, and drain again. Put the artichoke strips in a medium bowl.

3. Put the stock and water in a medium saucepan and bring to a boil. Reduce to a simmer, add the chicken, and cook, turning once, until just cooked through, about 12 minutes. Remove the chicken from the stock and let cool. Cut the chicken into matchstick strips and add to the artichokes.

4. In a small bowl, whisk together the remaining 1 tablespoon lemon juice, the salt, and ¼ teaspoon pepper. Add the oil slowly, whisking. Pour the dressing over the artichokes and chicken and toss to coat. Place five artichoke leaves around the edge of each of four plates, and put the artichoke mixture in the center. Sprinkle with the cheese and parsley and season with pepper.

—JOHN ROBERT MASSIE

TARRAGON CHICKEN SALAD WITH MELON AND CUCUMBER

Crisp cucumber and juicy melon make for a cooling and colorful salad. Not one to make too far ahead, though—if it sits too long before serving, the salad may become watery.

WINE RECOMMENDATION
A California sauvignon blanc from Napa or Sonoma would be a natural with this salad—but not a fumé blanc. Though the latter is made from the same grape as sauvignon blanc, and there's no legal difference, fumé blancs are traditionally oakier and richer. Stay with the leaner, more herbal sauvignon blanc.

SERVES 4

²⁄₃ pound boneless, skinless chicken breasts (about 2)

1   tablespoon tarragon vinegar

1   tablespoon minced fresh tarragon

½   teaspoon salt

¼   teaspoon fresh-ground black pepper

3   tablespoons olive oil

2   tablespoons minced red onion

½   cantaloupe, cut into ½-inch dice

1   cucumber, peeled, seeded, and cut into ¼-inch slices

Radicchio leaves, for serving

1. Put enough salted water in a medium saucepan to cover the chicken. Bring to a boil, reduce the heat, add the chicken, and simmer until just done, about 12 minutes. Remove the chicken breasts, let them cool, and then slice them.

2. In a large bowl, whisk together the vinegar, tarragon, salt, and pepper. Slowly add the oil, whisking. Add the onion and the chicken slices and toss gently.

3. Add the cantaloupe and cucumber to the bowl with the chicken and toss well. Serve the salad on a bed of radicchio leaves.

—BOB CHAMBERS

CHICKEN SALAD WITH CHILI DRESSING

Chilled chicken is mixed with shredded lettuce and cabbage, and then tossed with a thick chili-sauce dressing that's pungent with chopped watercress.

 **WINE RECOMMENDATION**
Easy-drinking pink wines don't get a lot of respect, but they're often perfect, such as with this salad in its chili dressing. Try a strawberry-scented, off-dry Cabernet d'Anjou, made from cabernet franc, or a white zinfandel.

SERVES 4

2¼ pounds bone-in chicken breasts (about 4)

½ egg yolk

Pinch dry mustard

2 tablespoons cider vinegar

½ teaspoon Worcestershire sauce

½ teaspoon salt

⅛ teaspoon fresh-ground black pepper

⅓ cup olive oil

½ cup chili sauce

½ cup coarse-chopped watercress

1 small head crisp lettuce, such as romaine or iceberg, shredded (about 1 quart)

1 pound green cabbage, shredded (about 1 quart)

Capers, for serving

1. Put the chicken breasts, skin-side down, in a saucepan just large enough to hold them. Add enough water to cover by 1 inch. Bring to a boil. Reduce the heat and simmer until the chicken is just cooked through, about 20 minutes. Remove from the pan and let cool. Remove the chicken meat from the bone and cut the meat into matchstick strips; discard the skin and bones.

2. In a medium bowl, whisk together the egg yolk, mustard, 1½ tablespoons of the vinegar, the Worcestershire sauce, salt, and pepper. Add the oil slowly, whisking. Whisk in the remaining 1½ teaspoons vinegar. Stir in the chili sauce and watercress.

3. In a large salad bowl, toss the chicken with the lettuce and cabbage. Add the dressing and toss well. Put the capers in a small bowl and serve with the salad.

TEST-KITCHEN TIP

The easiest way to measure an odd quantity of egg yolk is to whisk first and then measure out the quantity you need. Figure about four teaspoons per yolk.

Chicken, Mushroom, and Napa-Cabbage Salad with Cilantro

Marinating the mushrooms lets them absorb the flavor of the tangy dressing. The cabbage, on the other hand, shouldn't be mixed with the dressing until the last moment, or it will lose its crispness.

WINE RECOMMENDATION
This simple, earthy salad works beautifully with a dry chenin-blanc-based wine. Vouvray sec, with its floral and apple flavors, is a promising choice. Be sure the label includes the word *sec*. If it just says *Vouvray*, the wine will be off-dry, not dry.

SERVES 4

2   scallions with green tops, cut into thin slices

Juice of ½ lemon

1   tablespoon chopped cilantro, plus cilantro sprigs for serving

½   teaspoon salt

¼   teaspoon fresh-ground black pepper

¼   cup olive oil

¼   pound firm white mushrooms, stems removed and caps cut into ⅛-inch slices

3   cups diced cooked chicken

¾   pound napa cabbage (about ½ head), quartered lengthwise and cut crosswise into ⅛-inch slices

1. In a large bowl, whisk together the scallions, the lemon juice, the chopped cilantro, the salt, and the pepper. Add the oil slowly, whisking. Add the mushrooms and toss well. Cover and set aside for 1 hour, stirring occasionally.

2. Add the chicken and toss well. Add the cabbage and toss again. Serve the salad topped with the cilantro sprigs.

—Bob Chambers

Make It Ahead

Add the chicken to the marinated mushrooms, cover, and refrigerate for up to four hours. Bring to room temperature and then toss in the cabbage just before serving.

TUSCAN CHICKEN-AND-BEAN SALAD

White beans are a feature of many Tuscan dishes. Here they're cooked without being soaked first, which makes for a longer cooking time but a shorter preparation time overall.

WINE RECOMMENDATION
This rustic Tuscan salad begs for a native Tuscan Chianti Classico as its rightful mate. The earthy, slightly herbal flavors of the Chianti marry well with the beans, and its lean, dried-cherry fruit harmonizes with the red pepper and wine vinegar.

SERVES 4

1 pound dried white beans (about 2 cups), such as Great Northern

1 onion, chopped

1 bay leaf

1¼ pounds bone-in chicken breasts (about 2)

3 cloves garlic, unpeeled

1 red bell pepper

1½ teaspoons salt

2 tablespoons red-wine vinegar

½ cup extra-virgin olive oil

2 tablespoons minced fresh thyme, or 1 teaspoon dried thyme

3 tablespoons minced flat-leaf parsley
   Fresh-ground black pepper

3 scallions with green tops, minced

1. Put the white beans, onion, and bay leaf in a large pot. Add enough water to cover by at least 2 inches. Bring to a boil, reduce the heat, and simmer, partially covered, until tender, about 1½ hours. Drain and let cool. Discard the bay leaf.

2. Heat the oven to 350°. Lightly oil a medium baking pan. Put the chicken, garlic, and bell pepper in the baking pan and bake for 15 minutes. Turn the garlic and bell pepper and cook until the chicken is golden brown and cooked through, about 20 minutes longer.

3. When the bell pepper is cool enough to handle, peel off the skin. Remove the stem, seeds, and ribs. Cut the pepper into ½-inch dice.

4. Squeeze the roasted garlic from its skin into a large bowl. Using a fork, mash the garlic with 1 teaspoon of the salt. Whisk in the vinegar and then add the oil slowly, whisking. Add the thyme, parsley, and ½ teaspoon pepper.

5. Remove the chicken from the bones and shred it; discard the skin and bones. Add the chicken to the vinaigrette and toss well to coat. Add the beans, bell pepper, scallions, and the remaining ½ teaspoon salt. Season with black pepper. Serve warm or chilled.

—MOLLY O'NEILL

THAI CHICKEN SALAD

Inspired by a dish from Bangkok, this exotic, sophisticated chicken salad is crunchy with toasted wonton strips, bean sprouts, and chopped peanuts.

 WINE RECOMMENDATION
German rieslings often don't work well with food because of their sweetness, yet it's just that quality that makes them such a good match for spicy Asian flavors. Try a Mosel kabinett such as an Urziger Wurzgarten or Wehlener Sonnenuhr.

SERVES 4

2　cups vegetable oil

15　wonton wrappers, cut into ¼-inch strips

¼　pound mixed salad greens, shredded (about 5 cups)

2½　cups diced cooked chicken

⅔　cup bean sprouts

1　small yellow bell pepper, cut into matchstick strips

½　English cucumber (about 5 ounces), cut into matchstick strips

¼　cup lime juice

2½　tablespoons Asian fish sauce (nam pla or nuoc mam)*

2½　tablespoons light brown sugar

3　small serrano chiles, seeded and minced

¼　teaspoon grated nutmeg

2　teaspoons minced lemongrass* (optional)

2　teaspoons minced fresh ginger

2½　tablespoons minced fresh mint

2　tablespoons minced fresh basil

2½　tablespoons unsalted dry-roasted peanuts, chopped

*Available at Asian markets and some supermarkets

1.　In a large frying pan, heat the oil over moderately high heat until a strip of wonton added to the pan bounces across the surface of the oil. Add the wonton strips in batches and fry, stirring, until crisp and golden, about 1 minute. Transfer to paper towels to drain.

2.　In a large bowl, combine the salad greens, chicken, bean sprouts, bell pepper, and cucumber.

3.　In a medium bowl, whisk together the lime juice, fish sauce, brown sugar, chiles, nutmeg, lemongrass, if using, ginger, mint, and basil. Add this dressing to the salad and toss well. Gently fold in the wonton strips. Sprinkle with the peanuts.

—HUGH CARPENTER

LEMON CHICKEN SALAD WITH WILD RICE AND GRAPES

Easy to put together and hard to resist, this medley of juicy grapes, chewy wild rice, tender chicken, and crisp celery is perfect picnic fare. It's good warm or at room temperature.

WINE RECOMMENDATION
The grapes in the salad provide plenty of sweetness, so try a rich, dry riesling from Alsace. It will have the required zip to stand up to the tart lemon and a mineral undertow to echo the wild rice.

SERVES 4

½ cup wild rice

1½ cups warm water

2 cups Chicken Stock, page 61, or canned low-sodium chicken broth

½ teaspoon herbes de Provence, or a mixture of dried thyme, rosemary, marjoram, oregano, and savory

½ teaspoon salt

½ teaspoon fresh-ground black pepper

2½ tablespoons lemon juice

½ teaspoon Dijon mustard

1 tablespoon olive oil

1½ cups diced cooked chicken

½ rib celery, minced

¼ pound seedless red grapes, halved lengthwise

¼ pound seedless green grapes, halved lengthwise

Red leaf lettuce, for serving

1. In a medium bowl, soak the rice in the water for 1 hour. Drain, rinse well, and put in a heavy saucepan. Add the stock and bring to a boil over high heat, skimming occasionally.

2. Add the herbes de Provence, ¼ teaspoon of the salt, and ¼ teaspoon of the pepper. Reduce the heat, cover, and simmer for 25 minutes. Uncover and continue to cook until the rice is tender and the liquid has been absorbed, about 30 minutes longer. Add water if the stock evaporates before the rice is done. Put the rice in a medium bowl and let cool slightly.

3. In a small bowl, whisk together the lemon juice, mustard, and the remaining ¼ teaspoon salt and ¼ teaspoon pepper. Add the oil slowly, whisking. Add this dressing to the rice along with the chicken, celery, and grapes. Toss well to combine. Serve the salad warm or at room temperature, on a bed of red leaf lettuce.

—BOB CHAMBERS

CHICKEN SALAD
WITH SHRIMP AND FENNEL

Fennel, endive, and a light lemony dressing make this a refreshing salad for a hot summer day. To make life even easier, prepare the shrimp and the chicken a day ahead and refrigerate them until you're ready to put the salad together.

WINE RECOMMENDATION
Muscadet was once one of America's most popular imported wines, but it fell out of favor in the early '90s. Too bad—it's ideal with shellfish and other light foods. A good Muscadet de Sèvre-et-Maine *sur lie* will mesh deliciously with the fennel and shrimp here.

SERVES 4

¾ pound large shrimp, shelled and deveined, shells reserved

1½ cups water

1 pound boneless, skinless chicken breasts (about 3)

1 bulb fennel with fronds

3 tablespoons lemon juice

½ teaspoon salt

¼ teaspoon fresh-ground black pepper

¼ cup olive oil

2 large heads Belgian endive

1. Put the shrimp shells and the water in a saucepan and bring to a boil over high heat. Reduce the heat; simmer for 5 minutes. Strain the broth and return it to the pan.

2. Add the shrimp and cook over high heat just until opaque throughout, about 3 minutes. Drain, reserving the broth. Let the shrimp cool, and then cover and refrigerate until chilled.

3. Put the broth in a medium frying pan, add the chicken, and bring to a simmer over moderate heat. Cover and simmer until just cooked through, about 10 minutes. Remove the chicken and let cool. Cover the chicken and refrigerate until chilled.

4. Cut the fennel in half lengthwise and remove the core. Cut the bulb into thin slices. Chop the feathery fronds, reserving a few sprigs for garnish.

5. In a large bowl, whisk the lemon juice with the salt and pepper. Add the oil slowly, whisking. Add the shrimp, the fennel slices, and the chopped fennel tops and toss well.

6. Cut the chicken breasts into ¼-inch slices and toss them with the shrimp mixture. Place the endive spears around the edge of a platter, tips pointing out. Mound the salad on top and garnish with the reserved fennel sprigs.

—BOB CHAMBERS

Cashew Chicken Salad

Pureed cashews flavor the salad dressing, and chopped cashews add extra crunch.
If you prefer, sauté the chicken breasts whole and slice them just before serving.

WINE RECOMMENDATION
Tokay Pinot Gris from Alsace in France is among the beefiest of white wines, with deep nutty flavors and a dense, often unctuous, texture. Though the popular wisdom has it that Alsace wines are totally dry, they often have a bit of sweetness, which would be a virtue here.

SERVES 4

1⅔ pounds boneless, skinless chicken breasts (about 5), cut into ¼-inch slices

Salt and fresh-ground black pepper

1 tablespoon cooking oil, more if needed

⅔ cup dry white wine

⅓ pound smoked bacon

⅔ cup whole cashews, plus 1½ tablespoons chopped

2 cloves garlic, minced

2 tablespoons cider vinegar

1 teaspoon Dijon mustard

1 teaspoon anchovy paste

Pinch cayenne pepper

1 pound red cabbage, cut into thin slices (about 1 quart)

2 carrots, cut into 2-inch matchstick strips

1 small cucumber, peeled, halved, seeded, and cut into ¼-inch slices

1 hard-cooked egg, quartered

1. Sprinkle the chicken with salt and black pepper. In a large frying pan, heat the oil over high heat until it starts to smoke. Add the chicken and cook until browned, about 2 minutes. Turn and brown well on the other side, about 2 minutes longer. (If necessary, do this in two batches.) Transfer the chicken to a plate.

2. Add the wine to the pan and scrape up any browned bits from the bottom of the pan. Boil until the wine is reduced to ⅓ cup, about 1 minute. Stir in any accumulated juices from the chicken.

3. In a large frying pan, cook the bacon over moderate heat until crisp, about 7 minutes. Drain on paper towels. Break the bacon into small pieces.

4. Put the whole cashews, the garlic, vinegar, mustard, anchovy paste, and cayenne in a food processor; puree until smooth. Add the reduced wine, ⅛ teaspoon salt, and ⅛ teaspoon black pepper. Process until blended.

5. Put the cabbage on a platter. In a large bowl, toss the chicken, carrots, cucumber, and cashew dressing. Spoon the mixture over the cabbage and sprinkle with the bacon and chopped cashews. Place the egg quarters around the edge.

—Marcia Kiesel

POTATO AND CHICKEN SALAD
WITH SHREDDED ZUCCHINI

Make roast chicken and potatoes one night, and whip up this salad out of the leftovers the next. Or make good use of a bird you've simmered for making stock, and boil some potatoes to go with it (see box, below).

(see box, below)

WINE RECOMMENDATION
Chardonnay is a good choice for this informal salad. A bottle from California's Anderson Valley, whose wines have vibrant acidity and an herbal edge, would be perfect. Chablis (the real one, from France) is another excellent selection.

SERVES 4

  3 cups diced cooked red potatoes

1½ cups shredded cooked chicken

  2 small zucchini, shredded (about 2 cups)

  3 hard-cooked eggs, chopped coarse

  2 tablespoons minced fresh tarragon or parsley

  ½ teaspoon salt

 ⅛ teaspoon fresh-ground black pepper

    Scant ½ cup mayonnaise

  2 tablespoons Chicken Stock, page 61, or canned low-sodium chicken broth

1½ teaspoons white-wine vinegar

1. In a large bowl, toss together the cooked potatoes, cooked chicken, zucchini, hard-cooked eggs, minced tarragon or parsley, salt, and pepper.

2. In a small bowl, whisk together the mayonnaise, stock, and vinegar. Pour over the salad and toss well.

—ANNE DISRUDE

USING UNCOOKED POTATOES

If you don't have cooked potatoes to use in this recipe, it's easy to boil some. Cut one pound of red potatoes into half-inch dice and put them in a medium saucepan of salted water. Bring to a boil, reduce the heat, and simmer until tender, about fifteen minutes. Drain the potatoes and let cool before adding them to the salad.

CHICKEN SALAD WITH NEW POTATOES AND DILL

The chicken makes the broth, the broth cooks the potatoes, and the potatoes are tossed into a salad with chunks of the chicken and a zingy dill dressing.

WINE RECOMMENDATION
An interesting choice for this surprisingly rich salad would be a white Bordeaux, whose herbal sauvignon blanc will echo the dill and whose opulent sémillon contributes a hint of aromatic mustard seed. For this dish, avoid a heavily oaked version.

SERVES 4

½   chicken (about 1½ pounds)
1   carrot, chopped
1   rib celery, chopped
1   large onion, chopped
1   small bay leaf
5   peppercorns
2   cloves
2   cups Chicken Stock, page 61, or canned low-sodium chicken broth
1   pound small new potatoes
1   tablespoon grainy mustard
1½   teaspoons Dijon mustard
1½   tablespoons lemon juice
1   tablespoon red-wine vinegar
2   tablespoons heavy cream
½   teaspoon salt
¼   teaspoon fresh-ground black pepper
1   tablespoon chopped fresh dill
¼   cup extra-virgin olive oil

1. Put the chicken, skin-side up, in a large pot. Add the carrot, celery, onion, bay leaf, peppercorns, cloves, and stock. Add water to cover and bring to a boil. Reduce the heat and simmer for 25 minutes. Turn the chicken over and simmer for 20 minutes longer. Let the chicken cool to room temperature in the liquid, and then refrigerate until the fat solidifies on the surface of the broth, about 5 hours, or overnight.

2. Scrape the fat from the broth and remove the chicken. Bring the broth to a boil. Strain, pressing the vegetables firmly to get as much liquid as possible. Return the broth to the pan, add the potatoes, and bring to a boil. Reduce the heat and simmer until the potatoes are tender, 15 to 20 minutes. Drain (save the broth if you like) and let cool slightly.

3. Meanwhile, in a small bowl, whisk together both mustards, the lemon juice, vinegar, cream, salt, pepper, and dill. Add the oil slowly, whisking.

4. Discard the chicken skin and cut the meat into 1-inch chunks. Cut the potatoes into 1-inch chunks. In a large bowl, toss the chicken with the warm potatoes and the mustard dressing. Serve at room temperature.

—BOB CHAMBERS

CHICKEN SALAD WITH ONIONS AND POTATO CRISPS

Though it has just three major ingredients—sweet browned onions, roasted potato slices, and diced chicken—this salad is a feast of tastes and textures.

WINE RECOMMENDATION
Coteaux du Layon, from the Loire Valley, is often served as a dessert wine, but it's just moderately sweet. Its nuances of caramel and quince will match the onions well.

SERVES 4

- 1 pound small red potatoes, cut into ⅛-inch slices
- 7 tablespoons olive oil
- 1 teaspoon salt
- ½ teaspoon fresh-ground black pepper
- 1 pound Spanish onions, halved lengthwise and cut into ¼-inch slices
- 1 clove garlic, crushed
- 1 tablespoon Dijon mustard
- 1½ teaspoons grainy mustard
- 2½ tablespoons lemon juice
- 3 tablespoons chopped flat-leaf parsley
- 1 teaspoon minced fresh rosemary
- 3 cups diced cooked chicken
- 1 bunch watercress (about 5 ounces), tough stems removed
- 1 tomato, quartered

1. Heat the oven to 450°. Toss the potatoes with 1½ tablespoons of the oil and ¼ teaspoon each of the salt and pepper.

2. Spray two baking sheets with vegetable-oil cooking spray. Put the potatoes in a single layer on the baking sheets. Roast until the potatoes are nicely browned and crisp, 15 to 17 minutes. Put the potatoes on paper towels to drain.

3. Heat another 1½ tablespoons of the oil in a saucepan over moderate heat. Add the onions and ¼ teaspoon of the salt, cover, and cook, stirring occasionally, until translucent, about 10 minutes. Uncover, raise the heat to moderately high, and cook, stirring frequently, until well browned, about 10 minutes. Add the garlic; cook 2 minutes longer.

4. In a bowl, combine both mustards, the lemon juice, parsley, rosemary, and the remaining ½ teaspoon salt and ¼ teaspoon pepper. Add the remaining 4 tablespoons oil slowly, whisking. Set aside 2 tablespoons of this dressing; add the rest to the onions. Stir well, scraping up any browned bits from the bottom of the pan. Put the onions in a bowl, add the chicken and potatoes, and toss well.

5. In a bowl, toss the watercress with the reserved dressing. Put the watercress on a platter, mound the salad on top, and garnish with the tomato wedges.

—BOB CHAMBERS

85

Broiled Chicken Salad with Cellophane Noodles

The marinade—a mixture of cilantro, soy sauce, and fish sauce—gives this first-course salad its special flavor. Try the same marinade with thin slices of pork for an unusual and delicious barbecue.

■ **WINE RECOMMENDATION**
The traditional Asian combination of salty and piquant calls for the mediating influence of a fruity, high-acid riesling. Instead of looking to the more traditional regions of Alsace and Germany, seek out a taut, off-dry example from New York's up-and-coming Finger Lakes region.

SERVES 4

2½ ounces cellophane noodles (bean threads)

3 cloves garlic, chopped

1¼ teaspoons peppercorns

3 tablespoons chopped cilantro

3½ tablespoons soy sauce

1 tablespoon plus ½ teaspoon Asian fish sauce (nam pla or nuoc mam)*

⅔ pound boneless, skinless chicken breasts (about 2), cut into 1-inch cubes

2½ cups Chicken Stock, page 61, or canned low-sodium chicken broth

2 tablespoons lime juice

1 teaspoon sugar

Leaf lettuce, for serving

3 tomatoes, cut into wedges

2 scallions including green tops, chopped

½ English cucumber, cut into 1-inch dice

1 tablespoon chopped roasted peanuts

½ lime, cut into thin slices

*Available at Asian markets and some supermarkets

1. Break the noodles into short pieces. Put them in a bowl, add hot water to cover, and let soak until softened, about 30 minutes.

2. In a blender or food processor, blend the garlic, peppercorns, and 1½ tablespoons of the cilantro to a paste. Add 2½ tablespoons of the soy sauce and 1 tablespoon of the fish sauce. Pour into a shallow bowl and add the chicken. Toss well and marinate for 30 minutes at room temperature.

3. Heat the broiler. Bring the stock to a boil in a medium saucepan. Drain the noodles and add them to the stock. Boil until just done, about 5 minutes. Drain well.

4. Put the chicken in a single layer on a baking sheet. Broil, stirring occasionally, until browned and just cooked through, about 5 minutes.

5. In a small bowl, stir together the lime juice, the sugar, the remaining 1 tablespoon

soy sauce, and the remaining ½ teaspoon fish sauce.

6. Line a platter with lettuce leaves. Put the noodles on the lettuce and top with the tomatoes, scallions, and cucumber. Put the chicken on top and pour the dressing over it. Sprinkle the remaining 1½ tablespoons cilantro and the peanuts on top, and garnish with the lime.

—JEFFREY ALFORD

CELLOPHANE NOODLES

These clear Asian noodles are made from threads of mung-bean starch; they are also called bean threads or Chinese vermicelli. When fried, they puff up and become crisp. When soaked and boiled, as in this recipe, they become soft, but still add an interesting texture to the finished dish.

FISH SAUCE

Made from fermented fish, this pungent condiment is a mainstay of many Asian cuisines. The names may vary—*nam pla* in Thailand, *nuoc mam* in Vietnam, *patis* in the Philippines, *petis* in Indonesia, *tuk trey* in Cambodia, and *ngan-pya-ye* in Myanmar—but the sauces are virtually the same, and may be used interchangeably.

MINTED CHICKEN AND
RAW-ARTICHOKE SALAD IN PITAS

It's not unusual to find artichokes in a salad, but uncooked artichoke leaves are a bit of a surprise. Far from being unpalatable, they contribute a special flavor and texture to this cross between a salad and a sandwich. The secret is cutting the artichoke into very, very thin slices.

WINE RECOMMENDATION
Try a fino or manzanilla sherry here. Both are bone-dry and lean, with yeasty, floral aromas and a salty sea-breeze tang. Serve the sherry chilled with the pitas for a perfect summer medley of flavors and textures.

SERVES 4

¼ cup lemon juice

⅓ cup minced fresh mint

½ teaspoon salt

½ teaspoon fresh-ground black pepper

¼ cup extra-virgin olive oil

1 large artichoke

3 cups 1-inch chunks cooked chicken

⅓ cup fine-chopped or coarse-grated Parmesan cheese

½ cup mayonnaise

4 pitas

1. In a large bowl, whisk together the lemon juice, mint, salt, and pepper. Add the oil slowly, whisking.

2. Using a sharp knife, remove the tough outer leaves from the artichoke. Peel the stem. Cut the artichoke into quarters. Using a teaspoon, remove the purple inner leaves and the hairy choke. Using a very sharp stainless-steel knife, cut the artichoke quarters crosswise into thin slices. (Alternatively, slice the artichoke quarters in a food processor fitted with a slicing disk, putting them into the feed tube stem-end down.)

3. Toss the artichoke slices with the mint dressing. Add the chicken and Parmesan and mix well. Stir in the mayonnaise and blend thoroughly.

4. Cut a 1-inch slice from the top of each pita and stuff the pockets with the salad.

—MOLLY O'NEILL

chapter *4*

RICE & PASTA

Panfried Noodles with Chicken and Chinese Vegetables, page 109

ARROZ CON POLLO WITH SHRIMP AND ARTICHOKE

Rice with chicken is a traditional Spanish dish, but we've thrown in a few not-so-traditional extras—spicy sausage, whole shrimp, peas, fresh artichoke—for a one-dish meal that's even heartier than the original.

WINE RECOMMENDATION
A Rías Baixas from Galicia in northern Spain is a good match for this Spanish classic. Made from the albariño grape, it has sharp acidity to refresh the palate and enough weight and richness to partner the dish well.

SERVES 4

2   teaspoons lemon juice

1   large artichoke

4   chicken thighs
    Salt and fresh-ground black pepper

1   tablespoon plus 1 teaspoon olive oil

1   onion, chopped

½   pound chorizo or hot Italian sausage, cut into 1-inch pieces

1   clove garlic, minced

1⅓ cups canned tomatoes with their juice

¾   cup beer

½   cup Chicken Stock, page 61, or canned low-sodium chicken broth

1   bay leaf

½   teaspoon dried oregano
    Generous pinch saffron
    Generous pinch dried red-pepper flakes

1   cup rice

½   pound medium shrimp, shelled

⅔   cup frozen peas, thawed

1   roasted red pepper, cut into strips, (see "Roasting Red Peppers," next page), for serving

1. Fill a bowl with cold water and add 1 teaspoon of the lemon juice. Cut the stem and the top two-thirds of the leaves off the artichoke; remove the tough outer leaves. Drop the artichoke into the lemon water.

2. Bring a large saucepan of salted water to a boil. Add the artichoke and the remaining 1 teaspoon lemon juice and cook until tender, 15 to 20 minutes. Drain and rinse with cold water. Scrape out the choke and then cut the artichoke into eight to twelve wedges.

3. Heat the oven to 350°. Season the chicken thighs with salt and pepper. Heat 1 tablespoon of the oil in a Dutch oven over moderately high heat. Add the chicken thighs, skin-side down, in a single layer, and brown on both sides, 6 to 10 minutes in all. Transfer the thighs to a plate.

4. Pour off all but 1 tablespoon of the fat from the Dutch oven. Add the onion; cook over moderate heat, stirring occasionally,

until softened and beginning to brown, about 10 minutes.

5. Meanwhile, heat the remaining 1 teaspoon oil in a large frying pan over moderate heat. Add the chorizo and cook, turning occasionally, until lightly browned, about 5 minutes.

6. Add the garlic to the Dutch oven and cook, stirring, until fragrant, about 1 minute. Add the tomatoes with their juice, the beer, stock, bay leaf, oregano, saffron, red-pepper flakes, $\frac{1}{2}$ teaspoon salt, and black pepper to taste. Bring to a boil over high heat. Stir in the rice.

7. Using a slotted spoon, transfer the chorizo from the frying pan to the Dutch oven. Add the chicken and any accumulated juices. Cover the Dutch oven tightly and bake until the rice has absorbed most of the liquid, about 25 minutes.

8. Add the shrimp to the Dutch oven, burying them in the rice. Bake for 5 minutes. Add the peas and the artichoke wedges and bake until the shrimp are pink, 5 to 10 minutes. Garnish with the roasted red pepper.

—SUSAN WYLER

ROASTING RED PEPPERS

You can roast red bell peppers over a gas flame or grill or broil them four inches from the heat, turning with tongs until the peppers are charred all over, about ten minutes. When the peppers are cool enough to handle, pull off the skins and remove the stems, seeds, and ribs.

TIME-SAVING TIP

You can use canned artichoke hearts in place of the fresh artichoke and skip steps 1 and 2 altogether. Use about a third of a cup, and cut each piece in half. An equivalent amount of frozen artichoke hearts is another option; cook them according to package directions and then cut them in half before adding to the dish in step 8.

ASOPAO DE POLLO

From the island of Puerto Rico comes this sublime stew that's a country cousin to Spain's paella. There's no shellfish here, though, just chicken, ham, and bacon, with some fresh vegetables thrown in for good measure.

 WINE RECOMMENDATION
With its smoky, salty ham and bacon and piquant olives and capers, this dish dares a wine like a bully in a schoolyard. To meet the challenge, send in a rugged but fragrant Côte Rôtie from the northern Rhône. It's got power to spare, yet has some of the most complex aromas and flavors you will find anywhere in the world of wine.

SERVES 4

¾ teaspoon dried oregano

1 small clove garlic, minced

Salt

2 pounds chicken parts

1 strip thick-sliced bacon

1 ounce smoked ham, chopped coarse

1 tomato, chopped

½ onion, chopped

½ green bell pepper, chopped

4¼ cups water

3 tablespoons diced pimiento-stuffed olives

2 teaspoons capers

1⅓ cups medium-grain rice, such as Valencia

¾ cup fresh or frozen peas

3½ pimientos, cut into thin slices

⅓ cup grated Parmesan cheese

1. Combine the oregano, garlic, and ¼ teaspoon salt in a small bowl. Rub the seasonings all over the chicken parts.

2. In a large Dutch oven, cook the bacon over moderately low heat until it has rendered its fat; remove the bacon and reserve for another use. Increase the heat to moderately high, add the chicken, and brown well on both sides, about 8 minutes in all. Add the ham, tomato, onion, and bell pepper. Cover and simmer over low heat until the chicken is just cooked through, about 25 minutes. Let cool.

3. Remove the chicken meat from the bones and discard the skin and bones. Return the meat to the pot and add the water, olives, and capers. Bring to a simmer and cook for 5 minutes. Stir in the rice and 1 teaspoon salt and simmer until the rice is tender, about 15 minutes.

4. Meanwhile cook the peas in a small saucepan of boiling, salted water until tender, about 4 minutes for fresh, 1 minute for frozen.

5. Season the stew with salt. Top with the peas and pimientos, sprinkle with the Parmesan, and serve immediately.

—JESSICA B. HARRIS

CURRIED CHICKEN AND RICE

Sautéed chicken and delicate basmati rice simmer together in this spicy pilaf. Chutney and *raita* (the Indian yogurt and cucumber salad) would be excellent condiments to serve alongside.

WINE RECOMMENDATION
Today's spicier cuisines often demand sweeter wines. This aromatic dish, with its crushed pepper, is a case in point—the heat will turn a dry wine bitter. Opt instead for a Vouvray demi-sec; the lovely floral aromas will complement the spice.

SERVES 4

2   tablespoons cooking oil

1   chicken (3 to 3½ pounds), cut into 8 pieces

    Salt and fresh-ground black pepper

1   onion, chopped

1½ cups basmati or Texmati rice

3   tablespoons curry powder

1   teaspoon dried dill

1   teaspoon ground cumin

½ to ¾ teaspoon dried red-pepper flakes

2½ cups Chicken Stock, page 61, or canned low-sodium chicken broth

2   tablespoons fine-chopped cilantro

1. Heat the oven to 375°. Heat the oil in a large ovenproof frying pan over moderately high heat. Season the chicken with salt and pepper. Add the chicken, skin-side down, to the pan and brown well on both sides, about 8 minutes in all. Remove the chicken.

2. Pour off all but 2 tablespoons of the fat from the pan. Add the onion, reduce the heat to moderate, and cook until barely soft, about 3 minutes. Stir in the rice, curry powder, dill, cumin, red-pepper flakes, and 1 teaspoon salt.

3. Return the chicken to the pan and add the stock. Cover and bake for 20 minutes. Transfer the chicken breasts and wings to a plate, cover, and leave to rest in a warm spot. Cover the pan again and bake until the rice is tender, about 20 minutes longer. Spoon the rice onto a platter, put the chicken on top, and sprinkle with the cilantro.

—MICHAEL ROBERTS

CHICKEN WITH RICE AND OLIVES

Green olives, red pimientos, and a cup and a half of beer add a special tang to this easy chicken-and-rice meal. It's colorful, casual, and packed with flavor.

WINE RECOMMENDATION
Red wines of the Northern Rhône are made from the syrah grape; its suggestions of smoke and green olives will meld beautifully with the smoked ham and olives here. These wines can be very powerful, though, so avoid the big Hermitages or Côte Rôties in favor of a more modest Crozes-Hermitage or St-Joseph.

SERVES 4

3 tablespoons olive oil

3 cloves garlic, lightly crushed

1 chicken (3 to 3½ pounds), cut into 8 pieces

½ pound smoked ham, cut into ¼-inch dice

2 onions, chopped

½ green bell pepper, chopped

1½ cups rice

1¾ cups canned tomatoes (one 14-ounce can), drained and chopped

1½ cups Chicken Stock, page 61, or canned low-sodium chicken broth

1½ cups beer

½ cup pitted green olives, chopped

¼ cup chopped pimientos

1 teaspoon salt

½ teaspoon fresh-ground black pepper

1. Heat the oven to 375°. Heat the oil with the garlic in a large frying pan over moderate heat. Add the chicken and brown well on both sides, about 10 minutes in all. Transfer the chicken and the garlic to a Dutch oven.

2. Add the ham, onions, and bell pepper to the frying pan. Cook, stirring occasionally, until the vegetables are softened, 5 to 7 minutes. Transfer the vegetables and the ham to the Dutch oven.

3. Add the rice to the frying pan and cook, stirring constantly, until translucent, 2 to 3 minutes. Add the rice to the Dutch oven along with the tomatoes, stock, beer, olives, pimientos, salt, and pepper; stir to combine. Bring to a boil over moderate heat. Stir once, cover, and bake until the rice and chicken are tender, about 25 minutes.

—MARY LYNN MONDICH

CHICKEN OMELET DOMBURI

In Japanese this rice dish is called *oyako domburi*. The first word means mother and child, a culinary joke celebrating that famous question, "Which came first, the chicken or the egg?" Here the chicken comes first, simmered with bamboo shoots in a smoky amber broth. Then comes the egg, poached in the broth with green beans. They're served together over steaming rice.

 WINE RECOMMENDATION Chardonnay can work well with eggs, and a fruity, lightly oaked California version is just the ticket here. Usually the taste of charred oak runs roughshod over food, but with this dish it's a plus. It highlights the bamboo shoots and echoes the smokiness of the soy sauce.

SERVES 4

2 cups short-grain rice

2⅓ cups cold water

1⅔ cups drained canned bamboo shoots (one 15-ounce can)

1½ cups Chicken Stock, page 61, or canned low-sodium chicken broth

3 tablespoons soy sauce

2 tablespoons sugar

1 tablespoon sake or dry white wine

⅔ pound boneless, skinless chicken breasts (about 2)

4 eggs, beaten with a pinch of salt

2 ounces green beans, cut into diagonal 1-inch lengths

1 5-inch square nori,* cut into ⅛-inch strips (optional)

*Available at Asian markets

1. Rinse the rice in a strainer under cold water until the water runs clear. Drain well, then put the rice in a deep 3-quart saucepan with a tight-fitting lid. Add the 2⅓ cups water, cover, and soak for 10 minutes.

2. Set the saucepan over high heat and bring the water to a boil. Reduce the heat and simmer until the rice has absorbed all the water, about 6 minutes. Keep the pan tightly covered while cooking and steaming; if you must check the rice, do so quickly to lose as little steam as possible. Increase the heat to high and cook, still covered, for 20 seconds. Remove the pan from the heat and let steam, covered, for 15 minutes.

3. Meanwhile, cut the bamboo shoots into lengthwise strips. Rinse well and remove any white deposits on the rippled edges (these are harmless but unpleasantly gritty). Drain and pat dry.

4. In a large frying pan, bring the stock, soy sauce, sugar, and sake to a simmer over low heat, stirring to dissolve the sugar. Add the bamboo shoots and simmer for 5 minutes.

5. Meanwhile, cut the chicken breasts into ½-inch diagonal slices. Cut the slices

into 1-inch pieces. Add the chicken to the frying pan, cover, and raise the heat to moderate. Cook until the chicken is just done, about 4 minutes.

6. Pour the eggs into the pan and reduce the heat to moderately low. Scatter the beans on top, cover, and cook for 2 minutes. Remove from the heat and let steam, tightly covered, for 1 to 3 minutes, according to desired firmness. Cut the omelet into four wedges.

7. Divide the rice among four bowls. Top each serving with a wedge of omelet and a small mound of nori strips, if using.

—ELIZABETH ANDOH

NORI

Nori is seaweed—dried, processed, and pressed into paper-thin sheets. Usually it's used to wrap other foods, such as sushi, but it can also be sliced thin, as it is here, and used as a garnish. It gives a distinctly Japanese touch to the finished omelet.

ORANGE CILANTRO CHICKEN WITH RICE

Most supermarkets now sell broiled chickens in their deli section. That makes this flavorsome Asian dish particularly well suited to last-minute entertaining—pick up a chicken, toss it with the seasonings, and serve it atop ginger-spiced rice as a homemade masterpiece. If you have it on hand, you can use leftover roast pork instead of chicken.

WINE RECOMMENDATION
A riesling from Alsace makes a fine match here; the fruity acidity foils the saltiness and the citrus flavors complement the lemon juice and orange zest. Since a lighter wine might be overpowered, try a weighty grand cru or *vendange tardive*.

SERVES 4

¼ cup lemon juice

2 tablespoons tamari or soy sauce

1¼ teaspoons grated fresh ginger

Dash hot-pepper sauce

2 small broiled chickens, cut into serving pieces

2 tablespoons olive oil

1 small onion, cut into thin slices

1 clove garlic, minced

½ pound mushrooms, cut into thin slices

¼ teaspoon ground ginger

¼ teaspoon salt

Pinch fresh-ground black pepper

1⅓ cups rice

1⅓ cups Chicken Stock, page 61, or canned low-sodium chicken broth

⅔ cup dry white wine

⅓ cup water

⅓ cup minced cilantro

2 teaspoons grated orange zest

1. Put the lemon juice, tamari, grated ginger, and hot-pepper sauce in a large bowl. Add the chicken and turn to coat.

2. Heat the oven to 375°. Heat the oil in a large Dutch oven over moderate heat. Add the onion and garlic and cook until softened, about 5 minutes. Add the mushrooms; cook, stirring, until softened, about 5 minutes. Stir in the ground ginger, salt, and pepper.

3. Add the rice and raise the heat to moderately high. Cook, stirring constantly, until the rice is translucent, about 3 minutes. Stir in the stock, wine, and water. Bring to a boil, cover, and bake for 10 minutes. Uncover and put the chicken with any remaining marinade on top of the rice. Sprinkle with the cilantro and zest. Cover and bake until the chicken is heated through and the rice is tender, about 10 minutes.

—W. PETER PRESTCOTT

103

CHICKEN LASAGNE

Lasagne is a favorite party dish, especially for buffets. This version mixes chicken and chicken livers with fresh tomatoes. The fact that you can bake it a day ahead makes your entertaining that much easier.

WINE RECOMMENDATION
This intensely flavored dish requires a wine of substance. Go for a Brunello di Montalcino, Chianti's brawnier cousin. Brunellos are made from a special type of sangiovese grape and have rich dried-cherry and earth flavors. Look for one with a few years of age.

SERVES 12

- 10 tablespoons butter
- 4 tablespoons olive oil
- 3 onions, minced
- 2 small cloves garlic, minced
- ½ cup plus 2 tablespoons flour
- 2½ cups milk
- 2½ cups Chicken Stock, page 61, or canned low-sodium chicken broth
- 1 tablespoon fresh tarragon, or 1 teaspoon dried tarragon
- 1½ teaspoons salt
- ½ teaspoon white pepper
- ½ teaspoon grated nutmeg
- 4 large eggs
- 3 pounds tomatoes, peeled, seeded, and chopped (about 6)
- 2 tablespoons tomato paste
- ½ cup dry red wine
- 1 tablespoon dried basil
- ½ teaspoon sugar
- ½ teaspoon red-wine vinegar
- 2 pounds boneless, skinless chicken breasts (about 6)
- 1½ pounds chicken livers, separated into lobes
- 1 tablespoon fresh oregano, or 1 teaspoon dried oregano
- 1 pound lasagne noodles
- 2 cups grated Parmesan cheese

1. In a large saucepan, melt 5 tablespoons of the butter with 1 tablespoon of the oil over moderate heat. Add the onions and garlic and cook, stirring occasionally, until the onions are translucent, about 5 minutes.

2. Stir in the flour. Reduce the heat to low and cook, stirring, for 3 minutes. Remove from the heat and slowly whisk in the milk and stock. Bring to a boil over moderate heat and cook, stirring, for 5 minutes. Add the tarragon, 1 teaspoon of the salt, the pepper, and the nutmeg. Remove from the heat and briskly whisk in the eggs one at a time. Cover partially and set the béchamel sauce aside.

3. In a large stainless-steel frying pan, combine the tomatoes, tomato paste, wine, basil, sugar, vinegar, and the remaining ½

teaspoon salt. Cook, stirring frequently, over moderate heat until thick, about 15 minutes. Set the tomato sauce aside.

4. In another large frying pan, melt the remaining 5 tablespoons butter with 1 tablespoon of the oil over moderate heat. Add the chicken, cover, and cook for 5 minutes. Turn the chicken and cook for 5 minutes longer. Remove the chicken from the pan, let cool, and cut into ½-inch slices.

5. Add the chicken livers to the frying pan and cook over moderately high heat, tossing, until browned on all sides, 3 to 4 minutes. Add the oregano and let cool slightly. Mince the livers.

6. Bring a large pot of water to a boil and add the remaining 2 tablespoons oil. Cook the lasagne noodles until almost tender but slightly underdone, about 10 minutes. Drain and return the noodles to the pot. Add warm water to cover.

7. Heat the oven to 375°. Butter a 9-by-13-inch baking dish. Removing the noodles one at a time from the water, arrange a single layer in the dish. Cover with about 1¼ cups of the béchamel sauce. Top with half of the sliced chicken and then with ⅓ cup of the Parmesan. Add another layer of noodles, all of the tomato sauce, and ⅓ cup of the Parmesan. Add another layer of noodles. Spread the chicken livers over them and cover with 1¼ cups of the béchamel. Add the remaining chicken and ⅓ cup Parmesan. Top with a final layer of noodles,

the remaining béchamel, and the remaining 1 cup Parmesan.

8. Bake the lasagne until the top is golden brown and somewhat crusty, 45 minutes to 1 hour. Let stand for 15 minutes before cutting into squares.

—W. PETER PRESTCOTT

MAKE IT AHEAD

You can assemble the lasagne early in the day. Cover and refrigerate; let return to room temperature before baking. Or, bake the lasagne a day ahead, let it cool completely, and then cover and refrigerate. Bring to room temperature and reheat in a preheated 300° oven for thirty minutes. Let stand for fifteen minutes before serving.

TOMATO RAVIOLI WITH CHICKEN FILLING

Treat your guests to handmade ravioli. Serve the pasta with a red tomato sauce or a white béchamel sauce—or make both sauces and let your guests decide.

WINE RECOMMENDATION
The wine you drink will depend on the sauce you choose. With the béchamel, opt for a Tuscan chardonnay; with the tomato, a Valpolicella Classico.

SERVES 6

2 tablespoons plus 2 teaspoons olive oil

⅔ pound boneless, skinless chicken breasts (about 2)

1¼ pounds mild Italian sausage, casings removed

2 cloves garlic, minced

¼ cup heavy cream

Salt and fresh-ground black pepper

2½ cups all-purpose flour or bread flour, more if needed

5 tablespoons tomato paste

2 large eggs

1 egg yolk

Ravioli sauces, next page

1. In a medium frying pan, heat the 2 tablespoons oil over moderate heat. Add the chicken and cook until browned, about 5 minutes. Turn and cook until just done, about 4 minutes longer. Remove the chicken from pan and let cool.

2. Add the sausage to the pan. Cook, stirring to break up the meat, for 4 minutes.

Add the garlic and cook until there is no trace of pink in the meat, 2 to 3 minutes longer. Remove the sausage mixture with a slotted spoon and let cool.

3. Cut the chicken into chunks. Put the chicken, sausage, and cream in a food processor. Process until well blended. Season with salt and pepper.

4. Put the flour in a medium bowl and make an indentation in the center. Add the tomato paste, eggs, egg yolk, the remaining 2 teaspoons oil, and a pinch of salt. Using your fingers or a fork, mix the ingredients in the center of the flour. Gradually work in the flour until the dough pulls away from the side of the bowl. The dough should be slightly sticky. If it is too dry, add up to 2 tablespoons water, 1 teaspoon at a time. If it is too wet, add more flour, 1 tablespoon at a time. Transfer the dough to a lightly floured surface and knead until smooth, about 10 minutes.

5. Set the rollers of a pasta machine on the widest notch. Divide the dough into six pieces. Working with one piece of dough at a time, flatten it with your hands and pass it through the rollers of the pasta machine two or three times, until smooth and no longer sticky. Continue to pass the piece of dough through the machine, reducing the

setting by one notch each time, until the rollers are on the thinnest setting.

6. Cut the dough crosswise in half. Put one strip on a work surface. Spoon or pipe 1½-teaspoon mounds of the filling onto the dough, about ½ inch from the edges and 1½ inches apart. Brush the exposed areas of dough lightly with water. Put the second strip of dough on top; press firmly around each mound of filling, getting rid of the air and sealing the edges. Cut the ravioli apart with a sharp knife, a pastry wheel, or a ravioli stamp. Repeat with the remaining dough and filling.

7. In a large pot of boiling, salted water, cook the ravioli, in batches, until just done, about 7 minutes. Drain. Serve with one or a choice of sauces.

—JOHN ROBERT MASSIE

RAVIOLI SAUCES

EACH MAKES ABOUT 1½ CUPS

BÉCHAMEL SAUCE WITH PARMESAN

2 cups milk

Bouquet garni: 5 sprigs parsley, ¼ teaspoon dried thyme, and ½ bay leaf

2 tablespoons butter

3 tablespoons flour

½ teaspoon salt

Pinch of white pepper

Pinch grated nutmeg

½ cup grated Parmesan cheese

1. In a medium saucepan, bring the milk with the bouquet garni to a boil.

2. Meanwhile, in another medium saucepan, melt the butter over moderate heat. Add the flour and cook, whisking, for 1 to 2 minutes without browning. Whisk in the milk; discard the bouquet garni. Bring to a boil, whisking. Reduce the heat and simmer, stirring occasionally, 3 to 4 minutes. Season with the salt, pepper, and nutmeg. Stir in the Parmesan.

CREAMY TOMATO SAUCE

3½ cups canned tomatoes (one 35-ounce can), drained

Bouquet garni: 5 sprigs parsley, ½ teaspoon dried thyme, and 5 peppercorns,

¾ cup heavy cream

Salt and fresh-ground black pepper

1. Puree the tomatoes in a blender or food processor until smooth. Put the puree and the bouquet garni in a large frying pan. Bring to a boil over moderate heat; cook until slightly reduced, about 5 minutes.

2. Stir in the cream. Discard the bouquet garni. Season with salt and pepper.

PANFRIED NOODLES WITH CHICKEN AND CHINESE VEGETABLES

Originally from Shanghai, this traditional dish is often referred to as double-fried noodles. Though it's best with fresh water chestnuts, canned ones will do fine. If this is the only dish you're serving, you may want to double the quantities.

 WINE RECOMMENDATION
The panfried noodles have distinct nutty nuances from the sesame oil. Add salty, savory soy and spices, and you have a dish that's just right for a dry amontillado sherry. The wine's nuttiness is a good flavor match and its low acidity makes it pair well with the saltiness.

SERVES 4

- ½ pound fresh fine Chinese egg noodles* or fresh or dried capellini (angel hair)
- 2 teaspoons Asian sesame oil
- 1¾ teaspoons sugar
- 1½ teaspoons white vinegar
- 1½ teaspoons dry white wine
- ¾ teaspoon cornstarch
- 2½ teaspoons soy sauce
- ½ teaspoon salt
- ¼ teaspoon white pepper
- ⅓ pound boneless, skinless chicken breast (about 1), cut into thin strips
- ⅔ cup Chicken Stock, page 61, or canned low-sodium chicken broth
- 6 to 7 tablespoons peanut oil
- 1 teaspoon grated fresh ginger
- 1 clove garlic, minced

- ½ cup snow peas cut into thin diagonal strips (about 1¼ ounces)
- 3 water chestnuts, preferably fresh,* cut into thin slices
- ¼ cup bamboo shoots cut lengthwise into thin slices
- 2 scallions including green tops, white part quartered lengthwise, greens cut into ½-inch lengths

*Available at Asian markets and some supermarkets

1. Cook the noodles in a large pot of boiling, salted water until tender but still firm, about 15 seconds for fresh, 2 minutes for dried. Run cold water into the pot and drain the noodles. Return the noodles to the pot, add cold water, and drain again. Let drain, turning and separating them occasionally, until they are quite dry, about 30 minutes. Dry the noodles completely on paper towels.

2. In a medium bowl, combine 1 teaspoon of the sesame oil, ¾ teaspoon of the sugar, ½ teaspoon of the vinegar, 1 teaspoon of the wine, ¼ teaspoon of the cornstarch, ½ teaspoon of the soy sauce, the salt, and ⅛ teaspoon of the white pepper. Add the

strips of chicken breast, toss, and marinate for 30 minutes.

3. In a small bowl, combine the remaining 1 teaspoon sesame oil, 1 teaspoon sugar, 1 teaspoon vinegar, 1/2 teaspoon wine, 1/2 teaspoon cornstarch, 2 teaspoons soy sauce, 1/8 teaspoon white pepper, and the stock. Set this sauce aside.

4. Heat 4 tablespoons of peanut oil in a medium heavy frying pan over high heat. When a wisp of smoke appears, place the noodles in an even layer covering the bottom of the pan. Cook until the noodles are evenly browned and crisp on the bottom, about 4 minutes.

5. Slide the noodle cake onto a plate, invert, and slide back into the pan. Cook, adding another 1 tablespoon oil if needed, until the noodles are browned on the second side, about 2 minutes. Put on a plate and cover loosely.

6. Heat a wok or large frying pan over high heat for 30 seconds. Add 2 tablespoons of peanut oil and swirl to coat the pan. Add the ginger and garlic. Cook, stirring, until the garlic begins to brown, about 45 seconds. Add the chicken in a single layer and the marinade and cook for 2 minutes. Turn the chicken.

7. Add the snow peas, water chestnuts, bamboo shoots, and scallions. Cook, stirring occasionally, until the vegetables soften slightly, about 3 minutes. Make a well in the center and pour in the sauce. Cook until the sauce thickens, about 1 minute. Stir the mixture and spoon it over the noodle cake. Cut into wedges.

—Eileen Yin-Fei Lo

MALAYSIAN COCONUT-CHICKEN CURRY WITH TWO NOODLES

The Indian influence on Malay cooking is evident in the way this dish is served: Diners adorn the noodle curry to their taste with condiments served on the side. Refrigerate the can of coconut milk for at least four hours before using, and don't shake it—you want to be able to pour off the thick milk from the top.

 WINE RECOMMENDATION
Gewürztraminer is the usual choice for Asian or curried dishes, but riesling can be the better performer. Try an off-dry spätlese riesling from Germany's Pfalz or Rheingau.

SERVES 4

1 cup Chicken Stock, page 61, or canned low-sodium chicken broth

4 dried or 3 fresh kaffir lime leaves*

3 ¼-inch slices fresh galangal, or 5 slices dried (kha or laos)*

1 tablespoon seedless tamarind pulp*

¼ cup water

1 teaspoon coriander seeds

4 dried red Asian chiles*

1 tablespoon plus 1 teaspoon dried shrimp*

⅛ teaspoon white or black peppercorns

½ teaspoon ground turmeric

2 stalks lemongrass*

2 small cloves garlic

2 small red or green serrano chiles

⅔ cup minced shallots (about 6)

2½ tablespoons peanut or other cooking oil

1 13½-ounce can unsweetened coconut milk,* chilled

2½ teaspoons Asian fish sauce (nam pla or nuoc mam)*

½ teaspoon sugar

3 chicken thighs

⅔ pound boneless, skinless chicken breasts (about 2)

Salt

2 ounces cellophane noodles (bean threads)

1 pound fresh flat Chinese egg noodles*

2 teaspoons lime juice, plus 1 lime, cut into wedges, for serving

Cayenne pepper or hot-pepper sauce (optional)

1½ tablespoons cilantro leaves, plus cilantro sprigs for serving

Fresh basil leaves, preferably Asian*

Sliced red and green chiles, such as jalapeños

Crispy Shallots, page 113

Shrimp chips,* fried

Asian hot sauce* (see box, page 113)

*Available at Asian markets

1. In a small saucepan, bring the stock to a boil. Remove from the heat and add the lime leaves and dried galangal, if using. Let

soak. In a small bowl, combine the tamarind pulp with the water, breaking it up with a fork. Let soak.

2. In a small heavy frying pan, toast the coriander seeds over moderately high heat, shaking the pan, until fragrant, about 1½ minutes.

3. Using scissors, cut the dried chiles in half lengthwise. Shake out and discard one third of the seeds. Snip the chiles into small pieces. In a mortar with a pestle or in a spice grinder, grind the coriander seeds, dried chiles, dried shrimp, and peppercorns until pulverized. Stir in the turmeric.

4. Remove the tough outer leaves from the lemongrass and slice the stalks thin. Using a slotted spoon, remove the dried galangal, if using, from the stock and transfer it to a food processor. Add the lemongrass, garlic, serrano chiles, shallots, and fresh galangal, if using. Process until almost pureed. Add the ground spice mixture and the oil and pulse to blend.

5. In a large frying pan, cook the lemongrass mixture over moderate heat, stirring frequently, until very fragrant, about 10 minutes.

6. Remove the lime leaves from the stock and set them aside. Open the can of coconut milk and spoon off the thick milk at the top of the can; reserve. Blend the thin coconut milk with enough of the stock to make 2 cups.

7. In a large deep pot, combine the stock mixture, the lemongrass mixture, the lime leaves, the fish sauce, and the sugar. Add the tamarind pulp with any liquid and stir well. Add the chicken thighs and bring to a boil over high heat. Reduce the heat and simmer for 15 minutes.

8. Add the chicken breasts and simmer until the chicken is cooked through, about 30 minutes. Remove the chicken and let cool slightly. Remove the thigh meat from the bones and discard the skin and bones; shred all the chicken. Stir the thick coconut milk into the stock and add the shredded chicken. Simmer gently until the sauce is slightly thickened, about 15 minutes; do not boil. Stir in ¾ teaspoon salt.

9. Meanwhile, soak the cellophane noodles in warm water to cover for 20 minutes. Bring a large pot of water to a boil over high heat. Drain the noodles in a medium strainer, and then dip the strainer of noodles into the boiling water until the noodles are translucent, about 30 seconds. Immediately rinse with cold water and drain well. Put the noodles in a bowl and stir in about ¼ cup of the sauce.

10. Return the water to a boil and add the egg noodles. Cook until tender, about 2 minutes. Drain, rinse with cold water, and drain well.

11. Reheat the chicken and sauce over moderate heat. Remove the lime leaves. Add the lime juice and season with salt and

cayenne. Put the chicken and all but ¼ cup of the remaining sauce in a bowl.

12. Mix the cellophane noodles with the egg noodles and add them to the sauce remaining in the pot. Cook, stirring occasionally, until heated through, about 2 minutes.

13. Transfer the noodle mixture to a large platter or individual bowls. Spoon the chicken and sauce on top and sprinkle with the cilantro leaves. Put the cilantro sprigs, lime wedges, basil leaves, fresh chiles, Crispy Shallots, shrimp chips, and hot sauce in individual bowls and serve alongside.

—LINDA BURUM

MAKE IT AHEAD

Prepare the curry through step 8 up to three days ahead. Let cool to room temperature, cover, and refrigerate.

ASIAN HOT SAUCES

To accompany this Malaysian curry, we suggest Indonesian sambal olek, Thai sriracha sauce, or Vietnamese chile and garlic sauce.

CRISPY SHALLOTS

MAKES ABOUT ¹/₂ CUP

¼ cup peanut or other cooking oil, more if needed

4 shallots, cut into very thin slices

1. Heat ¼ cup oil in a medium frying pan over moderate heat. Add half the shallots and fry, shaking the pan almost constantly, until golden, about 4 minutes. Do not let them darken. Remove the shallots with a slotted spoon and spread them in a single layer on paper towels to drain.

2. Reheat the oil, adding more if needed, and repeat with the remaining shallots. (If the shallots are not crisp, bake in a 225° oven until they are.)

chapter 5

ROASTING

Roast Chicken with Corn-and-Pancetta Relish, page 127

A GOOD ROAST CHICKEN

Perfumed with rosemary and basted with butter, this roast chicken is elegant enough to be the centerpiece of a dinner party and easy enough to be a mainstay of weeknight family meals. For crisp skin, turn the oven up to 375° for the last ten minutes of roasting.

WINE RECOMMENDATION
Pair this rosemary-scented chicken with a peppery red Côtes-du-Rhône or Côtes-du-Rhône Villages. Made almost entirely from grenache, the world's most widely planted red grape, these wines are earthy, low in tannin, and redolent of lavender and thyme.

SERVES 4

1   chicken (3 to 3½ pounds)

3   sprigs rosemary, or 1½ teaspoons dried rosemary

3   tablespoons butter, at room temperature

1½   teaspoons coarse salt

¾   teaspoon coarse-ground black pepper

1. Heat the oven to 325°. Using your fingers, carefully loosen the skin of the chicken from the breast meat. Put one of the rosemary sprigs, or ½ teaspoon dried rosemary, and 1 tablespoon of the butter under the skin of each side of the breast. Put the remaining rosemary sprig or ½ teaspoon dried rosemary in the cavity. Twist the wings of the chicken behind the back and tie the legs together. Put the chicken, breast-side up, in a roasting pan. Rub with the remaining 1 tablespoon butter; sprinkle with the salt and pepper.

2. Roast the chicken for 45 minutes. Baste with the pan drippings and continue roasting, basting every 15 minutes, until the chicken is golden brown and the juices run clear when the thigh is pierced, about 1 hour longer. Leave the bird in a warm spot to rest for about 15 minutes.

—MOLLY O'NEILL

SIMPLE ROAST CHICKEN WITH PARSLEY AND LEMON

Basic roasted chicken gets a little lift from the refreshing taste of lemon. The bird is stuffed with lemon peel and parsley, which flavor the meat as it cooks.

WINE RECOMMENDATION
The strong mineral streak, racy acidity, and occasional touch of herbaceousness of Chablis make it a classic match for this aromatic chicken. Choose a premier cru or grand cru.

SERVES 4

- 1 lemon, cut in half
- 1 chicken (3 to 3½ pounds)
- ½ teaspoon salt
- ½ teaspoon fresh-ground black pepper
- 10 sprigs parsley
- 5 tablespoons butter, melted

1. Heat the oven to 400°. Squeeze the juice of the lemon into the cavity of the chicken; reserve the rinds. Turn the bird to moisten the cavity with the juice.

2. Sprinkle ¼ teaspoon each of the salt and pepper into the cavity and add the lemon rinds and parsley. Twist the wings of the chicken behind the back and tie the legs together. Put the chicken on its side on a rack in a roasting pan. Coat the chicken with about a third of the melted butter and sprinkle with the remaining ¼ teaspoon each salt and pepper.

3. Roast the chicken for 15 minutes. Baste with one third of the remaining butter and roast for another 10 minutes. Turn the bird onto its other side and roast for 15 minutes. Baste with half of the remaining butter and roast for another 10 minutes. Turn the chicken breast-side up, baste with the remaining butter, and roast until the juices run clear when the thigh is pierced, about 15 minutes longer. Leave the bird in a warm spot to rest for about 15 minutes.

—JOHN ROBERT MASSIE

Cantonese Roast Chicken

Rubbing a sesame-oil mixture over the chicken, inside and out, gives it a nutty taste and an Asian accent. Toss any leftover meat with greens and a sesame dressing for an impromptu Chinese chicken salad.

WINE RECOMMENDATION

East meets West when you pair this Asian-inspired chicken with a tocai friulano. Hailing from Italy's northeastern region of Friuli, the wine is among the most full-bodied of Italian whites and has both rich nuttiness and fresh herbal flavors.

SERVES 4

- 3 tablespoons dry white wine
- 1½ tablespoons white vinegar
- 1 tablespoon Asian sesame oil
- 1 teaspoon salt
- ¼ teaspoon fresh-ground black pepper
- 1 chicken (3 to 3½ pounds)
- 4 cloves garlic, cut into ¼-inch slices
- ¾ cup water

1. Heat the oven to 375°. In a bowl, stir together the wine, vinegar, oil, salt, and pepper. Rub this mixture all over the chicken, inside and out. Put half of the garlic slices inside the cavity. Put the chicken, breast-side up, on a rack in a roasting pan. Add the remaining garlic slices to the pan along with the water.

2. Roast the chicken for 30 minutes. Lower the oven temperature to 350° and roast for 15 minutes longer. Turn the chicken breast-side down and roast for 30 minutes. If the pan looks dry, add boiling water, ¼ cup at a time. Turn the chicken breast-side up and roast until the juices run clear when the thigh is pierced, about 15 minutes longer. Leave the bird in a warm spot to rest for about 15 minutes.

—Eileen Yin-Fei Lo

PROVENÇAL ROAST CHICKEN

Though this recipe may not be authentically Provençal, it certainly evokes the hill towns and hearty suppers of southern France. The cooked chicken is moist and aromatic, with juices that can be served au naturel or mixed with orange juice and cognac for a delightful sauce.

WINE RECOMMENDATION

Muscat's exotic floral muskiness and spicy orange-peel aromas perfectly mirror the fruitiness and herbs here. Uncork a sensuously fragrant version from Alsace—unlike other muscats, which can be delicate, those from Alsace have the richness and weight to match the chicken.

SERVES 4

- 1 tablespoon butter
- 1 tablespoon olive oil
- 1½ teaspoons salt
- ¾ teaspoon fresh-ground black pepper
- 4 oranges, 2 halved, 2 sliced, plus additional orange slices for serving
- 1 chicken (3 to 3½ pounds)
- 1 large onion, cut into thin slices
- 6 sprigs basil, plus basil leaves for serving
- 2 cloves garlic, unpeeled, smashed
- 1 tablespoon cognac or other brandy

1. Heat the oven to 375°. Melt the butter with the oil in a small saucepan over moderate heat. Add ½ teaspoon of the salt and ¼ teaspoon of the pepper.

2. Squeeze the juice from the halved oranges; you should have about 1 cup. Save the rinds from one of the oranges.

3. Using your fingers, carefully loosen the skin of the chicken from the breast and thigh meat. Put an orange slice under the skin of each thigh and two slices under the skin on each side of the breast. Season the cavity with ½ teaspoon of the salt and ¼ teaspoon of the pepper. Put the reserved orange rinds, four slices of the onion, and 1 basil sprig in the cavity. Twist the wings of the chicken behind the back and tie the legs together.

4. Lightly butter a flameproof casserole or Dutch oven. Add the garlic along with the remaining orange slices, onion slices, and basil sprigs. Season with the remaining ½ teaspoon salt and ¼ teaspoon pepper. Toss well.

5. Put the chicken, breast-side up, in the casserole and coat it with the melted-butter mixture. Add ¼ cup of the orange juice. Cover and roast the chicken for 15 minutes. Baste the chicken with another ¼ cup of the orange juice. Cover and roast, basting with the pan juices every 15 minutes, for 1 hour longer.

6. Remove the casserole from the oven and raise the heat to 425°. Strain the pan juices into a nonreactive saucepan. Return the chicken to the oven and roast, uncovered, basting once or twice, until the chicken is nicely browned and the juices run clear when the thigh is pierced, about 20 minutes. Transfer the bird to a plate and leave to rest in a warm spot for about 15 minutes.

7. Meanwhile, add the remaining orange juice to the reserved pan juices and boil over moderately high heat until reduced by half, about 7 minutes. Add the cognac and boil for 1 minute longer.

8. Carve or quarter the chicken and put on four plates. Pour a little sauce over each serving. Garnish with orange slices and basil leaves. Pass the remaining sauce separately.

—DORIE GREENSPAN

VARIATION

Fresh rosemary or thyme can be used in place of the basil. Use small sprigs of the same herb for garnish.

BUYING CHICKEN

When buying chicken, remember that the color (yellow or white) has no bearing on the quality of the meat. Color varies with the diet and breed of the bird. Do look for a well-shaped, plump body and smooth, slightly moist, soft flesh. Fresh chicken that has been stored at 35° is best. Frozen chicken is seldom as juicy, flavorful, or tender.

CARAWAY CHICKEN WITH LIGHT GRAVY

Savory and succulent, this buttery roast chicken is flavored by the ground caraway seeds tucked under its skin. The seeds also enhance the light, flavorful gravy. Make the caraway butter at least an hour and up to a day in advance so it has time to chill before you prepare the chicken.

WINE RECOMMENDATION
The richness and savory aromas of this dish will marry well with an opulent Napa Valley chardonnay. Try to find one with restrained oak, as too much wood tends to overwhelm most foods.

SERVES 4

1½ teaspoons caraway seeds

3 tablespoons butter, at room temperature

1 chicken (3 to 3½ pounds)

About ½ cup Chicken Stock, page 61, canned low-sodium chicken broth, or water

1½ teaspoons flour

2 tablespoons dry white wine

Salt and fresh-ground black pepper

1. Grind ¾ teaspoon of the caraway seeds in a mortar with a pestle or in a spice grinder. In a small bowl, beat the butter until fluffy. Stir the ground caraway into the butter. On a square of aluminum foil, form the caraway butter into a log 1 inch in diameter. Wrap tightly and refrigerate until solid, at least 1 hour.

2. Heat the oven to 350°. Using your fingers, carefully loosen the skin of the chicken from the breast meat. Cut three quarters of the caraway butter into thin slices and put them under the skin on each side of the breast. Toss the remaining ¾ teaspoon caraway seeds into the cavity. Twist the wings of the chicken behind the back and tie the legs together. Put the chicken, breast-side up, on a rack in a roasting pan.

3. Melt the remaining caraway butter in a small saucepan over low heat. Coat the chicken with half of the melted butter. Roast the chicken for 30 minutes. Baste with the remaining caraway butter and roast, basting with the pan drippings every 20 minutes, until the juices run clear when the thigh is pierced, about 1 hour longer. Pour the juices from the cavity into the roasting pan. Transfer the bird to a plate and leave to rest in a warm spot for about 15 minutes.

4. Meanwhile, pour the pan drippings into a bowl or large measuring cup. Spoon 1½ tablespoons of fat from the surface of the drippings and put the fat in a small nonreactive frying pan. Skim off and discard any remaining fat from the drippings; you should have about ½ cup of pan juices. Add any accumulated chicken juices from the plate and enough stock to make 1 cup.

5. Add the flour to the fat in the frying pan and stir over moderate heat until bubbling. Cook, stirring, for 2 minutes; do not allow the flour to brown. Whisk in the pan-juice mixture and the wine. Cook, whisking constantly, until the gravy boils and thickens slightly. Simmer, whisking occasionally, for 3 minutes. Remove from the heat and season with salt and pepper. Carve the chicken and serve the gravy separately.

—JIM FOBEL

TESTING FOR DONENESS

Some controversy exists regarding the correct way to test chicken for doneness. Many cooks use a meat thermometer and consider the bird done when it reaches anywhere from 165° (medium-well) to 180° (well-done). Others pinch or poke the thigh. We suggest piercing the thickest part of the thigh all the way to the bone to see if the juices run clear, but all these methods are viable. Wiggling the drumstick in the hip joint, on the other hand, is *not* a good test; by the time the leg moves in the socket, the bird is overcooked.

ROAST CHICKEN WITH GOAT CHEESE, HONEY, AND THYME

Basting apple and onion wedges with a honey glaze caramelizes them as they roast along with the chicken. They're then mashed into a creamy sauce with tangy goat cheese.

WINE RECOMMENDATION
In France's Loire Valley, particularly in Savennières, the chenin blanc grape is crafted into dry wines of surprising richness and complexity. An aged Savennières' full body, electric acidity, and hints of honey, herbs, quince, and flowers will blend beautifully with this dish.

SERVES 4

- 1 chicken (3 to 3½ pounds)
- 1 teaspoon coarse salt
- ½ teaspoon cracked black pepper
- 12 large sprigs thyme, or 2 teaspoons dried thyme
- 1 head garlic, cloves separated
- 1 tart green apple, such as Granny Smith, peeled and quartered
- 1 onion, quartered
- 4 shallots, unpeeled
- 4 tablespoons butter
- ¼ cup honey
- ¼ cup cider vinegar
- 1 cup dry white wine
- 2 ounces mild goat cheese, such as Montrachet
- ¼ cup heavy cream

1. Heat the oven to 450°. Sprinkle the cavity of the chicken with ¼ teaspoon each of the salt and pepper. Put half the thyme and half the garlic cloves in the cavity. Twist the wings of the chicken behind the back and tie the legs together. Put the chicken, breast-side up, in a roasting pan. Rub the remaining ¾ teaspoon salt and ¼ teaspoon pepper into the skin.

2. Scatter the apple and onion quarters, the shallots, and the remaining garlic cloves around the chicken. Roast for 30 minutes.

3. Meanwhile, in a small heavy saucepan, melt the butter with the honey and the vinegar over moderate heat, stirring frequently. Baste the chicken with this mixture and continue roasting, basting every 10 minutes, until the juices run clear when the thigh of the chicken is pierced, about 30 minutes longer. Turn the vegetables and the apple pieces occasionally to coat them with the drippings.

4. Transfer the chicken, shallots, and garlic to a plate and leave in a warm spot to rest for 15 minutes. Set the roasting pan over moderate heat and add the wine. Bring to a boil, scraping the bottom of the pan to

dislodge any browned bits and mashing the apple and onion into the sauce.

5. Strain the sauce into a medium saucepan and return to a boil. Strip the leaves from the remaining thyme sprigs, if using, and mince them. Stir the minced thyme or the remaining 1 teaspoon dried thyme into the sauce along with the goat cheese and cream. Boil the sauce until it is slightly thickened, about 5 minutes.

6. Remove the thyme sprigs, if using, and the garlic from the cavity of the chicken. Carve the chicken, place it on a platter, and put the caramelized garlic and shallots around it. Pass the sauce separately.

—ROBERT DEL GRANDE

GRADING CHICKEN

The USDA inspects all chickens for wholesomeness. The grading of birds raised and sold within each state is voluntary, but all chickens transported across state lines must, by law, be graded. Grading is based on cosmetic factors, not on size, tenderness, or age. Chickens that are whole, plump, and pretty—with no rips or missing parts—will be graded A. Others will fall into the B or C categories; these, however, are not generally available to the public.

ROAST CHICKEN WITH CORN-AND-PANCETTA RELISH

Corn, bell peppers, and pancetta combine in a piquant relish that's a lively companion for luscious, tender roast chicken. Creamy mashed potatoes make an excellent accompaniment.

 WINE RECOMMENDATION
With its high acidity and assertive flavors, chenin blanc has the authority and complexity to go the distance with the savory relish. Choose a demi-sec Vouvray, which will have enough sweetness to balance the relish's sugar and peppery heat.

SERVES 4

1 chicken (3 to 3½ pounds)

5 cloves garlic

Zest of 1 lemon, cut off in strips

2 sprigs rosemary

Coarse salt and fresh-ground black pepper

¼ cup dry white wine

½ cup water

Corn-and-Pancetta Relish, next page

1. Heat the oven to 475°. Stuff the cavity of the chicken with the garlic, lemon zest, and rosemary; season with salt and pepper. Twist the wings behind the back of the chicken and tie the legs together. Put the chicken, breast-side down, on a rack in a roasting pan.

2. Roast the chicken for 20 minutes. Turn the bird breast-side up and reduce the heat to 400°. Roast, basting occasionally, until the juices run clear when the thigh is pierced, about 45 minutes longer. Transfer the bird to a plate and leave to rest in a warm spot for about 15 minutes.

3. Meanwhile, set the roasting pan over moderate heat and add the wine and water. Bring to a boil, scraping the bottom of the pan to dislodge any browned bits. Reduce the heat and simmer for 5 minutes. Strain the gravy and skim off the fat. Season with salt and pepper.

4. Carve the chicken and spoon some of the relish over each serving. Pass the gravy separately.

—LANCE DEAN VELASQUEZ

MAKE IT AHEAD

Prepare the relish (next page), without the cilantro, up to one day ahead and refrigerate. Bring to room temperature and stir in the cilantro before serving.

CORN-AND-PANCETTA RELISH

MAKES ABOUT 1½ CUPS

1½ teaspoons slivered lime zest

1½ teaspoons extra-virgin olive oil

¼ pound pancetta, cut into ½-inch cubes

1 onion, cut into fine dice

½ red bell pepper, cut into fine dice

½ green bell pepper, cut into fine dice

1½ teaspoons minced garlic

1½ teaspoons minced fresh ginger

Coarse salt and fresh-ground black pepper

½ cup plus 2 tablespoons lime juice

¼ cup packed dark-brown sugar

¼ teaspoon cayenne

⅛ teaspoon dried red-pepper flakes

1 heaping cup fresh corn kernels (cut from about 2 ears)

½ cup chopped cilantro

1. In a small saucepan of boiling water, blanch the lime zest for 1 minute. Drain.

2. Heat the oil in a medium nonreactive saucepan over moderately low heat. Add the pancetta and cook, stirring, until lightly browned and crisp, about 10 minutes. Using a slotted spoon, transfer the pancetta to paper towels to drain.

3. Add the onion to the pan and cook, stirring occasionally, until translucent, about 5 minutes. Add the bell peppers, garlic, ginger, and a pinch each of salt and black pepper. Raise the heat to moderate and cook, stirring, until fragrant, about 2 minutes. Add the lime juice, brown sugar, cayenne, red-pepper flakes, and the blanched lime zest. Bring to a simmer. Add the corn and cook until just tender, about 5 minutes. Stir in the pancetta and transfer the relish to a bowl to cool. Season with salt and pepper. Stir in the cilantro.

ROAST CHICKEN WITH FIG GIBLET SAUCE

Figs take the place of the traditional giblets in the sauce for this roast chicken.
The tarragon and chives in the herb butter add to the sauce's complexity.

WINE RECOMMENDATION
The rich, sweet fig sauce—plus the pinot noir called for in the recipe—make this an easy choice. Try a snappy pinot noir from California's Santa Maria Valley, whose wines are packed with ripe, juicy fruit. Use the same wine in the sauce, as it creates a natural synchronicity of flavors.

SERVES 4

½ lemon, cut in half

1 chicken (3 to 3½ pounds)

2 tablespoons butter, at room temperature

   Salt and fresh-ground black pepper

½ cup pinot noir or other dry red wine

1 cup water

8 cloves garlic, unpeeled

2 large or 3 small dried figs, preferably Calimyrna

1 teaspoon chopped fresh tarragon

2 teaspoons chopped fresh chives

1. Heat the oven to 400°. Put the lemon in the cavity of the chicken. Twist the wings behind the back of the chicken and tie the legs together. Put the chicken, breast-side up, in a roasting pan just large enough to hold it. Coat the chicken with 1 tablespoon of the butter. Sprinkle lightly with salt and pepper. Add the wine and ½ cup of the water to the pan. Scatter the garlic and figs around the chicken and roast until the chicken is browned, about 30 minutes.

2. Meanwhile, in a small bowl, blend together the remaining 1 tablespoon butter, the tarragon, chives, and a pinch each of salt and pepper. Cover the herb butter and refrigerate.

3. Reduce the oven temperature to 350° and baste the chicken with the pan drippings. Roast for 10 minutes longer. Add the remaining ½ cup water to the pan and continue to roast, basting the chicken and turning the figs occasionally, until the juices run clear when the thigh is pierced, about 40 minutes longer.

4. Pour the juices from the chicken cavity into the roasting pan. Transfer the bird to a plate and leave to rest in a warm spot for about 15 minutes. Using a slotted spoon, remove the figs and garlic to a plate.

5. Pour the pan juices into a measuring cup and skim the fat from the surface. Set a coarse strainer over a small stainless-steel saucepan. Put the garlic cloves in the strainer and pour the pan juices over them. Press the garlic pulp through the strainer into the juices. ➤

6. Carve the chicken and add any accumulated juices to the sauce. Cover the chicken loosely with aluminum foil.

7. Cut the figs into ¼-inch dice and add them to the sauce. Warm the sauce over moderate heat, stirring, until heated through. Remove from the heat and whisk in the herb butter, bit by bit, until the sauce is smooth and slightly thickened. Season the sauce with salt and pepper and serve with the chicken.

—MARCIA KIESEL

PREPARING CHICKEN FOR COOKING OR STORING

Remove the store packaging and rinse the chicken thoroughly. If the chicken is to be roasted or sautéed, it should be patted completely dry so it will brown properly. If you do not intend to use the chicken right away, pat it dry, wrap it loosely in waxed paper, and place it on a plate in the refrigerator. If there are giblets, wrap and store them separately. To store the chicken for longer than a day or two, rinse the chicken and pat dry, wrap in freezer paper or waxed paper and then foil, and freeze.

AROMATIC ROAST CHICKEN

Putting stuffing under the skin makes for more succulent breast meat. Lemon in the cavity of the chicken and in the stuffing, too, guarantees a light, fresh flavor.

WINE RECOMMENDATION

This relatively plain roast chicken calls for a rich white wine to highlight its lemony fragrance. Puligny-Montrachet has sophisticated lemony fruit with nuances of smoke and butter and a steely minerality that will mesh perfectly with this dish.

SERVES 4

1	chicken (3 to 3½ pounds)
1	teaspoon salt
	Fresh-ground black pepper
½	cup dry bread crumbs
¼	teaspoon grated lemon zest
1	tablespoon minced fresh parsley
1	small clove garlic, minced
1	tablespoon olive oil
1	small lemon, cut in half
2½	tablespoons butter, melted

1. Heat the oven to 450°. Using your fingers, carefully loosen the skin of the chicken from the breast meat. Rub the chicken inside and out with ¾ teaspoon of the salt and ¼ teaspoon pepper.

2. In a small bowl, stir together the dry bread crumbs, lemon zest, parsley, garlic, the remaining ¼ teaspoon salt, and ⅛ teaspoon of pepper. Stir in the oil. Using your fingers, spread the stuffing in an even layer under the skin of the chicken breast. Put the lemon halves in the cavity. Twist the wings behind the back of the chicken and tie the legs together. Put the chicken, breast-side up, on a rack in a roasting pan. Coat with 1 tablespoon of the melted butter.

3. Roast the chicken for 10 minutes. Reduce the heat to 375° and turn the chicken on its side. Baste with 1 teaspoon of the butter and roast for another 15 minutes. Turn the chicken on its other side, baste with another 1 teaspoon butter, and roast for another 15 minutes. Turn the chicken breast-side down, baste with another 1 teaspoon butter, and roast for another 15 minutes. Finally, turn the chicken breast-side up, baste with the remaining 1½ teaspoons butter, and roast until the juices run clear when the thigh is pierced, about 30 minutes longer. Transfer the bird to a plate and leave to rest in a warm spot for about 15 minutes.

4. Meanwhile, pour the pan juices into a small bowl and skim off most of the fat. Serve the chicken with the pan juices.

APRICOT-AND-SHIITAKE-STUFFED CHICKEN WITH TURNIPS

To save a little time, you can make this with four single chicken breasts. Cook the chicken and vegetables together in a 375° oven for forty minutes.

WINE RECOMMENDATION
If you have an old bottle of German auslese riesling tucked in a corner of your cellar, break it out now. As these wines mature, they lose some of their sweetness and take on complex, mellow flavors and a silken texture. The peachy fruit with nuances of mushroom will be exquisite here.

SERVES 4

- 4 tablespoons butter
- 3 onions, 1 minced, 2 quartered
- ¼ pound prosciutto, chopped coarse
- ½ cup dried apricots
- ¼ pound shiitake mushrooms, stems removed and caps sliced, or 1 ounce dried shiitakes, reconstituted, stems removed and caps sliced
- ⅔ cup fresh bread crumbs
- ¼ teaspoon salt
- 1 chicken (3 to 3½ pounds)
- 1 tablespoon cooking oil
- ½ teaspoon fresh-ground black pepper
- 1¾ pounds turnips, peeled and cut into 1-inch pieces
- 4 small carrots, cut in half on the diagonal

1. Heat the oven to 425°. Melt the butter in a small frying pan over moderately low heat. Add the minced onion and cook until the onion is softened, 3 to 4 minutes.

2. Put the prosciutto and apricots in a food processor. Pulse until finely chopped. Transfer to a bowl, add the mushrooms, the cooked onion, the bread crumbs, and the salt, and toss to combine.

3. Using your fingers, carefully loosen the skin of the chicken from the breast meat. Spread the stuffing in an even layer under the skin. Put the chicken in a large oval gratin dish or a roasting pan. Rub the chicken with the oil and sprinkle with the pepper.

4. Roast the chicken for 20 minutes. Remove the dish from the oven and reduce the heat to 375°. Scatter the turnips, the quartered onions, and the carrots around the chicken and toss the vegetables with the pan drippings. Return the pan to the oven and roast until the vegetables are tender and the juices run clear when the thigh of the chicken is pierced, about 50 minutes longer. Transfer the bird to a plate and leave to rest in a warm spot for about 15 minutes.

—MARY LYNN MONDICH

THYME-ROASTED CHICKEN WITH ONION AND POTATOES

A large cast-iron skillet is a good choice for cooking this succulent chicken. It can do stovetop duty to sauté the onions, then move to the oven to hold the chicken and potatoes as they roast.

WINE RECOMMENDATION Try this hearty meal with a supple merlot from Washington's Columbia Valley. Merlot is fruity enough to stand up to the onion and has a herbal component that will blend well with the thyme. In addition, merlots from Washington are a bit earthy, making them a good foil for the potatoes.

SERVES 4

8   tablespoons butter, at room temperature

1   large onion, chopped coarse

½   teaspoon salt

½   teaspoon fresh-ground black pepper

1   tablespoon fresh thyme leaves, or 1 teaspoon dried thyme

1   chicken (3 to 3½ pounds)

1⅓ pounds boiling potatoes (about 4), quartered

1. In a large ovenproof frying pan, melt 1 tablespoon of the butter over moderately high heat. Add the onion, ¼ teaspoon each of the salt and pepper, and a pinch of the thyme. Cook, stirring frequently, until the onion is lightly browned, about 10 minutes. Remove from the pan and let cool to room temperature. Set the pan aside.

2. Heat the oven to 400°. In a small bowl, blend together the remaining 7 tablespoons butter, ¼ teaspoon salt, ¼ teaspoon pepper, and thyme.

3. Using your fingers, carefully loosen the skin of the chicken from the breast, thigh, and leg meat. Rub 4 tablespoons of the thyme butter under the skin. Put the browned onion in the cavity. Twist the wings behind the back of the chicken and tie the legs together. Coat the chicken with 1 tablespoon of the thyme butter. Put the bird in the frying pan.

4. Melt the remaining 2 tablespoons thyme butter, toss with the potatoes, and put the potatoes around the chicken. Roast until the potatoes are tender and the juices run clear when the thigh of the chicken is pierced, about 1¼ hours. Transfer the bird to a plate and leave to rest in a warm spot for about 15 minutes.

—JOHN ROBERT MASSIE

ROASTED CHICKEN WITH POTATOES AND CHORIZO

Potatoes, onions, red bell peppers, and chorizo sausage come together as a highly seasoned side dish for roast chicken. All you need to complete this hearty meal is a simple green salad.

WINE RECOMMENDATION
Regional foods really do taste better with local wines. Often the two have had many years to develop in harmony. So it is with chorizo and red Rioja. Their smoky, spicy flavors are made for each other, and the Rioja's soft, supple texture is heavenly with the chicken.

SERVES 4

- 1 chicken (3 to 3½ pounds)
- 1 tablespoon butter, at room temperature
- 1½ teaspoons salt
- 1½ teaspoons fresh-ground black pepper
- ½ cup plus 1 tablespoon olive oil
- 2 pounds small red potatoes, peeled and halved
- 2 onions, chopped coarse
- 2 red bell peppers, cut into 1-inch pieces
- ½ pound chorizo or other firm paprika-flavored pork sausage, cut into ⅓-inch pieces
- 2 cups Chicken Stock, page 61, or canned low-sodium chicken broth

1. Heat the oven to 425°. Coat the chicken with the butter. Sprinkle 1 teaspoon each of the salt and pepper over the chicken, inside and out. Twist the wings behind the back of the chicken and tie the legs together. Put the chicken, breast-side up, in a roasting pan. Roast until the chicken is golden brown and the juices run clear when the thigh is pierced, about 55 minutes. Remove from the oven and leave in a warm spot to rest.

2. Meanwhile, heat the ½ cup oil in a large heavy frying pan over moderately high heat. Add the potatoes. Cook, turning occasionally, until golden brown but not quite tender, about 20 minutes. Pour off the oil and leave the potatoes in the pan.

3. Heat the remaining 1 tablespoon oil in a medium frying pan over moderate heat. Add the onions and peppers and cook, stirring occasionally, until softened and starting to brown, 12 to 15 minutes. Add the chorizo and cook for 5 minutes longer.

4. Transfer the chorizo mixture to the pan of potatoes. Add the stock and bring to a simmer over moderate heat. Cook until the potatoes are tender and the stock has reduced by half, about 10 minutes. Season with the remaining ½ teaspoon each salt and pepper. Serve immediately with the chicken.

—COLMAN ANDREWS

ROAST CHICKEN STUFFED WITH PORK AND ARMAGNAC PRUNES

The Armagnac-soaked prunes in this recipe from Brittany, France, impart a subtle perfume to the filling. If you prefer, cognac or another fine brandy can be substituted for the Armagnac.

WINE RECOMMENDATION

A wine that is too dry will taste sour next to the sweetness of the prunes, but the sausage calls for a rich, fruity red wine. Try a Valpolicella made in the ripasso method. These wines are refermented on the grape skins left over from making Amarone, giving them a flavor and weight halfway between Amarone and Valpolicella *normale*.

SERVES 4

1 cup pitted prunes (about 6 ounces), cut in half

½ cup Armagnac or other brandy

4 tablespoons butter, at room temperature

2 onions, chopped fine

3 ribs celery, chopped fine

8 cloves garlic, minced

2 tablespoons olive oil

½ pound lean ground pork

2 teaspoons chopped fresh thyme leaves, or ½ teaspoon dried thyme

1 teaspoon grated nutmeg

Salt and fresh-ground black pepper

1 chicken (3 to 3½ pounds)

1. Combine the prunes and Armagnac in a small bowl, cover, and set aside for at least 1 hour, or overnight.

2. Heat the oven to 475°. In a large saucepan, melt 2 tablespoons of the butter over moderately low heat. Add the onions and cook, stirring occasionally, until they are translucent, about 5 minutes. Add the celery and garlic and cook until softened, about 5 minutes longer. Transfer the vegetables to a medium bowl.

3. Wipe out the saucepan and add the oil. Add the pork and cook over high heat, breaking up the meat with a fork, until cooked through, 3 to 5 minutes.

4. Add the pork to the cooked vegetables. Stir in the thyme, nutmeg, and the prunes with Armagnac. Season the stuffing with salt and pepper. Let cool completely.

5. Sprinkle the cavity of the chicken with ¼ teaspoon each of salt and pepper. Fill the cavity with the stuffing. Twist the wings behind the back of the chicken and tie the legs together. Put the chicken, breast-side up, in a roasting pan. Coat the chicken with the remaining 2 tablespoons butter.

6. Roast the chicken for 10 minutes. Reduce the heat to 400° and cook until the chicken is golden brown and the juices run clear when the thigh is pierced, about 1 hour. Leave the bird in a warm spot to rest for about 15 minutes before serving.

—JOYCE GOLDSTEIN

SALMONELLA

One of the most common causes of food poisoning is salmonella bacteria, which is present in about half of the raw poultry sold in this country. Proper storage, handling, and cooking of poultry, however, eliminate the health hazard. Here are some simple guidelines for avoiding salmonella poisoning:

• Rinse chicken before cooking it.

• After handling raw poultry, thoroughly wash your hands in hot soapy water before handling any other food. Also wash any utensils and scrub any cutting boards you used.

• If you use a pastry brush to baste raw poultry and intend to use any leftover basting mixture as a sauce, be sure to bring the sauce to a boil and simmer it for at least three minutes to kill any bacteria you may have introduced by dipping the pastry brush in it.

• Do not stuff poultry until just before roasting.

chapter 6

BAKING

Spicy Stuffed Chicken Breasts, page 141

SPICY STUFFED CHICKEN BREASTS

Since the stuffing goes between the skin and the meat, you need to use breasts that are boneless but not skinless—which means you'll probably have to buy them bone-in and either remove the bone or have the butcher do it. Complement these zesty chicken breasts with plain rice or couscous and a green vegetable. Sweet sugar-snap peas would balance the spicy heat perfectly.

 WINE RECOMMENDATION
The spices and sun-dried tomatoes here call for a red wine with lots of richness and fruit. A California zinfandel, full of intensely concentrated ripe-blackberry flavors and redolent of Asian spices such as anise and sandalwood, makes a fine match.

SERVES 4

- 12   dry-pack sun-dried tomatoes
- 1   tablespoon cumin seeds
- 3   cloves garlic, minced
- 1   jalapeño pepper, seeds and ribs removed, minced
- 2   teaspoons grated lemon zest
- 1   teaspoon fresh-ground black pepper
- ¼   cup plus 1 tablespoon sour cream
- ¼   cup chopped cilantro
- 4   bone-in chicken breasts (about 2¼ pounds in all), bones removed, skin left on
- ½   teaspoon pure ground chiles
- 1   tablespoon olive oil

1. Put the tomatoes in a small saucepan and add just enough water to cover. Bring to a boil over moderately high heat. Reduce the heat and simmer until the tomatoes are tender but still slightly chewy, about 3 minutes. Drain, rinse well with cold water, and drain again. Cut into ¼-inch dice.

2. In a small frying pan, toast the cumin seeds over moderately high heat, shaking the pan occasionally, until they darken slightly and are very fragrant, about 1 minute.

3. Set aside ½ teaspoon of the toasted cumin seeds. Crush the remaining 2½ teaspoons seeds. In a bowl, combine the chopped seeds with the garlic, jalapeño, lemon zest, black pepper, sour cream, cilantro, and the sun-dried tomatoes. Alternatively, grind the 2½ teaspoons toasted seeds in a mortar with a pestle. Blend in the garlic, jalapeño, lemon zest, and black pepper to form a paste, and then stir in the sour cream, the cilantro, and the sun-dried tomatoes.

4. Heat the oven to 450°. Divide the stuffing into four portions. Using your fingers, carefully loosen the skin of the chicken from the meat. Put one portion of the stuffing under the skin of each breast and press gently on the skin to spread it evenly. Sprinkle the breasts on both sides with the reserved ½ teaspoon cumin seeds and the chili powder. ➤

5. In a large ovenproof frying pan, heat the oil over high heat. When it begins to smoke, add the stuffed chicken breasts, skin-side down, and cook until the skin is crisp and browned, about 5 minutes. Turn the breasts over and put the frying pan in the oven. Bake until the chicken is just cooked through, about 8 minutes. Let rest for 5 minutes and then cut each breast into ¼-inch diagonal slices; or serve the chicken breasts unsliced, if you prefer.

—MARCIA KIESEL

MAKE IT AHEAD

You can stuff the chicken breasts one day in advance. Cover and refrigerate. Allow to return to room temperature before cooking.

SUN-DRIED TOMATOES

Tomatoes are naturally high in sodium. Drying them concentrates their flavor and intensifies the impact of their acidic sweetness. Some brands of dry, unmarinated sun-dried tomatoes contain small amounts of residual salt from the drying process. Blanching and rinsing the tomatoes well, as in step 1 here, removes most of the added salt.

CHICKEN BREASTS STUFFED WITH MORELS

Dried morels are soaked, sautéed, and stuffed into pockets cut in the chicken breasts. The sauce that tops the chicken packs double-barreled flavor from fresh morels and the dried-mushroom soaking liquid.

 WINE RECOMMENDATION

Any good Burgundy will be spectacular here, but a Gevrey-Chambertin, with its slightly earthy flavor, has a particular affinity for mushrooms.

SERVES 4

½   ounce dried morels

1   cup boiling water

4   boneless, skinless chicken breasts (about 1⅓ pounds in all)

     Salt and fresh-ground black pepper

¼   pound plus 3 tablespoons butter

4   shallots, minced

½   cup crème fraîche (see box, page 148) or heavy cream

½   pound fresh morels, stems trimmed

1   teaspoon lemon juice

1½   tablespoons flour

1   cup Chicken Stock, page 61, or canned low-sodium chicken broth

4   sprigs fresh tarragon, or ¼ teaspoon dried tarragon

1. Put the dried morels in a small bowl and pour the boiling water over them. Soak until softened, about 20 minutes. Remove the morels and strain the soaking liquid through a paper-towel-lined sieve into a bowl; reserve the liquid. Rinse the morels well to remove any grit and chop them.

2. Meanwhile, remove the tender (see box, page 200) from each chicken breast and reserve. With a sharp knife, cut a pocket in the thickest part of each breast. Sprinkle the chicken with ¼ teaspoon salt and ⅛ teaspoon pepper.

3. Heat the oven to 400°. Melt 2 tablespoons of the butter in a heavy medium frying pan over moderate heat. Add the shallots and cook, stirring occasionally, until translucent, 2 to 3 minutes. Add the chopped dried morels, a pinch each of salt and pepper, and ¼ cup of the crème fraîche. Cover and simmer until the morels are tender, about 10 minutes. Let cool.

4. Stuff one quarter of the shallot mixture into the pocket of each of the chicken breasts. Stuff a chicken tender into the opening of each pocket to close it.

5. Rinse the fresh morels and drain. Split or quarter the mushrooms, depending on their size. In a medium frying pan, melt 3 tablespoons of the butter over moderate

heat. Add 1 tablespoon of the morel-soaking liquid, a pinch each of salt and pepper, and the fresh morels. Cover and cook, stirring occasionally, until the mushrooms are tender, about 15 minutes.

6. Meanwhile, melt 4 tablespoons of the butter and pour into a medium baking dish. Put the chicken breasts in the dish in a single layer. Sprinkle with the lemon juice and 2 tablespoons of the morel-soaking liquid. Cover with aluminum foil and bake for 10 minutes.

7. While the chicken is baking, melt the remaining 2 tablespoons butter in a small saucepan over moderate heat. Add the flour and cook, stirring, for 2 minutes. Whisk in the stock, the remaining morel-soaking liquid, the remaining $1/4$ cup crème fraîche, and the tarragon. Bring to a boil, whisking constantly. Reduce the heat and simmer for 15 minutes. Remove the tarragon sprigs, if using, and stir in $1/4$ teaspoon salt and $1/8$ teaspoon pepper. Add the cooked fresh morels and heat through.

8. Put the baked chicken breasts on a platter and strain the cooking juices into the sauce. Pour the sauce over the chicken.

—LYDIE MARSHALL

NO FRESH MORELS?

If you can't find fresh morels, you can substitute additional reconstituted dried morels. You'll need an ounce and a half of the dried mushrooms to make half a pound when reconstituted. Soak them in three cups boiling water, but don't save this soaking liquid; the recipe requires only the one cup from the half-ounce of dried morels.

144

Papillotes of Chicken with Kale and Prosciutto

Sealed in parchment-paper packets, chicken breasts bake to a juicy tenderness. Bring the packets to the table unopened, letting each person enjoy the fragrant steam that bursts forth when the paper is slit open.

WINE RECOMMENDATION
The earthy, somewhat bitter bite of the kale will make a tannic wine taste medicinal. Instead, try a white that tends toward herbs, flowers, and nuts. Many Italian whites fill the bill nicely, but a nutty Greco di Tufo from Campania works particularly well.

SERVES 4

6 tablespoons extra-virgin olive oil

¼ pound kale, turnip greens, or mustard greens, stems removed, leaves washed well, dried, and chopped (about 4 cups)

Salt and fresh-ground black pepper

4 boneless, skinless chicken breasts (about 1⅓ pounds in all)

2 thin slices prosciutto

1. Heat the oven to 400°. Fold four 15-by-20-inch sheets of parchment paper in half to make 15-by-10-inch rectangles. Starting at the folded side, cut each rectangle into the shape of half a heart, so that when you unfold the sheet you have a heart with a fold running vertically down the center. Brush each heart with 1½ teaspoons of the oil.

2. In a large bowl, toss the kale with 2 tablespoons of the oil. Season lightly with salt and pepper. Put one quarter of the kale in the middle of one side of each heart.

3. Fold out the tender (see box, page 200) from each chicken breast to make an even thickness of chicken. Make four deep, evenly spaced diagonal cuts in each breast.

4. Cut the prosciutto slices in half. Roll up each half and cut it into four pieces. Tuck one spiraled piece of prosciutto into each cut in the chicken breasts. Put the chicken breasts on top of the kale and season lightly with salt and pepper. Drizzle the remaining 2 tablespoons oil on top.

5. Fold the other side of each parchment heart over the chicken to enclose it. Beginning at the top of each heart, fold over the edges of the parchment, making tight overlapping pleats to seal the packets. Put the packets on a baking sheet and bake for 10 minutes. Serve hot.

—ANNE DISRUDE

GINGERED CHICKEN BREASTS

Whether you serve these versatile chicken breasts whole or sliced into medallions, hot from the oven or cooled to room temperature, they're sure to be a hit. The accompaniments offer plenty of options, too—pick several different chutneys for a variety of tastes and textures.

WINE RECOMMENDATION
Light in alcohol and elegantly fruity, German rieslings have just the right piquancy and zing to mesh with these complex flavors and textures. Choose a kabinett from the Mosel or Nahe for some real excitement.

SERVES 4

2	tablespoons soy sauce
1	large scallion including green top, chopped
1	tablespoon cooking oil
2¼	teaspoons sherry vinegar
1	tablespoon chopped fresh parsley
1½	teaspoons ground ginger
¾	teaspoon Asian sesame oil
4	boneless, skinless chicken breasts (about 1⅓ pounds in all)
	Assorted chutneys, for serving

1. In a small bowl, mix together the soy sauce, scallion, cooking oil, vinegar, parsley, ginger, and sesame oil.

2. Put the chicken breasts in a shallow baking dish. Pour the soy-sauce mixture over the chicken and turn to coat. Marinate for 1 hour at room temperature.

3. Heat the oven to 350°. Bake the chicken breasts in the marinade until they are just cooked through, about 25 minutes. If the pan becomes dry, add a small amount of water. Serve the chicken with the chutneys alongside.

—PAUL GRIMES

MAKE IT AHEAD

You can marinate the chicken the day before and keep covered in the refrigerator overnight; return to room temperature before baking. Or, cook the chicken a day in advance; let cool, cover, and refrigerate. Return to room temperature before serving.

CHICKEN BREASTS WITH PROSCIUTTO AND LEMON

This flavorful dish would be great with buttered green beans tossed with pistachios. Add mashed potatoes or rice to complete the meal. If you have any chicken left over, cut it into thin slices and serve it cold.

 WINE RECOMMENDATION
Riesling, with its racy acidity and citrus tang, offers a good contrast to the salty and lemony flavors in this dish. Try one of the terrific dry rieslings from Austria; the best of them have tremendous concentration and complexity.

SERVES 4

6 tablespoons butter, at room temperature

2 ounces thin-sliced prosciutto, chopped

2 tablespoons minced fresh parsley

1½ teaspoons grated lemon zest
    Salt and fresh-ground black pepper

4 bone-in chicken breasts (about 2¼ pounds in all)

1 tablespoon olive oil

1 large shallot, minced

1 clove garlic, crushed

1 carrot, minced

½ small green bell pepper, minced

3 cups Chicken Stock, page 61, or canned low-sodium chicken broth
    Juice of ½ lemon

¼ cup crème fraîche (see box, next page)

¾ teaspoon arrowroot

1½ teaspoons water

1. Heat the oven to 450°. In a small bowl, beat together the butter, prosciutto, parsley, lemon zest, ½ teaspoon salt, and ½ teaspoon pepper. Divide the flavored butter into four portions.

2. Using your fingers, carefully loosen the skin of the chicken from the meat. Put one portion of the seasoned butter under the skin of each breast, spreading it evenly.

3. Put the chicken breasts on a rack set on a baking sheet. Bake, basting frequently with the drippings, until the chicken is golden brown and just cooked through, about 30 minutes. Cover loosely with aluminum foil and leave in a warm spot to rest.

4. Meanwhile, heat the oil in a large stainless-steel frying pan over moderate heat. Add the shallot and cook, stirring occasionally, until translucent, about 3 minutes. Add the garlic and cook for 1 minute more. Stir in the carrot and bell pepper and cook until slightly softened, about 2 minutes.

5. Add the stock, lemon juice, and crème fraîche and bring to a boil over high heat. Boil until the sauce has reduced to 1 cup, 8 to 10 minutes. ➤

6. In a cup, combine the arrowroot with the water and stir until dissolved. Stir the arrowroot mixture into the sauce and simmer, stirring constantly, until thickened, about 1 minute. Season with salt and pepper.

7. Using a long, thin, sharp knife, cut each stuffed chicken breast off the bone in one piece. Put the chicken breasts on plates and spoon the sauce on top.

—BOB CHAMBERS

CRÈME FRAÎCHE

This thickened cream—valued for its tangy, nutty flavor and the fact that it doesn't curdle when heated—is available at specialty-food stores and some supermarkets, but it's also easy to make at home. Heat one cup of heavy cream and one teaspoon of buttermilk until lukewarm. Transfer the mixture to a jar or plastic container and cover loosely. Let sit at room temperature until thick, about twenty-four hours, then refrigerate (it will continue to thicken as it chills) until ready to use, up to ten days.

CHICKEN WITH GARLIC, CAPERS, AND PARMESAN CHEESE

Sauté some garlic, brown some chicken, add capers and cheese, and bake until done—that's all it takes to make this simply delicious dish of chicken breasts with a tasty, tangy topping.

 WINE RECOMMENDATION
The sweet, salty flavors of the Parmesan call for a red wine, one with good acidity to counter the sharp capers. For ripe cherry fruit and some herbal accents as well, pour a Chianti Classico Riserva from a good recent vintage, such as 1985 or 1988.

SERVES 4

⅓ cup olive oil

8 large cloves garlic, cut into thick slices

8 chicken thighs

2½ teaspoons dried thyme

2½ teaspoons coarse-cracked black pepper

⅔ teaspoon salt

4 teaspoons capers, chopped

⅓ cup grated Parmesan cheese

1. Heat the oven to 350°. In a large heavy frying pan, heat the oil over moderate heat. Add the garlic and cook, stirring, until golden, about 3 minutes. Remove with a slotted spoon and chop fine.

2. Season the chicken thighs on both sides with the thyme and pepper. Reheat the oil in the pan over moderate heat. Add the chicken thighs and cook until golden, about 10 minutes on each side. Drain the thighs on paper towels and season with the salt. Put the thighs skin-side up on a baking sheet.

3. Combine the capers and the garlic and spread over the chicken thighs. Sprinkle the Parmesan on top. Bake until the chicken is just cooked through, about 15 minutes.

—ANNE DISRUDE

PEACH-GLAZED CHICKEN THIGHS

Summer, when peaches are at their best, is the perfect time for this slightly sweet chicken. Add rice, pasta, or simply bread, and dinner is ready.

WINE RECOMMENDATION

A California viognier has musky peach and apricot aromas and a voluptuous richness on the palate. Its exotic flavors can be tricky with food but make a great match here, as would a viognier-based Condrieu from the northern Rhône Valley of France.

SERVES 4

- 4 peaches
- 8 chicken thighs
- 1 teaspoon salt
- ½ teaspoon fresh-ground black pepper
- 1 tablespoon olive oil
- 1 tablespoon honey
- 1½ tablespoons red-wine vinegar
- ⅓ cup sliced scallion tops, for serving

1. Peel and chop two of the peaches, put them in a large bowl, and mash with a fork. Add the chicken thighs and turn to coat well. Cover and let stand at room temperature for 1 hour.

2. Heat the oven to 350°. Remove the chicken thighs from the marinade and pat dry with paper towels. Season the chicken with the salt and pepper.

3. In a large ovenproof frying pan, heat the oil over high heat. Add the chicken thighs, skin-side down, and cook until the skin is deep brown and crisp, about 5 minutes. Turn the thighs over and put the frying pan in the oven. Bake until just cooked through, about 15 minutes longer.

4. Meanwhile, peel and slice the remaining 2 peaches. Remove the chicken thighs from the frying pan and pour off any fat from the pan. Return the chicken thighs to the pan and cook over high heat until they begin to sizzle. Add the honey and turn the chicken to coat. Cook, stirring, until the honey begins to brown and stick to the pan, about 1 minute. Add the vinegar and the peach slices and scrape up any brown bits from the bottom of the pan. Cook, turning the chicken thighs once or twice, until glazed, about 1½ minutes. Put the chicken thighs on a platter and put the peaches in the middle. Sprinkle the scallions over the chicken.

—MARCIA KIESEL

MAKE IT AHEAD

Mix the chicken thighs with the peaches and leave in the refrigerator to marinate for up to 6 hours. Let the chicken return to room temperature before continuing with step 2.

CHICKEN THIGHS STUFFED WITH RICE, SAUSAGE, AND PECANS

Boning a chicken thigh creates a pocket in the dark meat that's just right for stuffing. Here, it's filled with a spicy mixture of *andouille* sausage, onion, green pepper, rice, and toasted nuts.

WINE RECOMMENDATION

Andouille is a powerful sausage that needs a sturdy red wine. Choose a rich yet surprisingly elegant and fragrant syrah-based Côte Rôtie or a less expensive, more rustic St-Joseph, both from France's northern Rhône Valley.

SERVES 4

¾   cup pecans

1½ cups water

¾   cup rice

2   ounces *andouille* or hot Italian sausage

1   tablespoon butter

½   small onion, chopped

2   tablespoons chopped green bell pepper

2   tablespoons minced scallion including green top

1   tablespoon minced fresh parsley

⅛   teaspoon thyme
     Salt

¼   teaspoon fresh-ground black pepper

1   egg, lightly beaten

8   boneless chicken thighs

¼   teaspoon paprika

1. In a small frying pan, toast the pecans over moderately low heat, stirring frequently, until golden brown, about 5 minutes. Or toast them in a 350° oven for about 8 minutes. Let cool and then chop coarse.

2. Bring the water to a boil in a small saucepan. Add the rice. Reduce the heat, cover, and simmer until the rice is tender and all the water is absorbed, about 25 minutes. Rinse the rice with cold water and drain.

3. Meanwhile, in a small saucepan of simmering water, cook the sausage for 10 minutes. Drain, cool slightly, and chop.

4. Melt the butter in a medium frying pan over moderately low heat. Add the onion and bell pepper and cook, stirring occasionally, until the onion is translucent, about 5 minutes. Remove from the heat and stir in the pecans, scallion, parsley, rice, sausage, thyme, ¼ teaspoon salt, and ⅛ teaspoon of the pepper. Mix in the egg.

5. Heat the oven to 375°. Season the chicken thighs on both sides with ⅛ teaspoon salt, the remaining ⅛ teaspoon pepper, and the paprika. Put a rounded tablespoon of the stuffing in the center of each

thigh and fold the meat and skin over to enclose it. Put the thighs, seam-side down, in two rows in a buttered baking dish, leaving a space down the center. Pack the leftover stuffing into the center space. Cover the stuffing with a strip of aluminum foil.

6. Bake the chicken for 35 minutes. Turn off the oven and let the chicken sit in the oven for 1 hour; do not open the door.

7. Put the stuffed chicken thighs and the extra stuffing on a platter. Skim the fat from the pan juices and pour the juices over the chicken.

—LEE BAILEY

MAKE IT AHEAD

These sausage-stuffed chicken thighs— as well as Baked Chicken with Celery Sauce, page 154—are perfect for making ahead because they're baked and then left to sit for an hour in a turned-off oven. This technique produces tender, moist pieces of chicken that are full of flavor. It also gives you plenty of time to make other dishes, prepare for a party, or just take a break. Resist the temptation, though, to open the oven door and see how the chicken's doing. You'll let out the heat that the chicken needs to finish cooking.

BAKED CHICKEN WITH CELERY SAUCE

Celery rarely gets a starring role in a main dish, but here it takes center stage: It's chopped to make a bed for the chicken as it bakes, then pureed and mixed with créme fraîche for a sublime sauce.

WINE RECOMMENDATION
Among the incredibly versatile wines of Alsace, perhaps none is more at home with food than pinot blanc. Its soft, nutty flavors, lemony lift, and light herbal accents will marry effortlessly with this juicy chicken. For a slightly richer wine, look for one labeled pinot d'Alsace.

SERVES 4

3 cups coarse-chopped celery
Salt
3½ pounds chicken parts
14 sprigs chervil, plus 1 teaspoon chopped fresh chervil or ½ teaspoon dried chervil
Fresh-ground black pepper
¼ cup crème fraîche (see box, page 148), more if needed

1. Heat the oven to 375°. Put the celery in a shallow baking dish just large enough to hold the chicken. Salt the chicken pieces very generously, including under the skin where possible. Tuck a sprig of chervil under the skin of each piece. Put the chicken, skin-side up, in the baking dish in a single layer; the celery should be completely covered. Sprinkle the chicken generously with pepper.

2. Put the chicken in the oven and bake for 30 minutes. Turn off the oven and let the chicken sit in the oven for 1½ hours; do not open the door.

3. Put the chicken on a platter. Using a slotted spoon, transfer the celery to a food processor. Pour the pan juices over the chicken and keep warm in the oven. Add the chopped chervil to the celery and puree. Drain the puree briefly if it seems too liquid. Put the puree in a small heavy saucepan, add the crème fraîche, and season with salt and pepper if necessary. Cook over moderate heat until warmed through. If the sauce is too thick, add more crème fraîche and some of the chicken juices from the platter. Serve the sauce with the chicken.

—LEE BAILEY

BAKED CHICKEN WINGS AND DRUMSTICKS WITH SEASONED SALT

Here's a dish as simple as any you'll come across, but that doesn't mean it lacks flavor. Two kinds of peppercorns—regular black and the more exotic Szechuan—provide plenty of punch.

WINE RECOMMENDATION
One of the guiding principles of matching food and wine is to pair similar flavors. Here, the nutmeg, cinnamon, and clove immediately call to mind a similarly spicy Coteaux du Layon. Though this is a sweet wine, its vibrant acidity stimulates the palate.

SERVES 4

2	teaspoons Szechuan peppercorns
1	teaspoon black peppercorns
1½	teaspoons salt
¼	teaspoon grated nutmeg
¼	teaspoon ground cloves
¼	teaspoon cinnamon
4	pounds mixed chicken wings and drumsticks
2	teaspoons peanut oil

1. Heat the oven to 400°. In a small heavy frying pan, toast the Szechuan and black peppercorns until very fragrant, 1 to 2 minutes.

2. Grind the toasted peppercorns in a mortar with a pestle or in a spice grinder and put them in a small bowl. Stir in the salt, nutmeg, cloves, and cinnamon.

3. Rub the chicken wings and drumsticks with the oil and put them in a single layer in a shallow roasting pan. Sprinkle the seasoned salt evenly over the chicken and bake until the chicken is crisp and golden, about 45 minutes.

SZECHUAN PEPPERCORNS

Despite the name, Szechuan peppercorns aren't really peppercorns at all. While black, white, and green peppercorns are all dried berries of the pepper plant, the berries known as Szechuan peppercorns come from the prickly ash tree. If your supermarket doesn't carry these, look for them at Asian markets.

PROVENÇAL CHICKEN WITH ROASTED GARLIC

The garlic in this traditional dish cooks so long that it becomes soft, mellow, and almost sweet. It's luscious squeezed from its skin and spread on slices of toasted French bread.

WINE RECOMMENDATION
The savory herbs and garlic make a southern Rhône red such as a Côtes-du-Rhône Villages or Vacqueyras a foolproof match. These husky wines are based on grenache, which gives them their signature flavors of roasted raspberry and herbs.

SERVES 4

- 1 chicken (3 to 3½ pounds), cut into 8 pieces
- ¼ teaspoon salt
- ½ teaspoon fresh-ground black pepper
- 6 tablespoons extra-virgin olive oil
- 1¼ teaspoons herbes de Provence, or a mixture of dried thyme, rosemary, marjoram, oregano, and savory
- 20 cloves garlic, unpeeled
- 1 loaf French or Italian bread, sliced and toasted

1. Heat the oven to 375°. Season the chicken pieces with the salt and ¼ teaspoon of the pepper.

2. In a flameproof casserole or Dutch oven, heat 1 tablespoon of the oil over moderately high heat. Add the chicken in batches and brown well on both sides, about 8 minutes in all. Remove the pot from the heat.

3. Add the herbes de Provence, garlic, and the remaining 5 tablespoons oil and ¼ teaspoon pepper. Turn to coat the chicken with the oil and seasonings. Cover the pot with aluminum foil and then with the lid. Bake, without removing the lid, for 1 hour and 10 minutes, until cooked through.

4. Serve the chicken with the garlic cloves, for spreading on the toasted bread.

—PETER KUMP

BAKED CHICKEN AND POTATOES WITH ROSEMARY AND LEMON

Bake chicken and potatoes together for an easy one-pot meal. A generous dose of lemon juice and dried rosemary enlivens the hearty mixture, and garlic gives it depth of flavor.

WINE RECOMMENDATION
Sauvignon blanc is an excellent foil for the flavors of lemon and rosemary. Try a Sancerre or Pouilly-Fumé or, if you can find one, a wine from nearby Menetou-Salon. While quite similar to its better known cousins, Menetou-Salon emphasizes pungent minerality over fruitiness.

SERVES 4

3 tablespoons olive oil

1 chicken (3 to 3½ pounds), cut into 8 pieces

3 baking potatoes, cut into 1½-inch chunks

1 clove garlic, minced

2 teaspoons dried rosemary, crumbled

¼ cup plus 2 tablespoons lemon juice (from about 2 lemons)

½ teaspoon salt

¼ teaspoon fresh-ground black pepper

1. Heat the oven to 400°. Coat a large baking pan with 1 tablespoon of the oil. Add the chicken pieces and the potatoes to the pan, toss them with the remaining 2 tablespoons oil, and spread them out in a single layer.

2. Sprinkle the garlic, rosemary, and the ¼ cup lemon juice over the chicken and potatoes. Cover loosely with aluminum foil. Bake for 30 minutes. Uncover and bake, turning the chicken occasionally so it browns evenly, until cooked through, about 15 minutes longer.

3. Put the chicken and the potatoes on plates and sprinkle with the remaining 2 tablespoons lemon juice, the salt, and the pepper. Spoon some of the pan juices over the chicken.

—JAMES W. BROWN

SPICY SPINACH CHICKEN

Feta cheese lends a predominantly Greek note to this mixed-heritage dish.
The chicken combines falling-off-the-bone tenderness with a crisp crust.

WINE RECOMMENDATION
This dish requires a rather neutral, but full-bodied, white wine to finesse the aggressive flavors. Try the wine grown on the high slopes of the Greek island of Santorini. Named for the island itself, it is surprisingly fresh and vibrant yet rich with Mediterranean earthiness.

SERVES 4

 5 tablespoons butter, at room temperature

 1 ounce feta cheese, crumbled (about ¼ cup)

 1 10-ounce package frozen chopped spinach, thawed and squeezed dry

 ½ teaspoon minced jalapeño pepper

 1 chicken (3 to 3½ pounds), cut into 8 pieces

 ¼ cup Dijon mustard

 1 cup fresh bread crumbs

 ½ teaspoon salt

 ¼ teaspoon fresh-ground black pepper

1. Combine 3 tablespoons of the butter, the feta cheese, spinach, and jalapeño pepper in a food processor and puree until smooth. Put the puree in a small bowl and refrigerate until slightly firm, about 10 minutes.

2. Using your fingers, carefully loosen the skin of the chicken from the meat. Stuff 1 tablespoon of the spinach mixture under the skin of each piece of chicken. Coat the chicken with the mustard and put, skin-side up, on a baking sheet. Refrigerate for 30 minutes.

3. Heat the oven to 350°. Mix the bread crumbs, salt, and pepper in a shallow bowl. Roll each piece of chicken in the crumbs and put on the baking sheet. Dot the pieces with the remaining 2 tablespoons butter. Bake until the skin is golden and crisp and the meat is falling off the bones, about 1½ hours.

—MOLLY O'NEILL

MUSTARD CHICKEN

Although this dish is delicious hot, it is even better at room temperature and can also be eaten cold. Make it a day ahead to give the flavors time to develop; the chicken can be reheated, if you like.

WINE RECOMMENDATION
Balance the spicy mustard, the lemon, and the tarragon in this dish with a powerful sauvignon blanc. Try one from New Zealand, where the fertile volcanic soils produce astonishingly ripe wines, while the cool climate helps them retain their palate-cleansing acidity.

SERVES 4

- 1 chicken (3 to 3½ pounds), cut into 8 pieces
- ½ cup Dijon mustard
- 2 eggs
- 2½ cups fresh bread crumbs
- 1 tablespoon paprika
- 1 teaspoon dried tarragon
- 1 teaspoon fresh-ground black pepper
- 3 tablespoons butter
- 3 tablespoons olive oil
- ⅓ cup lemon juice (from about 2 lemons)

1. Make a slit at the main joint of each chicken wing and remove the skin from the larger portion of the wing. Remove the skin from the remaining chicken pieces. In a large bowl, toss the chicken with the mustard to coat. Cover and marinate the chicken at room temperature, tossing occasionally, for 30 minutes.

2. Heat the oven to 375°. In a shallow bowl, lightly beat the eggs. In a shallow dish, combine the bread crumbs with the paprika, tarragon, and pepper.

3. One at a time, dip the chicken pieces into the eggs and then into the crumb mixture to coat evenly. Put the chicken pieces in a single layer in a shallow baking dish.

4. In a small saucepan, melt the butter with the oil over low heat. Remove the pan from the heat and stir in the lemon juice. Spoon half of the lemon butter over the chicken. Bake for 30 minutes. Spoon the remaining lemon butter over the chicken. Bake until the chicken is cooked through, about 30 minutes longer. Let rest in a warm spot for at least 15 minutes before serving.

—JIM FOBEL

CLAY-POT CHICKEN WITH OLIVES

Clay-pot cooking—in which the food is part baked, part steamed, in an unglazed pot that's been soaked in water—guarantees moist, tender meat.

WINE RECOMMENDATION
This rustic, earthy recipe offers an opportunity to showcase a northern Rhône red. These wines, made from syrah, often have a green-olive flavor to go along with their succulent cassis fruit and substantial tannins. Try a Crozes-Hermitage from a top producer.

SERVES 4

20 white boiling onions

1 tablespoon olive oil

1 chicken (3 to 3½ pounds)

2 bay leaves

Zest of 1 orange, cut off in strips

6 cloves garlic, crushed

2 sprigs rosemary, or ½ teaspoon dried rosemary

20 Kalamata olives, halved and pitted

20 green olives, halved and pitted

¼ teaspoon coarse-ground black pepper

¾ cup Chicken Stock, page 61, or canned low-sodium chicken broth

¼ cup dry vermouth

2 teaspoons arrowroot

2 tablespoons cold water

1. Soak the top and bottom of the clay pot in cold water for 15 minutes. In a large pot of boiling, salted water, cook the onions until almost tender, about 5 minutes. Drain well. Heat 1 teaspoon of the oil in a small frying pan over high heat. Add the onions and cook, shaking the pan, until well browned.

2. Stuff the chicken with one of the bay leaves, half the orange zest, two of the garlic cloves, and 1 rosemary sprig or ¼ teaspoon of the dried rosemary. Twist the wings behind the back of the chicken and tie the legs together. Coat the chicken with the remaining 2 teaspoons oil and put in the pot. (If the bottom is not glazed, line it with a piece of parchment or waxed paper.)

3. Put the onions, olives, and the remaining bay leaf, zest, garlic, and rosemary around the chicken. Sprinkle with the pepper; pour in the stock and vermouth. Cover and put in the center of the oven. Turn on the oven to 450°; bake for 1 hour. Remove the lid. Bake until the skin is browned, about 15 minutes longer.

4. Cut the chicken into serving pieces and put on a platter. Using a slotted spoon, remove the onions and olives and scatter over the chicken. Skim the fat from the cooking juices and pour the juices into a small saucepan. Stir the arrowroot into the water until dissolved, and then stir into the juices. Cook, stirring, until slightly thickened. Serve the gravy with the chicken.

—ANNE DISRUDE

161

SALT-BAKED CHICKEN WITH GINGER SAUCE

The most famous dish in the Hakka cuisine of China is this whole chicken "baked" in a cocoon of hot salt. It emerges exceedingly juicy and not at all salty.

WINE RECOMMENDATION

The intricate but heady aromas of this Chinese classic cry out for gewürztraminer, the signature flavors of which include rose petals, lychee, ginger, and spice. Look for a sleek version from Italy's Alto Adige.

SERVES 4

1 chicken (3 to 3½ pounds)

5 slices fresh ginger, each about the size of a quarter

2 scallions including green tops, cut into 1½-inch lengths

1½ tablespoons Chinese rice wine or dry sherry

5 sprigs cilantro, plus additional sprigs for serving

1 star anise, broken

1 tablespoon Rose Dew Liqueur or Wu Chia Pi Chiew,* extra-dry vermouth, or vodka

4½ pounds coarse salt

Hakka Ginger Sauce, opposite page

*Available in Asian liquor stores

1. Pat the chicken dry inside and out. Smash the ginger and scallions with the flat side of a heavy knife. Rub the cavity of the chicken with the rice wine and stuff it with the ginger and scallions, the cilantro sprigs, and the star anise. Truss the chicken tightly with string.

2. Brush the liqueur over the skin of the chicken. Put the chicken, breast-side up, on a rack and put in a cool, airy place until the skin is dry to the touch, about 2 hours.

3. Wrap the chicken in a single layer of cheesecloth, bringing the two sides up to overlap by ½ inch on top. Bring up the loose ends over the top of the bird and tie them tightly with cotton kitchen string. The chicken should be tightly wrapped in a neat ball.

4. Put the salt in a large heavy pot or spun-steel wok that will hold the chicken snugly. Heat the salt over moderately high heat, stirring frequently, until it is very hot to the touch, 5 to 10 minutes. Scoop out and reserve about 6 cups of the hot salt, all but a 1-inch layer. Put the chicken in the pot, breast-side up, and cover completely with the reserved hot salt.

5. Cover the pot and reduce the heat to moderate. Cook the chicken, undisturbed, until the juices run clear when the thigh is pierced, 1½ to 2 hours. Check for doneness

by brushing off the salt and piercing the thigh with a sharp knife. If the juices run pink, cover with the salt again and bake 15 to 30 minutes longer.

6. Push the salt aside and gently pull out the chicken, holding the knotted cheesecloth on top. Try not to tip the chicken, or the juices will spill out. Put the chicken on a platter and remove the cheesecloth. Untie the legs and use chopsticks or tongs to remove the seasonings from the cavity.

7. Serve the chicken hot, warm, or at room temperature. Chop it into bite-size pieces with a Chinese cleaver or carve it. Garnish with the additional cilantro sprigs and serve with the Hakka Ginger Sauce.

—BARBARA TROPP

CHINESE LIQUEURS

Rose Dew Liqueur (Mai Kuei Lu Chiew) and the untranslatable Wu Chia Pi Chiew are bottled in squat brown crocks. They have an inimitable flavor—the former heady with the aroma of roses—and are a walloping 99 proof.

HAKKA GINGER SAUCE

The traditional accompaniment to salt-baked chicken, Hakka Ginger Sauce is often made with a gingery powder that has a distinctly medicinal taste. This variation uses fresh ginger instead.

MAKES ABOUT 1/4 CUP

    2 tablespoons corn or peanut oil
    1 packed tablespoon minced fresh ginger
    1/4 teaspoon coarse salt

Heat the oil in a small saucepan over moderate heat until it sends up a wisp of smoke. Put the ginger in a small heavy dish. Scrape the hot oil over the ginger and stir to combine. Sprinkle with the salt and stir to blend. Serve warm or at room temperature.

CHICKEN WITH ARTICHOKES

Tarragon-flavored chicken bakes atop a bed of artichokes, shallots, and mushrooms. A final addition of Bel Paese cheese gives a touch of richness to the dish.

WINE RECOMMENDATION
Stick with a crisp, not too fruity white, since artichokes will make a fruity wine taste sweet. A Petit Chablis is a good selection, as its mineral flavors will harmonize well with the mushrooms and the effect of the artichokes will be to round out its sharp acidity.

SERVES 4

2	tablespoons butter
2½	teaspoons peanut oil
2	tablespoons minced shallots, or ¼ cup minced onions
	Salt
1	10-ounce package frozen artichoke hearts, thawed and patted dry
6	ounces mushrooms, sliced
⅛	teaspoon white pepper
1⅓	pounds boneless, skinless chicken breasts (about 4), cut into bite-size pieces
¼	cup dry white wine
¼	teaspoon dried tarragon
⅓	cup cubed Bel Paese cheese
1	teaspoon chopped fresh parsley

1. Heat the oven to 350°. In a large frying pan, melt 1 teaspoon of the butter with ½ teaspoon of the oil over high heat. Add the shallots and a pinch of salt and cook, stirring, until translucent. Using a slotted spoon, transfer the shallots to a medium baking dish.

2. Add 1 tablespoon of the butter to the frying pan. Add the artichoke hearts and ¼ teaspoon salt and cook over very high heat until the artichokes are light golden but not cooked through, about 3 minutes. Add the artichokes to the baking dish.

3. Add 1 teaspoon of the butter and 1 teaspoon of the oil to the frying pan. Add the mushrooms and the pepper and stir-fry until the mushrooms are lightly colored but have not started to give off any liquid. Add to the baking dish.

4. Melt the remaining 1 teaspoon butter with the remaining 1 teaspoon oil in the frying pan over moderately high heat. Add the chicken and ¼ teaspoon salt to the pan and cook, stirring occasionally, just until the chicken is lightly colored. Add the chicken to the baking dish.

5. Bring the cooking juices in the frying pan to a boil and boil until only the fat remains. Pour off the fat, add the wine, and bring to a boil, scraping up any brown bits from the bottom of the pan. Pour the juices over the chicken in the baking dish. Sprinkle with the tarragon.

6. Cover and bake, stirring occasionally, until the mixture is hot and the chicken is cooked through, 30 to 45 minutes.

7. About 5 minutes before the dish is ready, add the cheese and toss well. Cover and bake until the cheese is just soft but not melted, about 5 minutes. Sprinkle with the chopped parsley.

MAKE IT AHEAD

You can prepare the chicken through step 5 a day in advance. Cover and refrigerate. Bring to room temperature before baking.

PESTO CHICKEN WITH RED AND YELLOW PEPPERS

Pesto, crème fraîche, and Parmesan cheese create a smooth, flavorful sauce for chicken and vegetables. All you need to make a meal is some crusty bread or buttered noodles. Broiled tomatoes would also be nice.

 WINE RECOMMENDATION
Select a fresh, lively red wine to contrast with and highlight the vegetables and Parmesan. An interesting choice would be Saumur-Champigny, made from cabernet franc. The fruitiest of the Loire's top reds, it has a taste reminiscent of fresh strawberries, currants, and herbs.

SERVES 4

⅓ cup flour

1 teaspoon salt

1¼ teaspoons fresh-ground black pepper

4 chicken thighs

4 chicken drumsticks

1½ tablespoons olive oil

3 shallots, cut into thin slices

2 small cloves garlic, crushed

2 red bell peppers, cut into ¼-inch strips

2 yellow bell peppers, cut into ¼-inch strips

1 pound small zucchini, quartered lengthwise and sliced crosswise into ½-inch pieces

⅓ cup Pesto alla Genovese, next page, or store-bought pesto

¾ cup crème fraîche (see box, page 148)

½ cup grated Parmesan cheese

¾ cup fresh bread crumbs

¾ teaspoon dried thyme

⅛ teaspoon cayenne

1. In a shallow bowl, combine the flour, salt, and 1 teaspoon of the black pepper. Dredge the chicken thighs and drumsticks in the flour mixture and shake off any excess.

2. In a large flameproof casserole, heat 1 tablespoon of the oil over moderately high heat. Add the chicken and cook, turning often, until well browned, about 10 minutes. Drain the chicken on paper towels and wipe out the casserole.

3. Heat the oven to 375°. Heat the remaining 1½ teaspoons oil in a large frying pan over moderately high heat. Add the shallots and cook, stirring occasionally, until translucent, 2 to 3 minutes. Add the garlic and cook for 1 minute. Add the bell peppers and the zucchini and cook, stirring occasionally, until the vegetables are softened, 5 to 7 minutes. Remove the frying pan from the heat.

4. In a small bowl, whisk the pesto with the crème fraîche until blended. In another

small bowl, toss the Parmesan with the bread crumbs, thyme, cayenne, and the remaining 1/4 teaspoon black pepper.

5. Put the chicken in the casserole and spread the vegetables over the top. Spread the pesto cream over the vegetables. Sprinkle the Parmesan crumbs evenly over the top and bake for 45 minutes.

—Bob Chambers

Make It Ahead

You can assemble the dish up to two days in advance, but don't top with the crumbs; cover and refrigerate. Let return to room temperature before adding the Parmesan crumbs and baking.

Pesto alla Genovese

This recipe makes more than you'll need for the Pesto Chicken Cassoulet. Store the unused portion in the refrigerator for up to a week, or freeze it for future use.

MAKES ABOUT 1 CUP

- 2 cloves garlic, chopped
- 1 1/2 cups packed fresh basil leaves
- 3/4 teaspoon salt
- 1/2 cup olive oil
- 1/4 cup pine nuts
- 1/2 cup grated Parmesan cheese
- 1 tablespoon butter, at room temperature

1. In a food processor, mince the garlic and basil with the salt.

2. With the machine on, add the oil in a thin stream and continue processing until well blended. Add the pine nuts, Parmesan, and butter and process until the nuts are chopped fine.

CHICKEN PIES

Most chicken-pie recipes call for the chicken to be cooked twice: once before making the filling and then again within the pie. We have found that this is unnecessary—when raw chicken is used in the filling, the result is meat that is perfectly cooked and tasty.

WINE RECOMMENDATION
This classic American dish calls for a classic American wine. Though U.S. chardonnays can be tricky to pair with foods because they are strongly flavored and often oaky, an opulent, tropically fruity Napa Valley bottling will do well here.

SERVES 4

½ pound boneless, skinless chicken breasts (2 small)

1½ cups Chicken Stock, page 61, or canned low-sodium chicken broth, more if needed

1 carrot, cut into thin slices

1 small boiling potato, diced

½ cup frozen peas

½ turnip, peeled and diced

3½ tablespoons butter

½ onion, diced fine

3½ tablespoons flour

¼ cup dry sherry

Flaky Pastry, page 171

1 egg

1½ teaspoons water

1. Cut the chicken breasts lengthwise into thirds. Cut the chicken strips into ½-inch pieces. Put on a plate, cover, and refrigerate.

2. In a small saucepan, bring the stock to a boil over high heat. Add the carrot and potato, return to a boil, and cook for 3 minutes. Using a slotted spoon, transfer the vegetables to a large bowl.

3. Return the broth to a boil, add the peas and turnip, and cook for 3 minutes. Using the slotted spoon, add the peas and turnip to the carrot and potato. Measure the broth; if necessary, add stock or water to make 1 cup. Add the sherry to the broth.

4. Melt the butter in a small frying pan over moderately low heat. Add the onion and cook, stirring occasionally, until translucent, about 5 minutes. Stir in the flour and cook, whisking, for 2 minutes. Whisk in the sherry-broth mixture. Bring to a boil over moderate heat and continue boiling, whisking constantly, until the sauce thickens, about 1 minute. Remove from the heat, cover with a round of waxed paper, and let the sauce cool to room temperature (or cool in the refrigerator if desired).

5. On a lightly floured surface, roll out half the pastry to about ⅛ inch thick. Cut out four 7-inch rounds and fit them into four 5-inch pie pans or ceramic crocks. Cover the pans and refrigerate until needed. Roll out

the remaining dough and cut out four 6-inch rounds. Stack these between sheets of waxed paper and refrigerate.

6. Heat the oven to 400°. Add the chicken and sauce to the vegetables and toss until evenly mixed. Remove the rolled-out pastry from the refrigerator. Cut a ¼-inch steam hole in the center of each 6-inch round.

7. Divide the chicken mixture among the pie shells. Moisten the edge of one of the pie shells with water, center a 6-inch pastry round over the top, and press the edges together to seal. Tuck the excess pastry under itself and crimp the edge. Repeat with the remaining pie shells and pastry.

8. In a small bowl, beat the egg with the water. Brush the tops of the pies with egg glaze and put on a heavy baking sheet. Bake until the crust is crisp and golden brown, about 40 minutes.

FLAKY PASTRY

MAKES ENOUGH DOUGH FOR FOUR 5-INCH PIES

- 2 cups flour
- ½ teaspoon salt
- 3 tablespoons cold lard
- 4 tablespoons cold butter, cut into ½-inch pieces
- 4 tablespoons cold vegetable shortening
- 5 tablespoons ice water, plus more if needed

1. Combine the flour and salt in a large bowl. Using a pastry blender or two knives, cut in the lard, butter, and shortening until the mixture resembles coarse meal.

2. Sprinkle the ice water over the mixture and stir rapidly with a fork just to blend. If the pastry does not hold together when pressed, stir in up to 1 additional tablespoon of water. Do not overmix. Divide the dough in half, flatten each half into a disk, and wrap in waxed paper. Refrigerate for at least 30 minutes.

Baked Saffron Crêpes with Chicken Filling

The saffron appears as threads of crimson in these delicate pale-yellow crêpes. The creamy chicken filling is flavored with Pernod, and the dish is finished with a crunchy almond-and-butter topping.

WINE RECOMMENDATION
Select a simple, fairly neutral wine that won't compete with the multilayered flavors here, such as a Gavi from Italy's Piedmont region. Its crisp, limelike flavors and unusual (for Italy) steeliness will direct attention toward the crêpes.

SERVES 4

¼ pound plus 3 tablespoons butter

¾ teaspoon saffron threads

1½ tablespoons dry vermouth

3 large eggs

1⅓ cups milk

1 cup water, more if needed

½ teaspoon table salt

2½ cups flour

Cooking oil

Coarse salt and fresh-ground black pepper

1⅓ pounds boneless, skinless chicken breasts (about 4), cut into ¾-inch pieces

1½ teaspoons minced garlic

⅔ cup thin-sliced scallions, including green tops

¼ pound mushrooms, halved and cut into thick slices

1 teaspoon dried thyme or basil

3 tablespoons Pernod or other anise liqueur, more if needed

1½ teaspoons tomato paste

¼ to ½ cup sour cream

Pinch cayenne

½ cup sliced almonds

1. In a small saucepan, melt the 3 tablespoons butter. In a small bowl, soak the saffron in the vermouth for about 10 minutes.

2. Lightly beat the eggs in a food processor. Add the milk, the water, the saffron and vermouth, and the table salt and blend. Gradually add 2 cups of flour, blending thoroughly. Blend in the melted butter. Scrape the batter into a bowl, cover, and refrigerate for 1 to 2 hours.

3. Stir the batter. Add enough water (about ½ cup) to thin it to the consistency of heavy cream.

4. Heat a 6- to 7-inch crêpe pan over moderate heat. Brush with a little oil. Pour about 3 tablespoons of the crêpe batter into the center of the pan and swirl to cover the bottom evenly. Cook until the bottom of the crêpe is lightly browned, about 1 minute.

Turn the crêpe and cook until it is dry and spotted with brown on the other side, about 10 seconds. Repeat with the remaining batter, stacking the finished crêpes between paper towels. Regrease the pan as necessary.

5. In a medium bowl, combine the remaining ½ cup flour, ½ teaspoon coarse salt, and ¼ teaspoon black pepper. Toss the chicken in the mixture to coat lightly. Put the chicken in a sieve.

6. In a large frying pan, melt 4 tablespoons of the butter and heat until it stops foaming. Shake the excess flour from the chicken, add the chicken to the pan, and stir-fry for about 2 minutes. Add the garlic, scallions, mushrooms, and thyme and cook, stirring, until the mushrooms just lose their raw look, 1 to 2 minutes.

7. Add the Pernod, heat it for a moment, and then carefully light it with a match. Shake the pan until the flames die out. Add the tomato paste and toss to combine. Remove the pan from the heat.

8. Add just enough sour cream to bind the mixture lightly. Add the cayenne and enough additional coarse salt, black pepper, thyme, and/or Pernod to flavor the filling assertively. Cool slightly.

9. In a small frying pan, toast the almonds over moderately low heat, stirring frequently, until golden brown, about 5 minutes. Or toast them in a 350° oven for about 8 minutes.

10. Heat the oven to 375°. Lightly butter a shallow baking dish. In a small saucepan, melt the remaining 4 tablespoons butter.

11. On the spotty side of 1 crêpe, spoon a generous amount of filling about 1 to 2 inches from the edge nearest you. Fold the bottom edge of the crêpe up over the filling and carefully roll the crêpe up. Place, seam-side down, in the baking dish. Repeat with all the remaining crêpes and filling. Drizzle about a tablespoon of the melted butter over the crêpes, sprinkle the almonds on top, and then drizzle with the remaining butter. Bake until the crêpes are heated through and the butter is sizzling, 10 to 12 minutes.

Chicken Enchilada Casserole with Salsa Verde

Chicken enchiladas are great make-ahead food, and always a favorite. In this dish the tortillas are layered with the filling rather than rolled up around it.

WINE RECOMMENDATION
Any wine will be overwhelmed by the strong flavors and hot chiles in these enchiladas. Instead, try quenching the flames with a beer, the crisper and colder the better.

SERVES 4

1 chicken (3 to 3½ pounds)

1 small carrot, chopped

2 slices Spanish onion

2 small cloves garlic, chopped

1 teaspoon salt

1 cup corn oil

8 6-inch corn tortillas

⅔ cup heavy cream

⅓ cup sour cream

1⅔ cups Salsa Verde, next page

⅔ cup chopped scallions, including green tops

¼ pound Monterey Jack cheese, grated (about 1 cup)

¼ pound sharp cheddar cheese, grated (about 1 cup)

4 lettuce leaves

4 radish roses (optional)

1. Put the chicken, carrot, onion, garlic, and salt in a large heavy pot or flameproof casserole. Add water to cover and bring to a boil. Reduce the heat, cover, and simmer until the chicken is very tender, about 1½ hours. Remove from the heat, uncover, and let cool in the broth for 1 hour.

2. Separate the chicken meat from the skin and bones and shred it. Discard the skin and bones.

3. In a medium frying pan, heat the oil to 375°. Quickly fry the tortillas, two or three at a time, until crisp. Drain the tortillas well on paper towels.

4. Heat the oven to 375°. Lightly oil a large shallow baking dish. In a small bowl, combine the heavy cream and sour cream and blend well.

5. Spread ⅓ cup of the Salsa Verde over the bottom of the baking dish and cover with four of the tortillas. Drizzle the tortillas with ⅓ cup of the salsa and scatter the chicken on top. Spread half the sour-cream mixture over the chicken and sprinkle with ⅓ cup of the scallions and ⅔ cup of each cheese. Arrange the four remaining tortillas on top and cover with the remaining 1 cup salsa and ⅓ cup of each cheese. Spread the remaining sour-cream mixture

on top and sprinkle with the remaining ⅓ cup scallions.

6. Bake until the casserole is heated through and the cheeses are melted, 30 to 35 minutes. Accompany each serving with a lettuce leaf and a radish rose, if you like.

—JANE BUTEL

MAKE IT AHEAD

Prepare the casserole through step 5, cover well with plastic wrap, and refrigerate for up to three days or freeze for up to three months. Let the casserole come to room temperature before baking.

SALSA VERDE

This recipe makes more than you'll need for the enchilada casserole. Save the rest to use in other Southwestern dishes or on slices of leftover roast chicken.

MAKES ABOUT 2 ½ CUPS

- 1 13-ounce can tomatillos, drained
- 1 cup chopped scallions, including green tops
- 1 4-ounce can chopped hot green chiles, drained
- 1 large clove garlic, minced
- ½ teaspoon salt

Combine all the ingredients in a blender or food processor and puree.

chapter 7

GRILLING & BROILING

Grilled Deviled Chicken, page 189

GRILLED CHICKEN WITH GREEN-PEPPERCORN MUSTARD

The only thing in this recipe that takes any time is letting the chicken marinate—and that doesn't take any effort. If you like, substitute another kind of mustard for the green-peppercorn variety called for here.

WINE RECOMMENDATION
Serve these simple, unadorned chicken breasts with a crisp, mouth-watering Sancerre. Made from sauvignon blanc, Sancerre has grassy, herbal, and gooseberry flavors that will harmonize beautifully with the chicken.

SERVES 4

¼ cup lemon juice

¼ cup cooking oil

1½ tablespoons minced onion

⅛ teaspoon dried thyme

½ teaspoon salt

1 tablespoon green-peppercorn mustard

4 boneless, skinless chicken breasts (about 1⅓ pounds in all)

1. In a medium bowl, stir together the lemon juice, cooking oil, onion, thyme, salt, and mustard.

2. Cut a ⅛-inch-deep crosshatch pattern on each chicken breast. Pour half of the lemon-juice mixture into a shallow glass dish. Put the chicken breasts in a single layer in the dish and cover with the remaining marinade. Cover the dish with plastic wrap and refrigerate for 2 hours, turning occasionally. Let the chicken return to room temperature before cooking.

3. Light the grill. Grill the chicken for 3 minutes. Turn and cook until the chicken is just done, about 3 minutes longer.

—LEE BAILEY

179

SPICY GRILLED CITRUS CHICKEN

A luscious barbecue sauce—combining tomato, orange, and lime with a kick of hot pepper and a lick of honey—gives this grilled chicken a decidedly Mexican flavor. Start well ahead of time to give the chicken time to marinate.

WINE RECOMMENDATION

The multiple citrus influences in this sauce immediately call to mind the intricate citrus flavors of riesling. To counter the cayenne's zing, serve a German auslese from the Rheingau or Rheinhessen. Wines from these regions are more fruity than those of the Mosel or Nahe.

SERVES 4

- 1 6-ounce can frozen orange-juice concentrate, thawed
- ½ cup canned tomato puree
- ¼ cup honey
- 1 teaspoon minced orange zest
- 1 teaspoon minced lemon zest
- 1 teaspoon minced lime zest
- 3 tablespoons lemon juice (from about 1 lemon)
- 3 tablespoons lime juice (from about 2 limes)
- 4 cloves garlic, minced
- 1 teaspoon fresh thyme, or ¼ teaspoon dried thyme
- 1 teaspoon salt
- ¾ teaspoon cayenne
- ¾ teaspoon fresh-ground black pepper
- 4 bone-in chicken breasts (about 2¼ pounds in all)

1. In a large shallow bowl, combine the orange-juice concentrate, tomato puree, honey, orange zest, lemon zest, lime zest, lemon juice, lime juice, garlic, thyme, salt, cayenne, and black pepper. Mix well.

2. Add the chicken to the orange-juice mixture and turn to coat. Cover and refrigerate for at least 12 hours, or overnight. Bring back to room temperature before cooking.

3. Light the grill. Grill the chicken skin-side up for 5 minutes. Meanwhile, pour the marinade into a small stainless-steel saucepan and bring to a boil over moderate heat. Boil for 1 minute. Spoon some of the marinade over each chicken breast and turn. Grill, basting with the marinade and turning every 5 minutes, until the chicken is just done, 20 to 25 minutes.

—JIM FOBEL

GRILLED TANDOORI-STYLE CHICKEN

Tandoori chicken has two marinades—one of salt and citrus juice, and the other containing yogurt, onion, garlic, ginger, chile, and the Indian spice mix called *garam masala*. The hot-off-the-grill chicken can be eaten as is, with only lemon wedges as garnish, or topped with a spicy sauce and served as Chicken Makhani, page 183.

WINE RECOMMENDATION

Gewürztraminers are often recommended with Indian food because of their exotic, spicy character. But these wines also tend toward high alcohol and bitterness, which will be exaggerated by the hot chile here. Therefore, select a rich and fruity gewürztraminer, such as one from California, with some residual sugar.

SERVES 4

2½ pounds chicken drumsticks and thighs

2 teaspoons coarse salt

3 lemons, cut into quarters

¾ cup plain yogurt

½ onion, quartered

5 cloves garlic

1 ¾-inch chunk fresh ginger, peeled and quartered

½ hot green chile, sliced

2 teaspoons *garam masala* (see box, page 183)

½ pound butter, melted

1. Make two diagonal slits, about 1 inch long, down to the bone on each side of each chicken piece.

2. Put the chicken on a platter in one layer and sprinkle with 1 teaspoon of the salt and the juice from three of the lemon quarters. Lightly rub the salt and lemon juice into the slits in the chicken. Turn the chicken over and repeat on the other side, using the remaining salt and three more lemon quarters. Let marinate for 20 minutes.

3. In a food processor or blender, puree the yogurt, onion, garlic, ginger, chile, and *garam masala* to a smooth paste. Coat the chicken well with the paste, rubbing it into the slits. Cover and refrigerate for at least 5 hours and up to 24 hours.

4. Light the grill. Grill the chicken for 15 to 20 minutes, basting very frequently with the melted butter. Turn and grill, basting very frequently, until the chicken is just done, 15 to 20 minutes longer. Serve hot with the remaining lemon quarters.

—MADHUR JAFFREY

CHICKEN MAKHANI

While the Grilled Tandoori-Style Chicken, page 181, is cooking, whip up the tasty tomato sauce in this recipe. Like the chicken marinade, it contains ginger, hot green chile, and *garam masala*, so the finished dish is deeply spicy.

 WINE RECOMMENDATION
While gewürztraminer works just fine with unsauced tandoori-style chicken, the additional hot chile, herbs, and spices here are just too much for any wine. Instead, drink a rich, malty, dark beer.

SERVES 4

1 teaspoon cumin seeds

1 cup canned tomato sauce

1 1-inch chunk fresh ginger, peeled and grated fine

1 cup heavy cream

1 teaspoon *garam masala* (see box, right)

¼ teaspoon salt

¼ teaspoon cayenne

1 hot green chile, cut into very thin rounds

1 tablespoon minced cilantro

1 tablespoon lemon juice

¼ pound butter

Grilled Tandoori-Style Chicken, page 181

Cilantro sprigs, for garnish

1. In a small heavy frying pan, toast the cumin seeds over medium heat, shaking the pan, until they are a shade darker. Grind the seeds in a mortar with a pestle or in a spice grinder.

2. In a bowl, combine the tomato sauce, ginger, cream, *garam masala*, salt, cayenne, chile, cilantro, lemon juice, and the toasted cumin seeds.

3. Melt the butter in a large skillet over medium heat. Add the tomato mixture, bring to a simmer, and cook for 1 minute. Add the chicken pieces, stirring to coat and to re-warm if necessary. Serve the chicken and sauce topped with the cilantro sprigs.

—MADHUR JAFFREY

GARAM MASALA

Garam masala, a ground spice mixture, is available in Indian and other specialty-food stores, but tastes best when homemade. In a spice grinder, grind one tablespoon cardamom seeds, a one-inch cinnamon stick, one third of a whole nutmeg, one teaspoon cloves, one teaspoon peppercorns, and one teaspoon black cumin seeds. Store in a tightly closed jar.

SLOW-FIRE SMOKED CHICKEN

If you won't be eating the chicken immediately, let it cool and then set it on a plate and cover loosely with waxed paper to allow it to breathe.

 WINE RECOMMENDATION
The chicken's subtle smoky flavor and herbal aromas suggest a fruity but delicate pinot noir. Opt for Burgundy to echo the smoke and herbs but stay with a Bourgogne Rouge or district bottling such as an Hautes Côtes de Nuits so as not to overpower the chicken.

SERVES 4

1   chicken (3 to 3½ pounds)

1   lemon, halved

1   teaspoon salt

2   teaspoons fresh-ground Szechuan peppercorns, or 1 teaspoon fresh-ground black pepper

1   clove garlic, crushed

2   tablespoons butter

2   shallots

3   sprigs rosemary, or 1 teaspoon dried rosemary

1   tablespoon extra-virgin olive oil

1. Light the grill. Remove the fat from the tail end of the chicken. Squeeze the juice of one lemon half into the cavity. Sprinkle ½ teaspoon of the salt and 1 teaspoon of the Szechuan pepper or ½ teaspoon of the black pepper in the cavity. Put both lemon halves, the garlic, butter, shallots, and rosemary in the cavity. Rub the chicken with the oil and sprinkle with the remaining ½ teaspoon salt and 1 teaspoon Szechuan pepper or ½ teaspoon black pepper. Tuck the wings of the chicken behind the back and tie the legs together. Skewer the cavity and the neck closed.

2. Over a low fire, grill the chicken, breast-side up. Cover the grill, leaving all the vents wide open. Cook, turning the chickens every 15 to 20 minutes, until evenly browned and just cooked through, 1¼ to 1½ hours. Transfer the chicken to a plate and leave to rest in a warm spot for about 15 minutes before carving.

—KAREN LEE AND ALEXANDRA BRANYON

ALL-AMERICAN BARBECUED CHICKEN

Marinate the chicken in the cooled barbecue sauce for up to six hours before grilling it, if you have time. The longer it marinates, the more the meat will absorb the classic barbecue flavor.

 WINE RECOMMENDATION
Have this all-American chicken with the all-American red wine: zinfandel. Though the grape's origins are still debated by scientists, its wine is uniquely American. Zinfandel's blackberry fruit, exuberant spice, and massive body are ideal for the sweet and charry intensity of barbecue.

SERVES 4

1	6-ounce can tomato paste
1	cup dry vermouth
⅓	cup lemon juice
⅓	cup tarragon vinegar
⅓	cup honey
¼	cup Worcestershire sauce
3	tablespoons Dijon mustard
2	tablespoons soy sauce
1	tablespoon hot-pepper sauce
1	teaspoon ground cumin
2	tablespoons butter
1½	tablespoons olive oil
1	onion, minced
4	cloves garlic, minced
1	bay leaf
2½	pounds chicken parts

1. Light the grill. In a medium bowl, mix the tomato paste, vermouth, lemon juice, vinegar, honey, Worcestershire sauce, mustard, soy sauce, hot sauce, and cumin until blended.

2. In a medium stainless-steel saucepan, melt the butter with the oil over moderate heat. Add the onion and garlic and cook, stirring occasionally, until the onion is translucent, about 5 minutes.

3. Add the tomato mixture and the bay leaf and simmer over moderately low heat, stirring occasionally, until thickened, about 20 minutes.

4. Grill the chicken, turning once, for 5 minutes. Baste with the barbecue sauce and continue grilling, basting liberally and turning every 5 minutes, until the chicken is just done, 20 to 25 minutes longer.

SHERRIED CHICKEN WITH STICKY-LICK-IT BARBECUE SAUCE

The sherry marinade brings depth of flavor to the chicken, then is combined with honey, molasses, and tomato puree for a delectably sticky barbecue sauce.

WINE RECOMMENDATION
The sweet barbecue sauce calls for a fruity but very dry and tart red wine. Barbera d'Alba or Barbera del Monferrato, with their cherry and cassis flavors, strong acidity, and low tannin, will do splendidly.

SERVES 4

- 2 cups dry sherry
- ¼ cup lemon juice
- 2 bay leaves
- 2 large cloves garlic, crushed
- 1 small onion, chopped fine
- 1 chicken (3 to 3½ pounds), cut into 8 pieces
- 1¾ cups canned tomato puree
- ¼ cup honey
- 3 tablespoons light molasses
- ½ teaspoon dried thyme
- 1 teaspoon salt
- ½ teaspoon cayenne
- ¼ teaspoon fresh-ground black pepper
- 2 tablespoons white-wine vinegar

1. In a large bowl, combine the sherry, lemon juice, bay leaves, garlic, and onion. Add the chicken and toss well. Cover and marinate in the refrigerator for at least 6 hours, or overnight.

2. Drain the chicken, reserving the marinade. In a heavy stainless-steel saucepan, combine the marinade with the tomato puree, honey, molasses, thyme, salt, cayenne, and black pepper. Bring to a boil over moderate heat. Reduce the heat to moderately low and cook, stirring occasionally, until the sauce is reduced to 2 cups, 35 to 45 minutes. Remove from the heat and stir in the vinegar. Discard the bay leaves.

3. Light the grill. Grill the chicken, turning once, for 5 minutes. Baste with the barbecue sauce and continue grilling, basting liberally and turning every 5 minutes, until the chicken is just done, 20 to 25 minutes longer.

—JIM FOBEL

California-Style Barbe(

Salsa is the natural accompaniment for th:
own with chopped fresh pineapple, min(
juice, and chopped cilantro.

⬛ WINE RECOMMENDATION

A crisp, dry, but fruity wine will do
best with the intense sweet-tart flavors of
this dish. The delicious rosé produced by
the huge Sicilian firm Regaleali is just the
ticket. Consistently rich from year to year,
this wine is nonetheless brisk enough to cut
through the sweetness of the sauce.

SERVES 4

¾ cup pineapple juice or apricot
    nectar
½ cup packed light brown sugar
½ cup ketchup
½ cup cider vinegar
1 tablespoon cornstarch
2½ pounds chicken parts

1. Light the grill. In a stainless-steel
saucepan, bring ½ cup of the pineapple
juice, the brown sugar, ketchup, and vinegar to a boil over moderate heat, stirring
occasionally.

2. In a small bowl, dissolve the cornstarch in the remaining ¼ cup pineapple
juice. Whisk this mixture into the sauce
and simmer, stirring constantly, until the
sauce is thickened and slightly translucent,
about 3 minutes.

minutes
continue g
ing every 5 n.   n is
just done, 20 to 2.

SESAME CHICKEN

You may recognize this marinade, since it resembles the traditional sauce for cold sesame noodles. Broiling the marinated chicken breasts gives them an almost black, crusty exterior and a wonderful flavor. They need to marinate for twenty-four hours, so plan accordingly.

 WINE RECOMMENDATION
This is a great opportunity to let a mature Pfalz spätlese riesling strut its stuff. With age, these wines develop a complex nuttiness, and the sugar evolves toward the taste of caramel. The wines retain their acidity, which balances them much as this recipe balances sweet, sour, and rich flavors.

SERVES 4

½ cup Chinese sesame paste*

¼ cup brewed Chinese black tea

2½ tablespoons soy sauce

1 tablespoon Asian chili oil*

2 cloves garlic, crushed

4 teaspoons Asian sesame oil

4 teaspoons sugar

4 teaspoons red-wine vinegar

⅓ cup thin-sliced scallions, including green tops

1⅓ pounds boneless, skinless chicken breasts (about 4)

Watercress sprigs, for garnish

*Available at Asian markets and some supermarkets

1. In a small bowl, combine the sesame paste, tea, soy sauce, chili oil, garlic, sesame oil, sugar, and vinegar. Whisk until well blended. Stir in the scallions.

2. Put the chicken in a glass baking dish and pour the sesame mixture over it. Turn to coat. Cover and refrigerate for 24 hours. Let the chicken return to room temperature before cooking.

3. Heat the broiler. Broil the chicken breasts until slightly charred, about 5 minutes. Turn and cook until the chicken is just done, about 5 minutes longer.

4. Transfer the chicken to a plate and leave to rest in a warm spot for about 10 minutes. Cut the chicken into 1-inch chunks and serve warm or at room temperature, garnished with sprigs of watercress.

—KAREN LEE AND ALEXANDRA BRANYON

THYME-BROILED BUTTERFLIED CHICKEN

Butterflying the chicken allows you to broil the whole bird without cutting it into parts. Rubbing the skin all over with olive oil makes it especially crispy.

WINE RECOMMENDATION
This straightforward broiled chicken should be accompanied by a fairly light, herbal white wine. Experiment with one of the superb new-style sauvignon blancs from Italy's northeastern regions of Friuli and Trentino–Alto Adige.

SERVES 4

1 chicken (3 to 3½ pounds)
1 tablespoon olive oil
1 teaspoon cayenne
1 teaspoon dried thyme

1. Heat the broiler. Using poultry shears or a large knife, cut down along either side of the backbone of the chicken and remove the backbone. Cut off the wing tips. Spread the chicken open.

2. Rub the oil over the chicken skin. Broil the chicken, skin-side down, for 15 minutes. Turn the chicken over and sprinkle with the cayenne and thyme. Broil until the skin is crisp and the chicken is just done, about 5 minutes longer.

GOLDEN BROILED CHICKEN

Bring this broiled chicken along on your next picnic; it tastes wonderful at room temperature and holds up well if made the day before. The cornmeal coating gives the pieces a welcome crunch.

WINE RECOMMENDATION
Even if you don't take this dish on a picnic, serve it with a malvasia bianca from California. These crisp, light white wines are their own flower-strewn meadow on a sparkling, breezy day.

SERVES 4

- 1   clove garlic
- ¼   teaspoon salt
- ¼   teaspoon fresh-ground black pepper
- ¼   teaspoon cayenne
- ½   teaspoon minced fresh rosemary, or ¼ teaspoon crumbled dried rosemary
- 1½ tablespoons lemon juice
- 1   tablespoon cornmeal
- ¼   cup cooking oil
- 1   chicken (3 to 3½ pounds), cut into 8 pieces

1. In a small bowl, mash the garlic and the salt to a paste. Add the black pepper, cayenne, rosemary, lemon juice, and corn-meal and mash until fairly smooth. Stir in the oil until blended.

2. Put the chicken in a large shallow dish and spread the seasoned cornmeal over the pieces, coating them evenly. Let stand, uncovered, at room temperature for 1 hour.

3. Heat the broiler. Broil the chicken, pieces, skin-side up, for 20 minutes. Turn and cook until the chicken is just done, about 20 minutes longer.

—PHILLIP STEPHEN SCHULZ

Broiled Chicken with Caraway

A slightly sweet apple-flavored glaze contrasts with the savory onion and caraway seasoning of this butterflied chicken. For a beautiful accompaniment, sauté apple and red-onion slices in a little butter, paint them with some of the glaze, and sprinkle with caraway seeds.

 WINE RECOMMENDATION
Could there be a better occasion for an opulent, apple-and-tropical-fruit California chardonnay? The savory, nutty richness of the butter and caraway along with the sweetness of the glaze make for a perfect match. As always when pairing chardonnays with food, look for one with restrained use of oak.

SERVES 4

2   tablespoons butter

3   tablespoons minced onion

1   teaspoon caraway seeds

½   teaspoon salt

¼   teaspoon fresh-ground black pepper

1   chicken (3 to 3½ pounds)

1   6-ounce can frozen apple-juice concentrate, thawed

1.   Melt the butter in a small frying pan over low heat. Add the onion, caraway, ¼ teaspoon of the salt, and the pepper and cook until the onion is just softened, 2 to 3 minutes. Let cool.

2.   Using poultry shears or a large knife, cut down along either side of the backbone of the chicken and remove the backbone. Cut off the wing tips. Spread the chicken open. Using your fingers, carefully loosen the skin from the breast, thigh, and leg meat without detaching the skin. Cut into the thickest part of the thigh and leg, slicing down to the bone with a sharp knife.

3.   Heat the broiler. Stuff the onion mixture under the skin of the chicken, spreading it as evenly as possible. Sprinkle the remaining ¼ teaspoon salt over the skin. Broil the chicken, skin-side up, until well browned, about 10 minutes.

4.   Meanwhile, boil the apple-juice concentrate in a small saucepan until reduced to a syrupy glaze, about 5 minutes.

5.   Reduce the oven temperature to 375°, move the chicken to the middle of the oven, and roast for 10 minutes. Brush with the glaze and roast, basting twice, until the chicken is just done, about 10 minutes longer. Serve hot or at room temperature.

—Anne Disrude

chapter 8

SAUTÉING

Sesame Oat Chicken, page 199

SESAME OAT CHICKEN

Ground oats make a crunchy coating for chicken breasts. Sesame seeds add to the texture and also give good flavor. Try the combination on fish fillets, too.

 WINE RECOMMENDATION
The nutty oats will marry well with the toasty flavor of a chardonnay. A fairly light, crisp version, such as one from Chablis or from northeastern Italy, won't overwhelm this dish's clean, simple lines.

SERVES 4

2/3 cup old-fashioned rolled oats

1 teaspoon dried thyme

1/2 teaspoon white pepper

1 tablespoon sesame seeds

4 boneless, skinless chicken breasts (about 1 1/3 pounds in all)

6 tablespoons cooking oil

Salt

Lemon wedges, for serving

1. In a food processor, process the rolled oats until ground fine. Transfer to a shallow bowl and toss with the dried thyme, pepper, and sesame seeds. Dredge the chicken breasts in the oat mixture, pressing to coat well.

2. Heat the oven to 250°. In a large non-stick frying pan, heat 3 tablespoons of the oil over moderately high heat. Add two of the chicken breasts and cook until browned and cooked through, 3 to 4 minutes on each side. Drain on paper towels and blot lightly. Put the chicken on a plate and put in the oven to keep warm. Repeat with the remaining two chicken breasts and 3 tablespoons oil.

3. Sprinkle the chicken with salt. Serve the chicken breasts with the lemon wedges.

—TRACEY SEAMAN

VARIATION

Thyme is particularly good for seasoning poultry, but feel free to substitute another dried herb, such as marjoram or crumbled rosemary. Garnish with fresh sprigs of the same herb, if you like.

CHICKEN CUTLETS IN TARRAGON BREAD CRUMBS

Pounding boneless chicken breasts into cutlets makes them cook faster and more evenly. Here, they're coated with tarragon-flavored crumbs; chilling them in the refrigerator ensures that the crust stays intact as the cutlets cook.

WINE RECOMMENDATION
Enjoy this entrée with a crisp Italian pinot grigio from Collio or Alto Adige. Though made from the same grape as an Alsace pinot gris, these pinot grigios are much lighter in body and boast a vibrance that makes them a natural with chicken dishes.

SERVES 4

    4 boneless, skinless chicken breasts
       (about 1⅓ pounds in all)

    2 eggs

    1 cup dry bread crumbs

    2 teaspoons dried tarragon

   ¾ teaspoon salt

   ¼ teaspoon fresh-ground black pepper

 2½ tablespoons butter

 2½ tablespoons olive oil

    1 lime, cut into wedges

1. Fold out the tender from underneath each chicken breast. Place the chicken between two sheets of waxed paper; use a mallet, flat meat pounder, or rolling pin to flatten it to an even thickness of about ⅛ inch.

2. Beat the eggs in a shallow bowl. In another shallow bowl, combine the bread crumbs, tarragon, salt, and pepper. Dip each cutlet into the beaten egg and then into the bread-crumb mixture to coat. Put the cutlets on a wire rack set on a small baking pan and refrigerate, uncovered, for 1 hour.

3. Heat the oven to 250°. In a large heavy frying pan, melt the butter with the oil over moderate heat. Raise the heat to moderately high and heat until the butter and oil are almost smoking hot. Add two of the cutlets and cook just until the coating is crisp and golden brown and the meat is cooked through, about 1 minute on each side. Drain on paper towels and blot lightly. Put the cutlets on a plate and put in the oven to keep warm. Repeat with the remaining two cutlets. Serve hot, with the lime wedges.

CHICKEN TENDERS

The tender is the small strip of meat on the underside of a skinless, boneless chicken breast, also sometimes called the fillet. When making cutlets, you'll need to fold this piece of chicken out from under so that the breast can be pounded to an even thickness.

PEPPERED CHICKEN BREASTS WITH ROSEMARY AND GARLIC

The combination of red and black pepper in the marinade gives these chicken breasts a bit of a kick. We give a range on the spice quantities; use a little or a lot, depending on your taste. Serve the sautéed chicken hot or warm—it's delicious either way.

 WINE RECOMMENDATION

Red Riojas are among the world's most complex wines. Made mostly from the tempranillo grape and aged for long periods in oak barrels, Riojas are smoky and spicy, with rich cherry fruit and a gently tannic structure. A Reserva with a few years of age will be splendid alongside this peppery chicken.

SERVES 4

- 2 tablespoons lemon juice
- 2 tablespoons olive oil
- ½ teaspoon dried rosemary, crumbled
- ⅛ to ¼ teaspoon dried red-pepper flakes
- ½ to 1 teaspoon coarse-cracked black pepper
- 4 cloves garlic, crushed
- 4 boneless, skinless chicken breasts (about 1⅓ pounds in all)
- 1 teaspoon butter
- 1 teaspoon cooking oil
- ¼ teaspoon salt

1. In a medium glass dish, combine the lemon juice, olive oil, rosemary, red-pepper flakes, black pepper, and garlic. Add the chicken breasts, turn to coat, and marinate at room temperature, turning once or twice, for 1 hour.

2. Remove the chicken from the marinade and pat dry. In a large frying pan, melt the butter with the cooking oil over moderate heat. Add the chicken to the pan and cook until lightly browned, 4 to 5 minutes. Turn and continue cooking until the chicken is lightly browned on the other side and cooked through, 4 to 5 minutes longer. Season with the salt.

—ANNE DISRUDE

CHICKEN CUTLETS
WITH PINE NUTS AND LIME

Lime adds a refreshing tang to both the sauce and the coating for these quick-cooking chicken cutlets. Substitute thin slices of turkey breast for the chicken breasts, if you like.

WINE RECOMMENDATION
Try a sauvignon blanc from South Africa with this subtle dish. The wine's puckery acidity will match that of the lime.

SERVES 4

- 2 tablespoons minced fresh parsley
- 1 tablespoon chopped pine nuts
- 1½ teaspoons grated lime zest
- ½ teaspoon minced garlic
- ¼ cup flour
- 1 teaspoon dried tarragon
    Salt and white pepper
- 4 boneless, skinless chicken breasts (about 1⅓ pounds in all)
- 3 tablespoons butter
- 1½ tablespoons olive oil
- ¾ cup dry white wine
- 1 tablespoon lime juice
- 1 lime, cut into thin slices

1. In a small bowl, combine the parsley, pine nuts, ½ teaspoon of the lime zest, and the garlic. In a medium bowl, mix the flour with the remaining 1 teaspoon lime zest and the tarragon; season with salt and pepper.

2. Fold out the tender (see "Chicken Tenders," page 200) from underneath each chicken breast. Place the chicken between two sheets of waxed paper and use a mallet, flat meat pounder, or rolling pin to flatten the chicken to an even thickness of about ⅛ inch. Dredge the cutlets in the seasoned flour and shake off the excess.

3. Heat the oven to 250°. In a large frying pan, melt the butter with the oil over moderately high heat. Reduce the heat to moderate and cook two of the cutlets until lightly browned and cooked through, about 45 seconds on each side. Put the chicken on a plate and put in the oven to keep warm. Repeat with the remaining two cutlets.

4. Pour the wine into the frying pan and cook, scraping the bottom of the pan to dislodge any brown bits, until reduced to ½ cup, about 2 minutes. Stir in the lime juice and the pine-nut mixture.

5. Using tongs, remove a cutlet from the oven, dip it into the sauce, and place it on a plate. Repeat with the remaining cutlets. Spoon the remaining sauce over the cutlets and top with the lime slices.

MIXED SKILLET GRILL

The chicken and vegetables make a tasty and colorful combination when arranged on a platter. The slight bitterness of the radicchio is offset by the creamy mozzarella wrapped inside the leaves.

WINE RECOMMENDATION

The aromatic mustard and herbs combined with the emphasis on vegetables call for a crisp, herbal white such as one made from sauvignon blanc. Select a Pouilly-Fumé for its flinty aromas and broad, herb-inflected mineral flavors.

SERVES 4

4 boneless, skinless chicken breasts (about 1⅓ pounds in all)

½ cup olive oil

2 tablespoons Dijon mustard

½ teaspoon dried thyme

4 baby eggplants, halved lengthwise, or 2 small eggplants, quartered lengthwise

   Salt

8 1½-by-½-inch sticks mozzarella cheese, cut from about a 3-ounce piece

8 large radicchio leaves

4 fresh basil leaves, minced, or ½ teaspoon dried oregano

   Fresh-ground black pepper

4 small zucchini, halved lengthwise

2 large plum tomatoes, cut crosswise in half

1. Fold out the tender (see "Chicken Tenders," page 200) from underneath each chicken breast. Place the chicken between two sheets of waxed paper and use a mallet, flat meat pounder, or rolling pin to flatten the chicken to an even thickness of about ¼ inch. Put the cutlets on a plate.

2. In a small bowl, blend 4 teaspoons of the oil with the mustard and thyme. Brush this mixture over both sides of the chicken cutlets. Cover the cutlets and marinate in the refrigerator for 1 to 4 hours.

3. Using a sharp knife, score a diamond pattern in the cut side of the eggplant pieces and sprinkle with a little salt. Put the eggplant pieces cut-side down on a plate.

4. Put a mozzarella stick in the center of each radicchio leaf. Top with the basil and sprinkle with salt and pepper. Roll the cheese up in the radicchio.

5. Remove the chicken from the refrigerator. Heat a large heavy frying pan, preferably cast iron, over high heat for 5 minutes.

6. Pat the eggplant pieces dry and spread 2 tablespoons of the oil over the cut sides. Put the eggplant pieces in the frying pan, cut-side down, and cook, turning, until they are softened and well browned, about 10 minutes. Transfer the eggplant pieces to a

platter, cover loosely with aluminum foil, and put in a warm spot.

7. Brush 2 teaspoons of the oil over the cut sides of the zucchini. Put the zucchini, cut-side down, in the frying pan and cook over moderately high heat until browned, 3 to 4 minutes a side. Season with salt and pepper and transfer to the platter.

8. Brush 2 teaspoons of the oil over the cut sides of the tomatoes. Put the tomatoes in the frying pan, cut-side down, and cook until browned, about 1 minute. Transfer to the platter.

9. Add one tablespoon of the oil to the pan and heat. Put two of the chicken cutlets in the frying pan and cook for 2 minutes. Turn and cook until browned and cooked through, 1 minute longer. Season with salt and pepper and transfer to the platter. Repeat with another tablespoon of the oil and the remaining two cutlets.

10. Brush the radicchio rolls with the remaining 4 teaspoons oil. Put the rolls, seam-side down, in the frying pan and cook for 30 seconds. Turn and transfer to the platter. Serve immediately.

—ANNE DISRUDE

CHICKEN CUTLETS PARMESAN

Equally delicious hot or cold, these cutlets are good on their own or make tasty sandwiches. Just put them on crusty rolls with some mayonnaise, fresh-ground pepper, and slices of ripe tomato.

 WINE RECOMMENDATION
Rich, tangy Parmesan calls for a red to match its strong flavors, but you'll need one here that is very crisp and light. A perfect choice would be a young Chianti Rufina. Rufina is the most northerly of the seven Chianti growing zones, and its wines are loaded with lively fruit and acidity.

SERVES 4

    4   boneless, skinless chicken breasts
        (about 1⅓ pounds in all)
  ¼   cup flour
    2   eggs
    3   tablespoons milk
    1   cup dry bread crumbs
    1   cup grated Parmesan cheese
  ¼   cup olive oil, more if needed
    2   lemons, quartered

1. Fold out the tender (see "Chicken Tenders," page 200) from underneath each of the chicken breasts. Place the chicken breast between two sheets of waxed paper and use a mallet, flat meat pounder, or rolling pin to flatten it to an even thickness of about ⅛ inch.

2. Put the flour on a plate. Lightly beat the eggs and milk in a shallow bowl. Mix the bread crumbs and cheese together in another shallow bowl.

3. Dredge the chicken cutlets in the flour and shake off any excess. Dip them into the egg mixture and then into the bread-crumb mixture, patting the crumbs firmly so they adhere. Put the cutlets on a wire rack set on a small baking pan and refrigerate, uncovered, for 1 hour.

4. Heat the oven to 250°. Remove the cutlets from the refrigerator and let them sit at room temperature for 15 minutes. In a large heavy nonstick frying pan, heat the oil over moderate heat until almost smoking hot. Add two of the cutlets and cook until golden brown and just cooked through, about 45 seconds on each side. Drain on paper towels and blot lightly. Put the cutlets on a plate and put in the oven to keep warm. Repeat with the remaining two cutlets, adding more oil as needed. Serve with the lemon wedges.

CHICKEN TACOS

Simple, fresh-tasting, and low in fat, these soft tacos can be thrown together in practically no time. If you prefer, use turkey in place of the chicken.

 WINE RECOMMENDATION
Tannic wines are usually off-limits with Mexican-style foods because hot peppers and tannin combine to produce unpleasant bitterness. However, since there is no heat here, enjoy a Cahors from the southwest of France. Its spicy, roasted cherry fruit and rustic earthiness will mesh nicely with these tacos.

SERVES 4

2   teaspoons cooking oil

2   cloves garlic, minced

⅔   pound boneless, skinless chicken breasts (about 2), cut into 2-by-¼-inch strips

½   teaspoon ground cumin

½   teaspoon crumbled dried oregano
    Pinch salt

¼   teaspoon fresh-ground black pepper

1   onion, chopped fine

¼   cup chopped cilantro

8   corn tortillas

2   tomatoes, cut into fine dice

⅔   cup shredded romaine lettuce

1. In a large nonstick frying pan, heat the oil over moderate heat. Add the garlic and cook for 30 seconds. Add the chicken, cumin, oregano, salt, and pepper. Raise the heat to high and cook, stirring, until the chicken is almost cooked through, about 2 minutes. Add the onion and cook for 1 minute. Remove the pan from the heat and stir in the cilantro.

2. Heat a medium frying pan over moderate heat. Sprinkle drops of water on both sides of a tortilla and heat it in the pan, turning several times, until it is softened and the water has been absorbed. Repeat with the remaining three tortillas.

3. Spoon one eighth of the filling down the center of each tortilla. Top with the tomato and lettuce and fold in half.

—JIM FOBEL

CHICKEN CUTLETS WITH CURRIED CREAM SAUCE

You'll need less than thirty minutes to put together this simple dish of chicken and mushrooms in a creamy curry-spiced sauce. It's perfect for a busy weeknight.

WINE RECOMMENDATION
There are two ways to go with a cream sauce: try to match its richness with an equally rich wine, or contrast the sauce with a high-acid wine that will cut the fat and cleanse the palate. With this dish, a lean, minerally riesling from Austria will put the second principle to delicious effect.

SERVES 4

4 boneless, skinless chicken breasts (about 1⅓ pounds in all)

1 teaspoon salt

6 tablespoons butter

½ pound mushrooms, quartered

⅔ cup half-and-half or light cream

½ teaspoon curry powder

¼ teaspoon paprika

¼ teaspoon fresh-ground black pepper

2 tablespoons chopped fresh parsley
Lemon wedges, for serving

1. Fold out the tender (see "Chicken Tenders," page 200) from underneath each chicken breast. Place the chicken between two sheets of waxed paper and use a mallet, flat meat pounder, or rolling pin to flatten it to an even thickness of about ¼ inch. Season the cutlets on both sides with the salt.

2. In a large heavy frying pan, heat 2 tablespoons of the butter over moderately high heat. Add two of the chicken cutlets and cook just until lightly colored, about 1 minute per side. Remove the cutlets and repeat with another 2 tablespoons butter and the remaining two cutlets.

3. Melt the remaining 2 tablespoons butter in the pan. Add the mushrooms and cook, stirring, until softened, 1 to 2 minutes. Raise the heat to high and add the half-and-half, curry powder, paprika, and pepper. Boil until reduced to about ½ cup, about 5 minutes.

4. Reduce the heat to low and return the chicken cutlets to the frying pan, along with any accumulated juices. Simmer until the cutlets are hot and cooked through, about 2 minutes. Put the cutlets on plates and spoon the sauce on top. Sprinkle with the parsley and serve with the lemon wedges.

SAUTÉED CHICKEN BREASTS WITH COGNAC AND CREAM SAUCE

The cream sauce here leaves plenty of room for variation. Substitute bourbon for the brandy, add mustard or peppercorns for a spicier dish, or try a tarragon sauce (below) instead. However you serve it, it's sure to be delicious.

 WINE RECOMMENDATION Cognac has spicy and caramelized flavors that meld particularly well with those of a chardonnay that has also been aged in oak. Select a premier or grand cru white Burgundy, which will have enough weight to match the sauce.

SERVES 4

4   boneless, skinless chicken breasts (about 1⅓ pounds in all)
    Salt and fresh-ground black pepper
2   tablespoons butter
1   tablespoon cooking oil
2   tablespoons chopped shallots or scallions including green tops
¼   cup cognac or other brandy
1   cup Chicken Stock, page 61, or canned low-sodium chicken broth
1   cup crème fraîche (see box, page 148) or heavy cream

1. Sprinkle the chicken breasts lightly with salt and fresh-ground black pepper. In a large frying pan, heat the butter with the oil over moderately high heat until hot. Add the chicken breasts and immediately lower the heat to moderately low. Cook slowly, turning every 5 minutes, until the chicken is just tender, 12 to 16 minutes. Put on a plate; cover loosely to keep warm.

2. Pour off the fat from the frying pan. Add the shallots and cook until softened, about 1 minute. Add the cognac and carefully light it with a match. When the flames die down, scrape the bottom of the pan to dislodge any brown bits. Add the stock and boil over high heat until reduced to a thick, syrupy glaze, 5 to 10 minutes.

3. Add the crème fraîche and boil until the sauce is reduced to a thick golden cream, about 5 minutes. Do not let it scorch. Spoon the sauce over the chicken breasts.

VARIATIONS

- **Mustard Sauce:** Add one to two tablespoons of Dijon mustard with the crème fraîche.
- **Pepper Sauce:** Add one and a half tablespoons drained canned green peppercorns with the crème fraîche.
- **Tarragon Sauce:** Add one and a half tablespoons minced fresh tarragon at the end.

SAUTÉED CHICKEN BREASTS WITH GORGONZOLA AND FRESH HERBS

Cream and Gorgonzola cheese combine to form a rich, flavorful sauce for sautéed chicken breasts. Both the chicken and the sauce can be prepared ahead and then reheated at the last minute before serving.

WINE RECOMMENDATION

Gorgonzola is tricky to pair with wine. It requires high acid to cut its unctuousness, but significant sweetness as well to counter its high salt content. Try a young flower-and-herb-scented Vouvray demi-sec. Made from chenin blanc, it has tangy acidity and moderate sweetness that will be perfect here.

SERVES 4

4   boneless, skinless chicken breasts (about 1⅓ pounds in all)

Salt and white pepper

¼   cup flour

2   tablespoons butter

2   teaspoons peanut oil

⅓   cup plus 3 tablespoons Chicken Stock, page 61, or canned low-sodium chicken broth

3   ounces Gorgonzola cheese

1   cup heavy cream

Beurre Manié, opposite page (if needed)

2   tablespoons minced fresh tarragon

2   tablespoons minced fresh chives, for garnish

1. Season the chicken breasts lightly with salt and white pepper. Put the flour on a plate. Dredge the chicken breasts lightly in the flour and shake off the excess.

2. In a large heavy frying pan, melt the butter with the oil over high heat. Add the chicken breasts and cook until browned, 2 to 3 minutes per side.

3. Reduce the heat to moderately low. Add the 3 tablespoons stock, cover, and cook for 5 minutes. Using a slotted spoon, transfer the chicken to a plate. Cover loosely with aluminum foil and put in a warm spot.

4. Meanwhile, in a food processor or blender, puree the Gorgonzola with ¼ cup of the heavy cream.

5. Add the remaining ⅓ cup stock to the frying pan. Bring to a boil over high heat, scraping the bottom of the pan to dislodge any brown bits, and cook until the liquid is reduced to a glaze, about 2 minutes. Add the remaining ¾ cup heavy cream and cook, stirring, until reduced to ½ cup, about 5 minutes.

6. Whisk in the Gorgonzola cream. If the sauce seems thin, bring it to a boil and, bit by bit, whisk in enough of the Beurre

Manié so the sauce lightly coats a spoon. Add the tarragon and season with salt and white pepper.

7. Return the chicken breasts to the pan, cover, and cook over low heat just until heated through, about 2 minutes. Put the chicken on plates. Spoon the sauce over the chicken and sprinkle with the chives.

—PERLA MEYERS

MAKE IT AHEAD

You can prepare the chicken and the cream sauce up to two hours ahead; cover and refrigerate separately. When you are ready to serve the dish, bring the chicken to room temperature, bring the sauce to a boil in the frying pan, and proceed with step 7.

BEURRE MANIÉ

If the sauce is a little thin, this butter and flour mixture will thicken it nicely.

MAKES ABOUT 2 TABLESPOONS

1 tablespoon butter, at room temperature
1 tablespoon flour

In a small bowl, blend the butter and flour until they form a paste.

CHICKEN, SAUSAGE, AND SWEET-PEPPER SAUTÉ

The Mediterranean combination of bell peppers, black olives, and tomatoes makes a highly flavored and colorful background for sautéed chicken breasts and pork-sausage patties in this one-dish meal. A green salad with a mild vinaigrette is all you need to finish it off.

 WINE RECOMMENDATION
Savory from the sausage, acidic from the tomatoes—this is the kind of dish that Italian wines were made for. Try Barbaresco, Barolo's slightly lighter neighbor. Made in Piedmont from the nebbiolo grape, Barbarescos are powerful wines, high in both tannin and acid. Yet they are surprisingly complex and silky, too.

SERVES 4

1　pound boneless, skinless chicken breasts (about 3), cut lengthwise into ½-inch strips

⅔　cup milk

3　tablespoons hot-pepper sauce

¾　pound pork sausage meat

2　cloves garlic, halved and crushed

⅔　cup dry red wine

2¼　cups canned tomatoes, drained and chopped coarse (from a 28-ounce can)

⅓　cup Beef Stock, next page, or canned low-sodium beef broth

4　teaspoons olive oil

3　yellow bell peppers, cut into ½-inch dice

16　oil-cured black olives, pitted and halved

1. In a medium bowl, combine the chicken breasts, milk, and hot-pepper sauce. Cover and refrigerate for at least 6 hours, or overnight.

2. Form the pork-sausage meat into twelve patties. In a large stainless-steel frying pan, cook the sausage patties over high heat until they are well browned, 2 to 3 minutes on each side. Drain the patties on paper towels.

3. Pour off the fat from the frying pan and return the sausage patties to the pan. Add the garlic and wine. Cover, bring to a simmer, and continue simmering over moderate heat, turning the patties once, until the liquid is reduced to 3 tablespoons, about 12 minutes. Add the tomatoes and stock and simmer, uncovered, for 5 minutes.

4. Meanwhile, in a large heavy frying pan, heat 2 teaspoons of the oil over high heat. Add the bell peppers and toss to coat. Cook the peppers, stirring occasionally, until they are lightly browned and crisp-tender, about 5 minutes. Add the peppers to the pan with the sausage patties. Cover the pan and set aside in a warm spot. ➤

5. Drain the chicken and pat dry. Add the remaining 2 teaspoons oil to the heavy frying pan and heat the oil over high heat, Add the chicken and cook, turning frequently, until just cooked through, 3 to 5 minutes. Using a slotted spoon, add the chicken to the sausage and peppers. Stir in the olives.

—LEE BAILEY

BEEF STOCK

MAKES ABOUT 1 QUART

2 pounds beef bones, cut into pieces

1 onion, quartered

2 carrots, quartered

2 ribs celery, quartered

2½ quarts water

1¾ cups canned tomatoes, drained (one 14-ounce can)

8 parsley stems

4 sprigs fresh thyme, or ¾ teaspoon dried thyme

1 bay leaf

4 peppercorns

1. Heat the oven to 450°. Put the bones in a roasting pan. Brown in the oven for 40 minutes, stirring once or twice. Add the vegetables and cook until the bones and vegetables are well browned, about 20 minutes longer.

2. Put the bones and vegetables in a large pot. Pour off the fat in the pan; add 1 cup of water. Bring to a boil, scraping up any brown bits. Add to the pot with the remaining ingredients. Bring to a boil; skim off the foam. Reduce the heat. Simmer, partially covered, for 4 hours.

3. Strain, pressing the solids to get all the liquid. Skim the fat from the surface if using immediately. If not, refrigerate for up to a week or freeze. Scrape off the fat before using.

SAUTÉED GEWÜRZTRAMINER CHICKEN WITH CABBAGE AND LEEKS

The classic German combination of cabbage and bacon provides a bed for marinated chicken thighs. The chicken needs to marinate for twenty-four hours, so plan ahead. If you can't buy boneless chicken thighs with the skin still on, buy the bone-in kind and bone them yourself, or have the butcher do it.

WINE RECOMMENDATION

When cooking with gewürztraminer, it is hard to imagine serving any other wine, since gewürztraminer will stamp its signature so indelibly on the food. Go with a classic dry one from Alsace for its heady lychee and rose-petal aromas, full body, and apricot flavors.

SERVES 4

- 8 boneless chicken thighs, with skin
- ¾ teaspoon salt
- ¾ teaspoon fresh-ground black pepper
- 2 cups plus 4 teaspoons young Alsace gewürztraminer
- 7 slices smoked bacon
- 2 cloves garlic, minced
- 2 leeks, white part only, cut into matchstick strips and washed well
- 3 pounds Savoy, napa, or Chinese cabbage (about 1 large head), shredded
- ¼ teaspoon grated nutmeg
- 1 cup flour
- 7 tablespoons butter
- 1 cup Chicken Stock, page 61, or canned low-sodium chicken broth
- 1 tablespoon chopped fresh parsley

1. Sprinkle the chicken thighs with ½ teaspoon of the salt and ¼ teaspoon of the pepper. Put the thighs in a shallow glass baking dish just large enough to hold them. Pour in the 2 cups wine. Cover with plastic wrap and refrigerate, turning occasionally, for 24 hours.

2. Remove the chicken thighs from the marinade and pat dry. Reserve the marinade. Cut eight 2-inch-long pieces of bacon from two or three of the bacon slices. Loosen the skin of the chicken thighs and tuck one of these piece of bacon under the skin of each thigh.

3. Cut the remaining bacon crosswise into ½-inch strips. In a large deep heavy frying pan, preferably cast iron, cook the bacon pieces until crisp. Remove the bacon with a slotted spoon and drain on paper towels. Pour off all but 1 tablespoon of the fat from the frying pan.

4. Add the garlic and leeks to the pan and cook over moderately low heat until softened, about 5 minutes. Raise the heat to high and add the cabbage and nutmeg. Cook, tossing well, until the cabbage is

wilted, about 3 minutes; if the pan is too dry, add ¼ cup water.

5. Stir the remaining 4 teaspoons wine and ¼ teaspoon of the pepper into the cabbage. Transfer the cabbage mixture to a bowl, add the bacon, and toss well. Cover the bowl. Wipe out the frying pan.

6. Put the flour on a plate. Season the chicken thighs with the remaining ¼ teaspoon salt and ¼ teaspoon pepper. Dredge the thighs in the flour, shaking off the excess. Melt 3 tablespoons of the butter in the frying pan over moderately high heat. Put the chicken thighs in the frying pan, skin-side down, and cook over high heat until browned and cooked through, about 5 minutes. Turn and brown the other side, 3 to 4 minutes longer. Drain the chicken on paper towels and blot lightly.

7. In a small stainless-steel frying pan, boil the stock until reduced by half, about 3 minutes. Add ½ cup of the marinade and bring just to a boil. Remove from the heat and whisk in the remaining 4 tablespoons butter, 1 tablespoon at a time, moving the pan on and off the heat so the butter just softens and thickens the sauce but doesn't melt completely.

8. Divide the cabbage mixture among four plates and put the chicken thighs on top. Pour the sauce over the chicken and cabbage and sprinkle with the parsley.

—David Rosengarten

CHICKEN, SAUSAGE, AND GRITS WITH WILD MUSHROOMS

Don't try to save time by using quick-cooking grits in this recipe—the result will be less than satisfactory. You can, however, cut forty minutes from the cooking time (and skip the first step altogether) by using two cups of shredded leftover cooked chicken in place of the chicken thighs.

WINE RECOMMENDATION

An earthy red wine of medium body and good acidity is needed with this homespun dish. Try a Rosso di Montalcino from Italy's Tuscany region. Though made from the sangiovese grape, as is Chianti, Rosso di Montalcino comes from a slightly warmer area, and is thus a bit richer.

SERVES 4

- 4 chicken thighs
  Salt and fresh-ground black pepper
- 2¼ cups Chicken Stock, page 61, or canned low-sodium chicken broth
- ½ cup old-fashioned grits
- 6 ounces sage-flavored breakfast sausage, casings removed
- 4 teaspoons butter
- 1 onion, chopped
- 6 ounces mixed wild mushrooms, such as chanterelles, morels, porcini, and shiitakes, cut into thin slices
- 6 ounces white mushrooms, cut into thin slices
- ¼ teaspoon dried thyme
- 4 teaspoons cooking oil

1. Heat the oven to 375°. Put the chicken thighs in a roasting pan and season with salt and pepper. Bake until the juices run clear when a thigh is pierced, about 40 minutes. Let cool.

2. Meanwhile, lightly oil a small baking sheet. Bring the stock to a boil in a heavy medium saucepan. Add the grits in a slow stream, stirring constantly. Reduce the heat to low and simmer, stirring occasionally, for 15 minutes. Let cool slightly and then scrape the grits onto the prepared baking sheet and spread evenly to a ½-inch thickness with a rubber spatula. Let cool completely, about 30 minutes.

3. In a large heavy ovenproof frying pan, cook the sausage meat over moderately high heat, breaking up the meat with a fork, until well browned and crusty in spots, about 10 minutes. Using a slotted spoon, transfer the sausage to a bowl.

4. Reduce the heat to moderate and melt 2 teaspoons of the butter in the pan. Add the onion and cook, stirring, until softened and browned, about 8 minutes. If using shiitakes, remove and discard the stems. Stir

in all the mushrooms along with the thyme. Raise the heat to moderately high and cook, stirring occasionally, until the mushrooms are soft, browned, and dry, 10 to 12 minutes. Add them to the bowl with the sausage. Wipe out the pan and set it aside.

5. Cut the cooled grits into ¾-inch cubes. Using a spatula, transfer them to the bowl with the sausage and mushrooms.

6. Remove the chicken meat from the bones. Discard the skin and bones. Shred the meat into ¾- to 1-inch pieces. Add the chicken to the sausage mixture and season with ⅛ teaspoon salt and ⅓ teaspoon pepper. Toss gently.

7. In the frying pan, melt the remaining 2 teaspoons butter with the oil over moderately high heat. Add the chicken mixture, pressing it down lightly with the back of a spoon to pack it evenly. Cook, without stirring, for 10 minutes. Remove from the heat and let rest for 3 minutes.

8. Heat the broiler. Put the frying pan as close to the heat as possible and broil the hash for 3 minutes, rotating the pan as necessary, until the top is browned. Serve directly from the pan.

—LEE BAILEY

MAKE IT AHEAD

You can prepare the chicken and grits up to one day in advance. Cover and refrigerate separately. When you're ready to continue with the recipe, proceed with step 3.

SAUTÉED JAMBONNEAUX WITH MUSHROOM AND WILD-RICE STUFFING

Jambonneaux means little hams—which these chicken legs resemble after they're boned and stuffed. They do take a little time to prepare, but the result is a particularly elegant entrée.

 WINE RECOMMENDATION
Mushrooms, wild rice, and dark-meat chicken are a siren song for pinot noir. Those from the New World emphasize fruitiness, so for this recipe go for a more gamy Gevrey-Chambertin from Burgundy. Its earthy undercurrents will harmonize better with the rice and mushrooms.

SERVES 4

¼ cup wild rice

2 slices bacon

1 tablespoon butter

1 small shallot, minced

½ cup minced mushrooms (about 3 ounces)

½ tablespoon minced fresh parsley

¼ teaspoon salt

   Fresh-ground black pepper

4 large chicken legs (drumsticks and thighs), bones removed (see "Boning Chicken Legs," page 221)

1 tablespoon cooking oil

1. Rinse the rice in several changes of cold water. Drain. In a small pot, combine the rice and enough water to cover the rice by 2 inches. Bring to a boil over moderate heat. Cover, reduce the heat, and cook at a gentle boil until the rice is tender. The cooking time can vary from 35 to 60 minutes. Add more water if needed. Drain the rice and put it in a medium bowl.

2. In a heavy medium frying pan, cook the bacon until crisp. Drain on paper towels. Pour 1 tablespoon of the bacon fat over the rice; set the pan with the remaining fat aside.

3. In another medium frying pan, melt the butter over moderate heat. Add the shallot and mushrooms and cook, stirring, until the mushrooms have released their liquid and it has evaporated, about 5 minutes. Add the mushrooms to the wild rice.

4. Crumble the bacon and add it to the the rice along with the parsley, ⅛ teaspoon of the salt, and a pinch of pepper. Toss the stuffing lightly and let cool to room temperature.

5. Season the chicken with the remaining ⅛ teaspoon salt and a dash of pepper and turn the meat skin-side out. Spoon two rounded tablespoons of the stuffing into the cavity of each leg. Fold down the top flap of each thigh, wrapping the meat around

the stuffing so that the leg resembles a small ham, and tuck the thigh flap into the skin. Sew the skin together with a trussing needle and cotton kitchen string to secure the stuffing.

6. Add the oil to the bacon fat in the frying pan and heat over moderately high heat. Add the *jambonneaux* and sauté, turning frequently, until the skin is golden and lightly crisped and the chicken is cooked through, about 20 minutes. Drain on paper towels. Remove the string before serving.

—JOHN ROBERT MASSIE

BONING CHICKEN LEGS

1. Using a sharp, thin knife, cut down the inside of each chicken thigh to expose the bone.

2. Starting at the top of the thigh and scraping against the bone, gently work the meat down to expose the leg joint. Cut the tendons at the joint, being careful not to pierce the skin.

3. Continue scraping down the leg bone, turning the meat inside out as you go. At the lower part of the drumstick, use your fingers to pull the meat down around the end of the bone.

4. Cut through the skin at the bottom of the drumstick; remove the bones. Remove the white tendons by grasping them with small pliers or your fingers and pulling them out while you scrape against them with a small sharp knife.

CHICKEN HASH WITH EGGS

For this recipe, you poach the chicken for the hash and use the resulting stock to make the gravy. It's easier to degrease the stock if you refrigerate it overnight, which means that this is a good make-ahead dish. The potatoes can be baked in advance as well.

WINE RECOMMENDATION
This robust one-dish meal calls for a wine with the power to match its complex flavors. Look to an Australian chardonnay, which is typically lavishly oaked, with dense tropical-fruit flavors and overtones of butterscotch and caramel.

SERVES 4

- ¾ pound baking potato (about 1 large), scrubbed
- 2 pounds chicken parts
- 1 onion, half cut into 1-inch chunks, half chopped
- 1 rib celery with leaves, cut into 1-inch pieces
- 1 carrot, cut into 1-inch pieces
- 1 small clove garlic, crushed
- 1 small bay leaf
- ¼ teaspoon dried thyme
- 1 large sprig parsley, plus 1 tablespoon minced fresh parsley
- ½ teaspoon peppercorns
- 1 teaspoon salt
- 3 cups water, more if needed
- 3½ tablespoons butter
- 1 tablespoon cooking oil
- ½ teaspoon fresh-ground black pepper
- 4 large eggs
- 1 tablespoon flour
- 2 tablespoons heavy cream

1. Heat the oven to 400°. Pierce the potatoes in a few places with a fork. Bake until the potatoes are soft, about 1 hour. Set aside to cool. When the potatoes are cool enough to handle, peel, wrap in aluminum foil, and refrigerate.

2. Put the chicken in a flameproof casserole or small Dutch oven. Add the onion chunks to the casserole along with the celery, carrot, garlic, bay leaf, thyme, parsley sprig, peppercorns, and ½ teaspoon of the salt. Pour in the water and bring to a boil. Reduce the heat, cover, and simmer for 45 minutes. Using a slotted spoon, transfer the chicken to a plate. Let the chicken cool to room temperature.

3. Meanwhile, raise the heat to moderately high and boil the stock for 15 to 20 minutes. Strain the stock into a large measuring cup, pressing the vegetables firmly to get as much liquid as possible. If you have more than 1 cup, boil to reduce to 1 cup; if you have less, add enough water to make 1 cup. Refrigerate.

4. Remove the chicken meat from the bones and tear into bite-size pieces. Discard the skin and bones. Put the meat in a medium bowl, cover, and refrigerate.

5. In a medium ovenproof frying pan, melt 1 tablespoon of the butter over moderate heat. Add the chopped onion and cook, stirring occasionally, until softened, about 5 minutes. Using a slotted spoon, transfer the onion to a large bowl.

6. Raise the heat to moderately high and add ½ tablespoon of the butter to the frying pan. Heat until the butter is foamy. Add the chicken and cook until browned and crisp in spots, about 10 minutes. Add the chicken to the onions and mix well. Set the pan aside.

7. Heat the oven to 350°. Cut the potatoes into ½-inch dice. In the same frying pan, melt 1 tablespoon of the butter with the oil over moderately high heat. Raise the heat to high and add the potatoes. Cook, stirring occasionally, until golden and crisp, about 10 minutes. Season with the remaining ½ teaspoon salt and the pepper. Add the potatoes to the chicken and onions and mix well. Return the mixture to the pan and smooth the surface with the back of a spoon.

8. Using the spoon, make four indentations, about 2½ inches wide and ½ inch deep, in the hash. Crack 1 egg into each indentation. Cover the pan loosely with aluminum foil and bake the hash until the eggs are set, about 25 minutes.

9. Meanwhile, scrape off the fat from the stock. In a small frying pan, melt the remaining 1 tablespoon butter over moderately high heat. Whisk in the flour and cook, whisking constantly, for 3 minutes. Gradually whisk in the stock and cook, whisking frequently, for 3 minutes. Add the cream and bring to a boil. Reduce the heat to very low and stir in the minced parsley. Keep warm over very low heat; if the sauce gets too thick, stir in water a tablespoon at a time. Serve the hash with the sauce on the side.

—Tracey Seaman

Make It Ahead

You can prepare the stock and chicken through step 4 up to one day ahead.

chapter 9

FRYING & STIR-FRYING

Peanut-Coated Drumsticks with Curried Cucumbers, page 237

COUNTRY FRIED CHICKEN

Lard is the traditional medium for frying Southern-style chicken. If you like, substitute vegetable shortening—but don't skip the bacon fat, which adds its own special flavor.

 WINE RECOMMENDATION
There isn't a classic wine from the Deep South to pair with this regional icon, but a robust California chardonnay is the next best thing. Its deep tropical fruitiness, full body, and oaky overtones will harmonize beautifully with the nutty and slightly smoky taste of the chicken.

SERVES 4

- 1 cup flour
- 1 tablespoon salt
- 1 teaspoon fresh-ground black pepper
- 1 teaspoon paprika
- 1 large egg
- ⅓ cup milk
- 1 chicken (3 to 3½ pounds), cut into 8 pieces
- 1 pound lard
- ¼ cup bacon fat

1. Combine the flour, salt, pepper, and paprika in a paper or plastic bag. In a shallow bowl, lightly beat the egg with the milk.

2. Dip each piece of chicken in the egg mixture and allow the excess to drip off. One by one, put the chicken pieces in the bag with the seasoned flour and shake gently to coat. Shake off the excess.

3. In a large heavy frying pan, melt the lard over moderate heat. Add the bacon fat, raise the heat to moderately high, and wait until the fat is hot (375°).

4. Put the chicken pieces in the fat, skin-side down, and cook for 15 minutes. Turn the pieces and cook until the chicken is golden brown and cooked through, about 10 minutes longer. Remove the chicken pieces and drain on paper towels.

—JOHN ROBERT MASSIE

FRIED CHICKEN WITH THYME CREAM GRAVY

Rice serves as the secret thickening ingredient that makes this thyme-scented gravy especially creamy. Be sure to serve mashed potatoes or biscuits so you can soak up every last drop.

WINE RECOMMENDATION
A big, rich recipe requires a big, rich white wine. Tokay Pinot Gris from Alsace is a terrific choice. These, like gewürztraminers, can be downright huge, with deep color, full body, and high alcohol. But their spicy, nutty flavors are backed by fresh acidity that gives them liveliness and focus.

SERVES 4

- 4 chicken drumsticks
- 4 chicken thighs
- 2¼ cups milk
- 1 bunch fresh thyme
- 2 tablespoons butter
- 1 onion, sliced
- 2 tablespoons rice, preferably basmati
- ⅓ cup flour
- 1 teaspoon salt
- ½ teaspoon fresh-ground black pepper
- ⅔ cup corn oil
- 2 tablespoons heavy cream

1. Put the chicken drumsticks and thighs and 2 cups of the milk in a medium bowl. Strip enough thyme leaves from the sprigs to make 4 teaspoons minced; set the minced thyme aside. Rub the remaining thyme sprigs to release the oil and add them to the bowl. Cover and refrigerate overnight.

2. Let the chicken return to room temperature. Meanwhile, melt the butter in a medium saucepan over low heat. Add the onion and cook, stirring occasionally, until softened, about 10 minutes. Add the rice.

3. Remove the chicken from the milk. Strain the milk into the pan and bring just to a simmer over moderate heat. Reduce the heat, cover, and simmer, stirring occasionally, until the rice is soft, about 25 minutes.

4. Transfer the mixture to a blender and puree until smooth. Return the thyme gravy to the pan and then stir in 1 teaspoon of the minced thyme.

5. Heat the oven to 400°. Pat the chicken dry. In a shallow bowl, combine the flour, ½ teaspoon of the salt, ¼ teaspoon of the pepper, and the remaining 1 tablespoon minced thyme. Heat the oil in a large heavy frying pan over high heat. Dredge half the chicken pieces in the seasoned flour and add them to the pan. Reduce the heat to moderate and cook, turning once, until the

chicken is browned and crisp, about 5 minutes on each side. Transfer to a baking sheet and repeat with the remaining chicken.

6. Put the baking sheet in the oven and bake the chicken until cooked through, 12 to 15 minutes. Cover loosely with aluminum foil and put in a warm spot.

7. Add the remaining ¼ cup milk and the cream to the gravy. Season with the remaining ½ teaspoon salt and ¼ teaspoon pepper. Reheat and serve with the chicken.

—MARCIA KIESEL

LONG-GRAIN RICE

When it comes to flavor and texture in long-grain rice, basmati from India is tops. If an American-grown rice seems more appropriate for this down-home chicken, however, Texmati rice is similar to basmati and makes a fine substitute.

YAMATO'S SESAME CHICKEN

The combination of a ginger-spiked marinade and a crunchy sesame-flour coating gives this Japanese dish its character. Soy sauce and hot mustard serve as dipping sauces for the crunchy fried-chicken pieces.

WINE RECOMMENDATION
The gingery, sweet, and salty flavors invite the racy citrus tang of riesling. You'll want an off-dry example, so look to Germany's Mosel-Saar-Ruwer and select a light and elegant kabinett.

SERVES 4

⅓ cup soy sauce, plus more for serving

4 teaspoons sugar

4 teaspoons sake or dry sherry

½ teaspoon grated fresh ginger

1 chicken (3 to 3½ pounds), chopped into 1½-inch pieces

¼ cup sesame seeds

1 cup cornstarch

1⅓ cups peanut or other cooking oil

Strips of daikon and red radish, for garnish (optional)

Hot mustard, for serving

1. In a large bowl, blend the soy sauce, sugar, sake, and ginger. Add the chicken, toss to coat, and let marinate for 30 to 40 minutes at room temperature.

2. Meanwhile, in a small heavy frying pan, toast the sesame seeds over moderately high heat, shaking the pan, until the seeds are light brown, about 20 seconds. Remove from the pan to cool.

3. In a shallow bowl, combine the cornstarch with the sesame seeds. Dredge the chicken in the mixture and shake off the excess. Put the chicken on a plate and let sit for 10 minutes.

4. In a deep, heavy frying pan, heat the oil over moderate heat to about 360°. Fry the chicken, in batches, until it is golden brown and cooked through, 2 to 3 minutes for boneless pieces, 5 to 8 minutes for bone-in pieces. Drain on paper towels.

5. Put the chicken on a platter or individual plates. Scatter the radishes, if using, over the chicken. Serve with small bowls of soy sauce and hot mustard for dipping.

—YAMATO, SAN FRANCISCO

VARIATION

Hacking up a whole chicken is more authentic, and the bones in the chicken pieces provide extra flavor, but if you prefer, you can substitute three pounds of boneless chicken breasts and thighs for the whole chicken here.

CHICKEN IN WHOLE-WHEAT LEMON BATTER

Mixing whole-wheat and all-purpose flours adds a richness of flavor to this lemony batter. The chicken is wonderfully crisp on the outside, tender within.

WINE RECOMMENDATION
With their crisp acidity, light body, and little or no tannin, rosés act more like white wines than reds, yet they offer just a bit of extra red fruit that helps them go well with more intensely flavored foods. Here, try one of the classic tempranillo-based rosés for which Spain's Navarra region is famous.

SERVES 4

1¼ cups all-purpose flour

½ cup whole-wheat flour

½ cup cornstarch

2 teaspoons salt

1¼ cups ice water

¼ cup lemon juice (from about 1 lemon)

Cooking oil, for frying

¼ teaspoon fresh-ground black pepper

1 chicken (3 to 3½ pounds), cut into 8 pieces

1. In a large bowl, whisk together ½ cup of the all-purpose flour, the whole-wheat flour, cornstarch, and 1 teaspoon of the salt. Combine the water and lemon juice, pour over the flour all at once, and whisk until the batter is smooth. Cover the bowl tightly with plastic wrap and refrigerate for at least 1 hour. Just before using, whisk the batter again.

2. In a deep fryer or a deep heavy saucepan, heat about 3 inches of oil to 375°. In a bowl, combine the remaining ¾ cup all-purpose flour and 1 teaspoon salt with the pepper. Dip four pieces of the chicken into the flour and then into the batter, letting the excess drip off.

3. Put the chicken pieces into the hot oil. Cook until crisp, golden, and just cooked through, 10 to 12 minutes. Remove the chicken pieces and drain on paper towels. Repeat with the remaining chicken.

CHICKEN KIEV

When this classic dish is properly prepared, the coating is crisp, the meat is moist, and the hot herb butter gushes out when you cut into the chicken.

WINE RECOMMENDATION
Look for a wine with high acidity to balance the richness while matching the intensity of the buttery chicken. A grand cru Chablis, with its nuances of lemon, apple, butter, and mineral, will be perfect. Chablis should always be racy, but grand cru means the wine will be powerful and concentrated, too.

SERVES 4

¼ pound butter, at room temperature

2 tablespoons minced fresh parsley

2 teaspoons minced scallion including green top

¼ teaspoon dried tarragon

¼ teaspoon cayenne

½ teaspoon salt

2 teaspoons lemon juice

4 boneless, skinless chicken breasts (about 1⅓ pounds in all)

¼ cup flour

2 large eggs

½ cup dry bread crumbs

Cooking oil, for frying

1. In a small bowl, beat together the butter, parsley, scallion, tarragon, cayenne, salt, and lemon juice. Shape the herb butter into a 2-by-3-inch rectangle, wrap it in waxed paper, and put it in the freezer.

2. Fold out the tender (see "Chicken Tenders," page 200) from underneath each chicken breast. Place the chicken between two sheets of waxed paper and use a mallet, flat meat pounder, or rolling pin to flatten it to an even thickness of ⅛ to ¼ inch.

3. Cut the herb butter lengthwise into four slices. Place one slice of butter on each chicken breast. Fold the short edges of the chicken over the butter, and then fold over the long edges to form a roll.

4. Put the flour and bread crumbs in shallow bowls. In another shallow bowl, lightly beat the eggs. Gently roll the chicken breasts in the flour, then the eggs, and then the bread crumbs to coat evenly. Put the chicken breasts on a plate, seam-side down, and refrigerate for 1 hour.

5. In a deep fryer or deep heavy saucepan, heat about 3 inches of oil to 375°. Using a slotted spoon, lower two chicken rolls into the hot oil. Cook until golden brown, about 5 minutes, then remove and drain on paper towels. Repeat with the remaining two rolls.

SPICY CHICKEN WITH SPRING PEANUT SAUCE

Here's a recipe for fried chicken that's packed with peanuts, from the chopped nuts that make up the crust to the peanut-butter-based dipping sauce that gives the dish its finishing touch.

WINE RECOMMENDATION This spicy chicken has enough hot pepper to wipe out the flavor of most wines and leave only the taste of alcohol. So try something fun, fruity, off-dry, and definitely not serious, such as the ever-popular white zinfandel. Perfect for picnicking.

SERVES 4

  6 strips bacon

½ cup fine-chopped unsalted dry-roasted peanuts

¼ teaspoon coarse salt

½ to 1 teaspoon dried red-pepper flakes

  4 boneless, skinless chicken breasts (about 1⅓ pounds in all)

  2 large eggs, separated

½ cup corn oil

    Spring Peanut Sauce, opposite page

    Lemon wedges, for serving

1. In a large frying pan, cook the bacon until crisp, about 5 minutes. Drain on paper towels and then chop fine. Combine the peanuts, bacon, salt, and red-pepper flakes in a small bowl.

2. Fold out the tender (see "Chicken Tenders," page 200) from underneath each chicken breast. Place the chicken between two sheets of waxed paper and use a mallet, flat meat pounder, or rolling pin to flatten it to an even thickness of ⅛ to ¼ inch.

3. In a medium bowl, beat the egg whites until they hold soft peaks. Beat in the yolks. Spread a thick layer of egg on one side of each chicken breast. Sprinkle about 1½ tablespoons of the nut mixture over each breast and press firmly so it adheres. Put the chicken on a plate and refrigerate for 30 minutes. Repeat to coat the other side of each chicken breast. Chill for 15 minutes longer.

4. Heat the oil in a large heavy frying pan over moderately high heat. Add the chicken and cook until browned, about 5 minutes. Turn each chicken breast carefully and cook until browned on the other side, about 5 minutes longer. Drain on paper towels. Serve hot or at room temperature, with the peanut sauce and the lemon wedges.

—ANNE DISRUDE

SPRING PEANUT SAUCE

You can adjust the spiciness of the sauce by using more or less of the hot-pepper sauce and red-pepper flakes.

MAKES ABOUT 1 1/2 CUPS

- 3 tablespoons smooth peanut butter
- 1 cup Chicken Stock, page 61, or canned low-sodium chicken broth
- 1 tablespoon lemon juice
- 1 teaspoon Asian sesame oil
- 2 scallions including green tops, minced
- 1 large clove garlic, crushed
- 1/4 teaspoon coarse salt
- 1/4 teaspoon fresh-ground black pepper
- 1/8 to 1/4 teaspoon hot-pepper sauce
- 1/2 to 1 teaspoon dried red-pepper flakes

Put the peanut butter in a medium bowl and gradually stir in the stock until smooth. Add the lemon juice, sesame oil, scallions, garlic, salt, black pepper, hot-pepper sauce, and red-pepper flakes. Cover and let stand at room temperature for at least 1 hour.

MAKE IT AHEAD

The sauce can be prepared one day in advance. Cover and refrigerate. Let the sauce come to room temperature before serving.

SERVING SUGGESTION

Make an easy salad of radishes, scallions, tomatoes, and cucumbers to accompany the chicken. Sprinkle the vegetables lightly with coarse salt and fresh-ground pepper.

PEANUT-COATED DRUMSTICKS WITH CURRIED CUCUMBERS

Double-dipping the drumsticks ensures an even coating, and chopped peanuts give them a special crunch. They're started in a skillet and finished in the oven rather than deep-fried.

 WINE RECOMMENDATION

Want to try something completely different? Go for a spicy Torrontés from Argentina's Cafayate region. Even experts are fooled by its gewürztraminer-like body and exotic floral character; if you can't find it, an off-dry gewürztraminer from Washington State will make a fine substitute.

SERVES 4

⅔ cup flour

1½ tablespoons plus ¾ teaspoon curry powder

2¼ teaspoons dried dill

1 teaspoon salt

1¼ teaspoons fresh-ground black pepper

8 chicken drumsticks, skin removed

¾ cup unsalted dry-roasted peanuts

¾ teaspoon dried red-pepper flakes

1 large egg

1 tablespoon milk

½ cup olive oil

1 shallot, minced

1 English cucumber, cut lengthwise into eighths and then crosswise into 1½-inch pieces

½ teaspoon dill seeds

1. Heat the oven to 400°. In a medium bowl, combine the flour, the 1½ tablespoons curry powder, 2 teaspoons of the dried dill, ¾ teaspoon of the salt, and 1 teaspoon of the black pepper. Pat the drumsticks dry and dredge them in the seasoned flour, coating thoroughly. Shake off the excess and put the chicken on a wire rack set on a baking sheet. Reserve the flour mixture.

2. In a food processor, combine the peanuts, red-pepper flakes, and 1 tablespoon of the reserved seasoned flour. Pulse until the nuts are chopped fine, then transfer the mixture to a shallow bowl.

3. In another shallow bowl, beat the egg with the milk. Dredge the drumsticks again in the remaining seasoned flour, dip them in the egg mixture, and then dip them into the ground peanuts, turning to coat completely.

4. Set aside 1 tablespoon of the oil. In a large deep skillet, heat half of the remaining oil over moderately high heat until it is almost smoking hot. Add half of the drumsticks and fry, turning, until well browned, 10 to 12 minutes. Be careful not to break the delicate crust as you turn the chicken. Return

the drumsticks to the rack. Repeat with the remaining oil and drumsticks.

5. Put the baking sheet in the oven and bake the chicken until cooked through, 35 to 40 minutes.

6. Meanwhile, in a large skillet, heat the reserved ¾ tablespoon oil over moderate heat. Add the shallot and cook, stirring occasionally, until translucent, 2 to 3 minutes. Add the cucumber and sprinkle with the dill seeds and the remaining ¾ teaspoon curry powder and ¼ teaspoon each dried dill, salt, and black pepper. Cover and cook, stirring frequently, until the cucumber is tender, 4 to 6 minutes.

7. To serve, reheat the cucumber if necessary. Mound the cucumber on a serving platter; arrange the drumsticks all around.

—BOB CHAMBERS

CRISPY CHICKEN STRIPS WITH LEMON SOY DIPPING SAUCE

Strips of fried chicken are fast-food favorites, but they're easy to prepare at home. Dunk these in the zippy lemon dipping sauce for extra flavor.

 WINE RECOMMENDATION
Though almost unknown in the U.S., Germany's Nahe region produces some of the world's greatest rieslings, with winemakers such as Armin Diel, Helmut Dönnhöff, and Peter Crusius turning out wines of stunning complexity and finesse. Try a zesty spätlese for the right weight and balance.

SERVES 4

¼ cup flour

1⅓ pounds boneless, skinless chicken breasts (about 4), cut into 3-by-½-inch strips

2 tablespoons cooking oil, more as needed

½ teaspoon fresh-ground black pepper

Lemon Soy Dipping Sauce, right

1. Put the flour in a paper or plastic bag. Add the chicken strips to the bag and shake to coat. Shake off the excess.

2. In a large heavy frying pan, heat the oil over moderately high heat. Add as many of the chicken strips to the pan as will fit without crowding. Fry the chicken strips until golden brown, 1 to 2 minutes. Turn and cook on the other side until just cooked through, about 15 seconds. Drain on paper towels. Cook the remaining strips, adding more oil as needed.

3. Sprinkle the chicken strips with the pepper and serve with the dipping sauce.

—JIM FOBEL

LEMON SOY DIPPING SAUCE

MAKES ABOUT 1 CUP

½ cup soy sauce

¼ cup lemon juice

1 clove garlic, minced

1 tablespoon sugar

1 tablespoon Asian sesame oil

2 scallions including green tops, minced

Combine all the ingredients in a small bowl. Stir until the sugar dissolves.

DILLED CHICKEN-AND-VEGETABLE STIR-FRY IN PITAS

If the ingredients are cut up nice and small, a stir-fry makes a delicious hot filling for pitas. Topping the sandwiches with a cool mixture of tomato and dill makes this a perfect informal meal.

WINE RECOMMENDATION
A light and fruity red with good crisp acidity will highlight the earthy mushrooms and stand up to the tomatoes. Try a Bardolino or Valpolicella from Italy's Veneto. The region's reputation has been damaged by cheap, mass-produced wines, but many smaller estates produce excellent ones.

SERVES 4

3 tablespoons peanut oil

2/3 pound boneless, skinless chicken breasts (about 2), cut into 1/2-inch dice

1 small onion, cut into thin slices

1 large rib celery, cut into thin slices

1 clove garlic, minced

10 mushrooms, quartered

4 tablespoons minced fresh dill

3/4 teaspoon lemon juice

About 5 drops hot-pepper sauce

Salt

1/4 teaspoon fresh-ground black pepper

1 tomato, peeled, seeded, and chopped

4 pitas, warmed

1. In a wok or large heavy frying pan, heat 1 tablespoon of the oil over high heat. Add the chicken and toss to coat. Reduce the heat to moderate and cook, stirring, until the chicken is lightly browned, about 2 minutes. Using a slotted spoon, transfer the chicken to a bowl.

2. Add the onion to the pan and stir-fry until soft, about 3 minutes. Add the celery and garlic and cook for 30 seconds. Transfer to the bowl with the chicken.

3. Add the remaining 2 tablespoons oil to the pan and heat over moderately high heat. Add the mushrooms and stir-fry until well browned, about 3 minutes. Transfer the mushrooms to the bowl; stir in 2 1/2 tablespoons of the dill, the lemon juice, hot-pepper sauce, 1/2 teaspoon salt, and the pepper.

4. In another bowl, toss the remaining 1 1/2 tablespoons dill with the chopped tomato and a pinch of salt. Fill the pitas with the chicken mixture and top with the tomato mixture.

CHICKEN AND ASPARAGUS STIR-FRY

Stir-frying really brings out the best in vegetables, and the quick-cooking technique helps them retain their color and nutrients, too. Use asparagus stalks of standard thickness here; thicker stalks may not cook through.

WINE RECOMMENDATION
Sauvignon blancs from New Zealand's Marlborough region have a bit of asparagus flavor, and make an intriguing match here. Volcanic soils promote ripeness, while the cool climate keeps the acids fresh and vital.

SERVES 4

- 1 egg white
- 1 tablespoon dry vermouth
- 1 tablespoon cornstarch
- 1 teaspoon coarse salt
- 1 pound boneless, skinless chicken breasts (about 3), cut into 1-inch pieces
- 2 teaspoons cooking oil
- ¼ cup olive oil
- 2 tablespoons minced fresh parsley
- 2 tablespoons minced onion
- 4 cloves garlic, minced
- ⅛ teaspoon dried red-pepper flakes
- ¾ pound asparagus, cut into 2-inch pieces (about 2½ cups)
- Table salt
- ⅛ teaspoon sugar
- 1 tablespoon water, if needed
- 2 tablespoons minced pitted black olives
- 1 teaspoon grated orange zest
- ½ teaspoon dried basil
- Fresh-ground black pepper

1. In a medium bowl, whisk together the egg white, vermouth, cornstarch, and coarse salt. Add the chicken and toss to coat. Cover and refrigerate for at least 1 hour, or overnight.

2. Bring a medium pot of water to a simmer and add the cooking oil. Add the chicken and cook, stirring gently, until almost cooked through but still pink in the center, about 2 minutes. Drain and rinse the chicken with cold water. Pat dry.

3. Heat a wok or large heavy frying pan over high heat until a drop of water evaporates on contact. Pour in the olive oil in a thin stream around the edge of the pan (it should immediately smoke). Add the parsley, onion, garlic, and red-pepper flakes all at once. Cook, stirring, until fragrant, about 10 seconds; do not let the garlic color. Add the asparagus, sprinkle with ½ teaspoon table salt and the sugar, and stir-fry until almost crisp-tender, 1½ to 2 minutes. If the asparagus begins to dry out, add the water.

4. Add the chicken to the pan and stir-fry until just cooked through, about 30 seconds. Add the olives, orange zest, basil, and black pepper; stir-fry for about 20 seconds. Remove from the heat and season with table salt and black pepper.

CHICKEN STIR-FRY WITH SUMMER SQUASH

Light and summery, this colorful combination of green zucchini and yellow summer squash needs only some fresh tomatoes and good bread to make a meal.

WINE RECOMMENDATION
Spice up the squash with a grüner velt-liner from Austria. These light whites make up over a third of Austria's wines, but are produced almost nowhere else. Try one from the Wachau, Austria's finest winegrowing region.

SERVES 4

1⅓ pounds boneless, skinless chicken breasts (about 4)
  1 egg white
  1 tablespoon dry white wine
  1 tablespoon cornstarch
  ¾ teaspoon salt
  3 tablespoons olive oil
  ½ onion, chopped fine
  2 cloves garlic, minced
  2 small zucchini, cut into 2-by-¼-inch matchstick strips
  2 small yellow summer squash, cut into 2-by-¼-inch matchstick strips
  ¼ teaspoon fresh-ground black pepper
  ¼ cup fresh basil leaves

1. Remove the tender (see "Chicken Tenders," page 200) from underneath each chicken breast and cut it lengthwise into ¼-inch-thick strips. Cut the chicken breasts on the diagonal into long strips about ¼ inch wide.

2. In a medium bowl, whisk together the egg white, wine, cornstarch, and ½ teaspoon of the salt. Add the chicken and toss to coat. Cover and refrigerate for at least 1 hour, or overnight.

3. Bring a large pot of water to a simmer. Add the chicken, stirring gently to separate the pieces, and simmer until almost done but still pink in the center, about 1 minute. Do not let the water boil. Drain and rinse the chicken with cold water. Pat dry.

4. In a wok or large heavy frying pan, heat the oil over moderate heat. Add the onion and cook, stirring, for 1 minute. Add the garlic and cook for 30 seconds. Add the zucchini and yellow squash and stir-fry until just tender, about 3 minutes. Add the chicken and stir-fry until cooked through, about 1 minute. Add the remaining ¼ teaspoon salt, the pepper, and the basil and toss well. Serve the stir-fry on its own or over rice.

—ANNE DISRUDE

243

CHICKEN STIR-FRY WITH CELERY, CARROTS, AND DILL

An abundance of dill accents this stir-fry of chicken, carrots, and celery. Since the herb loses its flavor when heated, it is always added at the very last minute.

WINE RECOMMENDATION
The carrots, celery, and dill immediately suggest an herbal, light-bodied wine made from sauvignon blanc. A fresh Sancerre, with its mineral and citrus tones, will harmonize well.

SERVES 4

- 1   egg white
- 1   tablespoon dry vermouth
- 1   tablespoon cornstarch
- 1   teaspoon coarse salt
- 1   pound boneless, skinless chicken breasts (about 3), cut into 1-inch pieces
- 2   teaspoons cooking oil
- ¼   cup olive oil
- 2   tablespoons minced fresh parsley
- 2   tablespoons minced onion
- 4   cloves garlic, minced
- ⅛   teaspoon dried red-pepper flakes
- 2½ cups sliced celery
- 1   carrot, cut into matchstick strips (about ½ cup)
-     Table salt
- ⅛   teaspoon sugar
- 1   tablespoon water, if needed
- ¼   cup minced fresh dill
-     Fresh-ground black pepper

1. In a medium bowl, whisk together the egg white, vermouth, cornstarch, and coarse salt. Add the chicken and toss to coat. Cover and refrigerate at least 1 hour, or overnight.

2. Bring a medium pot of water to a simmer and add the cooking oil. Add the chicken; cook, stirring gently, until almost cooked through but still pink in the center, about 2 minutes. Drain and rinse with cold water. Pat dry.

3. Heat a wok or large heavy frying pan over high heat until a drop of water evaporates on contact. Pour in the olive oil in a thin stream around the edge of the pan (it should immediately smoke). Add the parsley, onion, garlic, and red-pepper flakes all at once. Cook, stirring, until fragrant, about 10 seconds; do not let the garlic color. Add the celery and carrots. Sprinkle with ½ teaspoon table salt and the sugar; stir-fry until almost crisp-tender, 1½ to 2 minutes. If the vegetables begin to dry out, add the water.

4. Add the chicken and stir-fry until just cooked through, about 30 seconds. Add the dill and black pepper to taste and stir-fry for about 20 seconds. Remove from the heat and season with table salt and black pepper.

—ANNE DISRUDE

Chicken in Sweet Wine Sauce

This wine-flavored dish, not typical of Chinese cuisine in general, is popular in the province of Fukien. Its special character comes from the wine paste—fermented wine lees left at the bottom of the crock when rice wine is put aside to age. Serve the chicken with rice or a loaf of good French bread.

WINE RECOMMENDATION
An off-dry German riesling makes a great accompaniment for piquant Asian flavors. The sauce for this chicken is quite sweet, so select a rich spätlese riesling from the Pfalz. The most southerly of the Rhein regions, the Pfalz produces the highest in alcohol and most full-bodied of all the Rhein wines.

SERVES 4

2 egg whites

2 teaspoons coarse salt

7 tablespoons Chinese rice wine or dry sherry

2 tablespoons plus 4 teaspoons cornstarch

1⅓ pounds boneless, skinless chicken breasts (about 4), cut into ¾-inch pieces

4 teaspoons Chinese wine paste*

1 cup plus 2 tablespoons Chicken Stock, page 61, or canned low-sodium chicken broth

½ teaspoon Asian sesame oil

¼ cup sugar, more if needed

¼ cup plus 2 teaspoons cooking oil, more if needed

⅔ cup thinly sliced scallions including green tops

2 tablespoons minced fresh ginger

2 tablespoons minced garlic

*Available at Asian markets

1. In a medium bowl, combine the egg whites, salt, 2 tablespoons of the wine, and the 2 tablespoons cornstarch. Add the chicken and toss to coat. Cover and refrigerate for at least 1 hour, or overnight.

2. In a small bowl, blend the wine paste, the remaining 5 tablespoons rice wine, the 1 cup stock, and the sesame oil. Mash the wine paste to dissolve it thoroughly. Add the sugar. The sauce should be sweet; add more sugar if necessary.

3. Bring a large pot of water to a simmer. Add the 2 teaspoons cooking oil and reduce the heat to just below a simmer. Add the chicken to the pan. Cook, stirring gently, until the chicken is almost entirely white, 15 to 20 seconds. Drain and rinse the chicken with cold water. Pat dry.

4. Heat a wok or large heavy frying pan over high heat until a drop of water evaporates on contact. Pour in the remaining ¼ cup of cooking oil in a thin stream around the edge of the pan (it should immediately

smoke). Reduce the heat to moderately high, add the scallions, ginger, and garlic, and stir-fry until fragrant, about 10 seconds; add more oil if needed to prevent sticking. Add the chicken and toss to combine. Add the sauce and bring to a boil, stirring; cook for 30 seconds.

5. Dissolve the remaining 4 teaspoons cornstarch in the remaining 2 tablespoons stock. Add to the pan and cook, stirring, until the sauce thickens and turns glossy, about 10 seconds.

—BARBARA TROPP

HOT-AND-SOUR CHICKEN WITH RED AND GREEN PEPPERS

As with most stir-fries, this dish is ready in a flash. The ingredients are added to the wok or frying pan at a brisk pace, so make sure they're all sliced up and measured out ahead of time so you won't have to stop the action.

WINE RECOMMENDATION
Port is one of the few red wines that has the right combination of flavor, sweetness, and viscosity to cope with this dish. A good ruby port is almost syrupy and loaded with roasted mulberry fruit and peppery spiciness.

SERVES 4

3 tablespoons rice-wine vinegar

2 tablespoons soy sauce

1 tablespoon sugar

2 teaspoons cornstarch

¾ teaspoon dried red-pepper flakes

1 teaspoon Asian sesame oil

1 pound boneless, skinless chicken breasts (about 3), sliced crosswise into ¼-inch strips

2 tablespoons peanut oil

1 tablespoon minced fresh ginger

1 large onion, cut into thin slices

1 large red bell pepper, cut into ¼-inch-wide strips

1 large green bell pepper, cut into ¼-inch-wide strips

⅓ cup Chicken Stock, page 61, or canned low-sodium chicken broth

½ teaspoon salt

¼ teaspoon fresh-ground black pepper

1. In a medium bowl, whisk together the vinegar, soy sauce, sugar, cornstarch, and red-pepper flakes. Whisk in the sesame oil. Add the chicken and toss to coat. Marinate for about 5 minutes.

2. Heat a wok or large heavy frying pan over high heat until a drop of water evaporates on contact, and then add the peanut oil. Add the ginger and onion and stir-fry until the onion is slightly softened, about 1 minute. Add the bell peppers and stir-fry until slightly softened, about 1 minute. Add the chicken with its marinade and the stock and stir-fry until the chicken is cooked through, about 3 minutes. Season with the salt and black pepper.

—JIM FOBEL

CHICKEN, RED-PEPPER, ARUGULA, AND PROSCIUTTO STIR-FRY

All the chopping, shredding, julienning, and marinating for this dish can be done in advance. To make the final frying fast and simple, put the various ingredients that will be added at the same time in a single bowl.

 WINE RECOMMENDATION With a peppery green such as arugula as a main ingredient, you'll want a wine that is light in alcohol, or the combination may be unpleasantly bitter. A crisp Soave from Italy's Veneto will make a fine counterpoint to the varied flavors of this dish.

SERVES 4

1 egg white

1 tablespoon dry vermouth

1 tablespoon cornstarch

1 teaspoon coarse salt

1 pound boneless, skinless chicken breasts (about 3), cut into 1-inch pieces

2 teaspoons cooking oil

¼ cup olive oil

2 tablespoons minced fresh parsley

2 tablespoons minced onion

4 cloves garlic, minced

⅛ teaspoon dried red-pepper flakes

2 large red bell peppers, diced

Table salt

⅛ teaspoon sugar

1 tablespoon water, if needed

¼ pound arugula, stems removed, leaves shredded (about 2½ cups)

2 tablespoons fine-chopped prosciutto

½ teaspoon dried oregano

Fresh-ground black pepper

1. In a medium bowl, whisk together the egg white, vermouth, cornstarch, and coarse salt. Add the chicken and toss to coat. Cover and refrigerate for at least 1 hour, or overnight.

2. Bring a large pot of water to a simmer and add the cooking oil. Add the chicken and cook, stirring gently, until the pieces are almost cooked through but still pink in the center, about 2 minutes. Drain and rinse with cold water. Pat dry.

3. Heat a wok or large heavy frying pan over high heat until a drop of water evaporates on contact. Pour in the olive oil in a thin stream around the edge of the pan (it should immediately smoke). Add the minced parsley, onion, and garlic and the red-pepper flakes all at once. Cook, stirring, until fragrant, about 10 seconds. Do not let the garlic color.

4. Add the bell peppers, sprinkle with ½ teaspoon table salt and the sugar, and

249

stir-fry until almost crisp-tender, $1\frac{1}{2}$ to 2 minutes. If the bell peppers begin to dry out, add the water.

5. Add the chicken to the pan and stir-fry until cooked through, about 30 seconds. Add the arugula, prosciutto, oregano, and black pepper to taste and stir-fry for about 20 seconds. Remove from the heat and season with table salt and black pepper.

—ANNE DISRUDE

MAKE IT AHEAD

In all our stir-fry recipes that call for cooking the chicken in a pot of water before stir-frying—Chicken and Asparagus Stir-Fry, page 241, Chicken Stir-Fry with Summer Squash, page 243, and Chicken Stir-Fry with Celery, Carrots, and Dill, page 244, as well as this one—you can precook the chicken up to three hours in advance and refrigerate it, covered. Let the chicken return to room temperature before proceeding with the recipe.

VIETNAMESE CHICKEN

The lemongrass, fish sauce, and hot pepper in this fragrant stir-fry reflect its Southeast Asian origins. Serve the chicken with steamed or boiled rice.

 WINE RECOMMENDATION
With its spiciness and exotic fruit flavors, including lychee nut and apricot, a gewürztraminer *vendange tardive* (late harvest) from Alsace is particularly well suited to Asian foods.

SERVES 4

1½   stalks lemongrass,* bottom third only, or 1 teaspoon grated lemon zest

 3   cloves garlic, minced

 2   tablespoons Asian fish sauce (nuoc mam or nam pla)*

 ¾   teaspoon plus 1½ tablespoons sugar

 ¼   teaspoon fresh-ground black pepper

 ½   pound boneless, skinless chicken thighs, cut into 1-inch pieces

 ⅔   pound boneless, skinless chicken breasts (about 2), cut into 1-inch pieces

 1   tablespoon cold water

 ½   teaspoon lemon juice

1½   teaspoons peanut oil

 ¼   teaspoon dried red-pepper flakes

   *Available at Asian markets and some supermarkets

1.   Mince 1 teaspoon of the bulblike part of the lemongrass's inner stalk and put it, or the lemon zest if using, in a large bowl. Add half the garlic, 1½ tablespoons of the fish sauce, the ¾ teaspoon sugar, and the black pepper. Add the chicken and toss to coat. Cover and marinate at room temperature for up to 1 hour.

2.   Meanwhile, in a small saucepan, combine the remaining 1½ tablespoons sugar with the water and cook over moderate heat until the mixture begins to brown, about 2 minutes. Stir constantly until the sugar is amber-colored, about 1 minute longer. Immediately remove the pan from the heat and stir the lemon juice into the caramel mixture. Be careful, it will spatter.

3.   In a wok or large heavy frying pan, heat the oil over high heat. Add the remaining garlic and stir-fry until fragrant, about 10 seconds. Add the chicken with its marinade and stir-fry for 3 to 5 minutes. Reduce the heat to moderate and add the remaining 1½ teaspoons fish sauce, the red-pepper flakes, and 1 teaspoon of the caramel mixture. Cook, stirring, for 5 minutes longer.

CHICKEN SOONG

A popular Cantonese dish, Chicken Soong is eaten much like *mu-shu* pork, with lettuce leaves replacing pancakes as wrappers for the filling. Spoon a serving of the chicken mixture onto a leaf, fold the bottom and sides over the mixture, and eat the roll with your fingers.

WINE RECOMMENDATION
A ripe, fruit-driven pinot noir from Napa or the Santa Barbara area is just the ticket with this sweet and savory dish. Go for the biggest, richest mouthful of fruit you can find. What you don't want is something too subtle; it will just get buried.

SERVES 4

1 egg white

2 tablespoons dry sherry

1½ teaspoons water-chestnut powder* or cornstarch

½ pound boneless, skinless chicken breast (2 small), partially frozen and cut into small dice

½ ounce dried Chinese mushrooms*

2 cups boiling water

¼ cup pine nuts

2 tablespoons hoisin sauce

1 tablespoon soy sauce

¼ teaspoon fresh-ground black pepper

2 cups peanut oil

⅓ cup minced shallots

¼ cup diced carrots

1 clove garlic, minced

1 teaspoon minced fresh ginger

¼ cup diced red bell pepper

½ cup diced water chestnuts, preferably fresh*

½ cup diced snow peas

1 teaspoon Asian sesame oil

1 head iceberg lettuce, cored and cut in half, with individual leaves loosened

*Available at Asian markets

1. In a medium bowl, whisk together the egg white, 1½ teaspoons of the sherry, and the water-chestnut powder. Add the chicken and toss to coat. Cover and refrigerate for at least 1 hour, or overnight.

2. Put the mushrooms in a small bowl and add the boiling water. Soak until the mushrooms are soft, about 20 minutes. Remove the mushrooms from the soaking liquid and squeeze out the excess moisture. Remove the stems and cut the caps into ¼-inch dice.

3. In a small frying pan, toast the pine nuts over moderately low heat, stirring frequently, until golden brown, about 5 minutes. Or toast them in a 350° oven for about 8 minutes.

4. In a small bowl, combine the remaining 1½ tablespoons sherry, the hoisin sauce, soy sauce, and black pepper. Blend well.

5. Heat a wok or large heavy frying pan over high heat until a drop of water evaporates on contact. Pour in the peanut oil in a thin stream around the edge of the pan (it should immediately smoke). Stir the chicken and add it to the pan. Cook, stirring, until the chicken is white, about 1 minute. Remove the chicken from the pan with a slotted spoon and drain. Pour off all but 1 tablespoon of oil from the pan.

6. Reduce the heat to moderate and add the shallots, carrots, and mushrooms. Stir-fry for 1 minute. Add the garlic and ginger and stir-fry for 1 minute. Raise the heat to high and add the bell pepper, water chestnuts, and snow peas. Stir-fry for 1 minute. Remove the vegetables from the pan.

7. Stir the soy-sauce mixture and add it to the pan. Cook, stirring, over high heat for 30 seconds. Return the chicken to the pan and stir-fry for about 30 seconds. Add the vegetable mixture; stir-fry until heated through, 30 seconds longer.

8. Remove the pan from the heat and stir in the sesame oil. Put the chicken mixture on a platter and sprinkle the pine nuts over it. Serve hot, with the lettuce leaves for wrapping.

—KAREN LEE AND ALEXANDRA BRANYON

CHICKEN SLICING AND DICING

When you need to cut raw chicken into thin slices or small dice, put it in the freezer first. Once the flesh firms up, it's ever so much easier to cut neatly.

GLAZED CHICKEN DOMBURI

In Japanese, *domburi* means big bowl, and it refers both to the deep ceramic dish and to the heaping portion of rice, meat, and vegetables that goes in it. In this example, richly sauced and glazed chicken is served with crisp snow peas over rice and sprinkled with toasted sesame seeds.

SERVES 4

2 cups short-grain rice

2⅓ cups cold water

1 pound boneless, skinless chicken breasts (about 3), cut into ½-inch-thick diagonal slices and then into 1-inch pieces

2 tablespoons sake or dry white wine

½ teaspoon salt

1 tablespoon sesame seeds

½ pound snow peas

1 tablespoon cornstarch

2 tablespoons cooking oil

¼ cup Chicken Stock, page 61, canned low-sodium chicken broth, or water

2 tablespoons soy sauce

2 tablespoons mirin (sweet Japanese cooking wine)*

1 teaspoon sugar

8 sweet pickled scallions (*rakko*)* or pickled pearl onions

*Available at Asian markets and some supermarkets

1. Rinse the rice in a strainer under cold water until the water runs clear. Drain well, then put the rice in a deep 3-quart saucepan. Add the water, cover, and soak for 10 minutes.

2. Set the saucepan over high heat and bring the water to a boil. Reduce the heat and simmer until the rice has absorbed all the water, about 6 minutes. Increase the heat to high and cook, still covered, for 20 seconds. Remove the pan from the heat and let steam, covered, for 15 minutes.

3. Meanwhile, put the chicken pieces in a small bowl and add the sake and salt. Marinate for 5 to 10 minutes.

4. In a small heavy frying pan, toast the sesame seeds over moderately high heat, shaking the pan, until the seeds are light brown, about 20 seconds. Remove the sesame seeds from the pan. When the seeds are cool enough to handle, mince them.

5. In a large a saucepan of boiling, salted water, cook the snow peas for 10 seconds. Drain, rinse the snow peas with cold water, and pat dry.

6. Remove the chicken from the marinade and pat dry. Put the chicken in a small bowl, sprinkle with the cornstarch, and toss lightly to coat.

7. In a large heavy frying pan, heat the oil over moderately high heat. Add the chicken and cook, stirring, until all the pieces are white. Add the stock and scrape the bottom of the pan to dislodge any brown bits. Reduce the heat to low, add the soy sauce, mirin, and sugar, and simmer until the sauce is reduced by two thirds, about 5 minutes. Raise the heat to high and cook, stirring, until the chicken is glazed with the sauce and just cooked through, about 10 seconds. Sprinkle half of the sesame seeds over the chicken and stir to mix them in.

8. Divide the rice among four bowls or soup plates. Cover the center of the rice with the chicken. Cover the remaining rice with the snow peas, standing them up at an angle at the edge of the chicken to look like leaves. Garnish with the pickled scallions and sprinkle the remaining sesame seeds over all.

—ELIZABETH ANDOH

STEAMING RICE

While the rice is steaming, be sure to keep the pan tightly covered. If you must check the rice, do so quickly in order to lose as little steam as possible.

chapter 10

STEWS

Chicken and Sausage Stew with Parsley and Lemon, page 279

CHICKEN-DRUMSTICK RAGOUT WITH BELL PEPPERS AND ARTICHOKES

A mixture of different-colored bell peppers makes this stew especially attractive, but you can use just one color if you like; the dish will be no less delicious. Serve it with white rice and hot garlic bread.

WINE RECOMMENDATION
The mix of herbs and vegetables in a creamy sauce strongly suggests a crisp white made from sauvignon blanc to harmonize with the flavors and balance the ragout's richness. Choose one of the many superb sauvignons from the Italian region of Friuli, which specializes in vivacious, varietally labeled white wines.

SERVES 4

12 chicken drumsticks
¾ cup flour
    Salt and fresh-ground black pepper
8 tablespoons butter
2 onions, chopped
3 cloves garlic, minced
¾ teaspoon dried thyme
¾ teaspoon dried basil
1 bay leaf
1½ cups Chicken Stock, page 61, or canned low-sodium chicken broth
¾ cup dry white wine
1 red bell pepper, cut into quarters
1 green bell pepper, cut into quarters
1 yellow bell pepper, cut into quarters
1 10-ounce package frozen artichoke hearts, thawed and drained
¾ cup heavy cream

1. Dredge the drumsticks in the flour, shaking off the excess. Season the drumsticks with ¾ teaspoon salt and ½ teaspoon black pepper. In a large pot or Dutch oven, melt 4 tablespoons of the butter over moderate heat. Add six of the drumsticks to the pot and cook, turning occasionally, until the drumsticks are lightly browned all over, about 10 minutes. Transfer the drumsticks to a large plate. Cook the remaining drumsticks.

2. Melt another 2 tablespoons of the butter in the pot. Add the onions, garlic, thyme, basil, and bay leaf. Reduce the heat to moderately low, cover, and cook, stirring occasionally, until the onions are soft, 10 to 15 minutes.

3. Return the drumsticks to the pot. Add the stock and wine and bring to a boil. Reduce the heat, cover, and simmer, turning occasionally, until the chicken is very tender, about 40 minutes. Remove the drumsticks. Strain the cooking liquid and return it to the pot. ➤

4. Meanwhile, in a medium frying pan, melt the remaining 2 tablespoons butter over moderately high heat. Add the bell peppers, season with a pinch each of salt and black pepper, and cook, stirring frequently, until lightly browned, about 5 minutes. Add the artichoke hearts and cook for 2 minutes.

5. Stir the cream into the strained cooking liquid and bring to a boil over high heat. Boil until the liquid is reduced by one third, about 15 minutes. Season with salt and black pepper. Add the chicken, bell peppers, and artichokes to the pot and simmer gently until heated through, about 5 minutes.

—MICHAEL MCLAUGHLIN

RAGOUT OF CHICKEN WITH BLACK OLIVES AND ONION JAM

Chicken pieces stay moist and pick up a heady aroma when they're braised with browned onions and olives. Serve the ragout with buttered egg noodles.

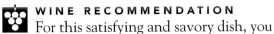 **WINE RECOMMENDATION**
For this satisfying and savory dish, you need a big white with some guts. Go for a premier cru Puligny-Montrachet, which has the steely backbone for which all wines from Puligny are known.

SERVES 4

1 cup black olives, such as Niçoise or Kalamata, pitted

1 cup flour

Salt and fresh-ground black pepper

1 chicken (3 to 3½ pounds), cut into 8 pieces

3 tablespoons butter

2 pounds large white onions, cut into thick slices

2 cups Chicken Stock, page 61, or canned low-sodium chicken broth

¼ cup dry sherry

1 tablespoon grated lemon zest

1 teaspoon dried thyme

1. If the olives taste very salty, put them in a saucepan, cover them with cold water, and bring the water to a boil over high heat. Drain and rinse the olives with cold water. Repeat if necessary.

2. Combine the flour, ½ teaspoon salt, and ¼ teaspoon pepper in a medium bowl. Dredge the chicken pieces in the seasoned flour. Shake off the excess. In a large pot or Dutch oven, melt 2 tablespoons of the butter over moderately high heat. Add the chicken, in batches if necessary, and brown well on both sides, about 8 minutes in all. Transfer the chicken to a bowl. Wipe out the pot.

3. Melt the remaining 1 tablespoon butter in the pot over moderate heat. Add the onions, cover, and cook until softened, about 15 minutes. Uncover and cook, stirring occasionally, until the onions are golden brown, about 25 minutes.

4. Heat the oven to 325°. Add the olives, stock, sherry, lemon zest, and thyme to the pot and bring to a boil. Return the chicken to the pot. Cover and bake, stirring occasionally, until the chicken is cooked through, about 1¼ hours.

5. Remove the chicken and boil the liquid until it thickens slightly, 5 to 10 minutes. Season with salt and pepper. Return the chicken to the pot and heat through.

—MOLLY O'NEILL

CHICKEN FRICASSEE WITH ARTICHOKES AND PEARL ONIONS

For this luscious stew, sautéed chicken cooks in a creamy sauce laced with artichokes, pearl onions, and mushrooms. If you like, serve it with rice or couscous.

WINE RECOMMENDATION

Since artichokes tend to make a wine taste sweeter, here it's best to employ the principle of using a dry, crisp wine to cut the richness of the dish, rather than matching it with a wine of equal size. Try a tocai friulano, from Italy's northeastern region of Friuli. The wine's touch of earthiness is an added plus since it will echo the taste of the mushrooms.

SERVES 4

½ cup lemon juice (from about 2 lemons)

6 artichokes

¾ pound pearl onions

1 chicken (3 to 3½ pounds), cut into 8 pieces

Salt and fresh-ground black pepper

2 tablespoons butter

2 tablespoons cooking oil

¾ pound mushrooms, quartered if large

½ cup dry white wine

½ cup Chicken Stock, page 61, or canned low-sodium chicken broth

1 cup heavy cream

1 bay leaf

2 tablespoons chopped fresh parsley

1. Add ¼ cup of the lemon juice to a large stainless-steel saucepan of water. Working with one artichoke at a time, break off and discard the tough outer leaves until you reach the tender pale-yellow leaves. Cut 1 inch off the tops of the leaves. Using a small sharp knife, trim the dark-green areas from the bottom of the artichoke. To prevent darkening, put each artichoke into the lemon water when you finish trimming it.

2. Bring the water to a boil over moderately high heat and cook until the artichokes are just tender when pierced with a knife, about 25 minutes. Let the artichokes cool in the cooking liquid. Then drain, scoop out the fuzzy chokes, and cut the artichokes into quarters.

3. Meanwhile, in a saucepan of boiling water, blanch the onions for 1 minute. Drain, cool, and peel.

4. Season the chicken with ½ teaspoon salt and ¼ teaspoon pepper. In a large pot or Dutch oven, melt the butter with the oil over moderately high heat. Add the chicken and brown well on both sides, about 8 minutes in all. Transfer the chicken to a large bowl.

5. Transfer the peeled onions to the pot and cook, stirring frequently, until evenly browned, about 10 minutes. Using a slotted spoon, transfer the onions to the bowl.

6. Add the mushrooms to the pot and cook, stirring frequently, until they are lightly browned, about 8 minutes. Using the slotted spoon, transfer the mushrooms to the bowl.

7. Pour off the fat from the pot and add the wine. Bring to a boil, scraping the bottom of the pan to dislodge any brown bits. Add the stock and cook until the liquid is reduced to 3 tablespoons, about 5 minutes.

8. Add the cream, the artichokes, the chicken, onions, and mushrooms, and the bay leaf. Reduce the heat and simmer for 35 minutes.

9. Stir the remaining ¼ cup lemon juice into the stew and season with salt and pepper. Remove the bay leaf. Sprinkle the stew with the parsley.

—JOHN ROBERT MASSIE

MAKE IT AHEAD

You can prepare the artichokes up to two days in advance. Put the quartered artichokes in a bowl and cover with their cooking liquid. Cover the bowl and refrigerate.

CHICKEN FRICASSEE WITH CHERRIES AND SHERRY VINEGAR

Turnips, carrots, and green beans are familiar fricassee ingredients, but cherries aren't so common. Their tartness gives a nice zing to the vegetables and the tarragon-flavored sauce.

♣ WINE RECOMMENDATION
In 1985, Austria's wine industry was nearly destroyed by a fraud scandal. Since then, a new breed of dedicated young winemakers has been producing wines of stunning quality and diversity. Search for a red made from, and called, Zweigelt. Its fresh, lip-smacking cherry fruit will be perfect with this dish.

SERVES 4

3 carrots, cut into 1½-inch pieces

3 small turnips, peeled and quartered lengthwise

Salt

¼ pound green beans, halved

4 bone-in chicken breasts (about 2¼ pounds in all), or 4 whole chicken legs, or 2 of each

¼ cup plus 2½ teaspoons flour

2 tablespoons olive oil

Fresh-ground black pepper

1½ tablespoons butter

1 small shallot, minced

¼ cup plus 2 tablespoons sherry vinegar

¼ cup plus 2 tablespoons Brown Chicken Stock, opposite page

¾ cup cherries preserved in sherry vinegar, drained,* or ¾ cup canned pitted dark sweet cherries marinated in sherry vinegar to cover (about ½ cup) for 12 to 24 hours and drained

½ teaspoon dried tarragon

*Available at specialty-food stores

1. Put the carrots and turnips in separate small saucepans. Add water to cover and ¼ teaspoon salt to each. Bring to a boil over moderate heat. Reduce the heat; simmer until just tender, 5 to 10 minutes. Drain thoroughly.

2. In a medium saucepan of boiling, salted water, cook the beans until crisp-tender, 4 to 6 minutes. Rinse with cold water and drain thoroughly.

3. Heat the oven to 450°. If using chicken legs, separate the thighs and drumsticks. Dredge the chicken in the ¼ cup flour, shaking off the excess. Heat the oil in a large pot or Dutch oven over high heat. Add the chicken, sprinkle with salt and pepper, and brown well on both sides, about 8 minutes in all. Drain the chicken on paper towels.

4. Pour off the fat from the pot. Return the chicken to the pot and bake, turning once or twice, until just cooked through, 20 to 25 minutes. Transfer the chicken to a plate. Cover loosely with aluminum foil and put in a warm spot.

5. Blend ½ tablespoon of the butter with the remaining 2½ teaspoons flour to form a paste. Pour off any fat from the pot. Add the shallot and vinegar and bring to a boil over moderately high heat. Add the stock and, bit by bit, whisk in enough of the paste so the sauce lightly coats a spoon.

6. Reduce the heat, add the cherries and tarragon, and simmer for 2 to 3 minutes. Season the sauce with salt and pepper. Remove from the heat and stir in the remaining 1 tablespoon butter, in small pieces.

7. Meanwhile, reheat the carrots, turnips, and green beans in a steamer or in the oven. Divide the chicken and vegetables among four plates; spoon the sauce over the chicken.

—ANNE WILLAN

BROWN CHICKEN STOCK

MAKES ABOUT 1 QUART

3 to 4 pounds chicken carcasses, backs, wings, and/or necks

1 onion, quartered

1 rib celery, sliced

1½ cups dry white wine

2 tomatoes, quartered

1 sprig fresh thyme, or ¼ teaspoon dried thyme

1 bay leaf

½ teaspoon peppercorns

1. Heat the oven to 500°. Put the chicken, onion, and celery in a roasting pan and roast, turning the bones once or twice, until they are a dark, golden brown, about 30 minutes.

2. Put the chicken and vegetables in a large pot. Pour the wine into the roasting pan and bring to a boil, scraping the bottom of the pan to dislodge the brown bits. Pour into the pot. Add the tomatoes, thyme, bay leaf, peppercorns, and enough water to cover by 1 inch. Bring to a boil over high heat; skim the foam from the surface. Reduce the heat and simmer, partially covered, skimming occasionally, for 3 hours.

3. Strain the chicken stock into a large saucepan; there should be about 2 quarts. Skim off the fat and boil the stock until reduced by half, about 1 hour and 50 minutes.

MARESCA FAMILY CHICKEN CACCIATORE

In this version of an old favorite, bell peppers are added to the cacciatore basics—mushrooms, onions, and tomatoes. If you prefer the traditional version, just leave them out.

 WINE RECOMMENDATION
Italian reds shine with tomato-based dishes because they are high enough in acid to match the tomato's natural tartness. For the best effect, serve this dish with a top-quality Chianti Classico or Chianti Classico Riserva with a few years of age.

SERVES 4

- 1 cup flour
- ¾ teaspoon salt
- ½ teaspoon fresh-ground black pepper
- 1 chicken (3 to 3½ pounds), cut into 8 pieces
- 3 tablespoons olive oil
- ½ pound mushrooms, cut into ¼-inch slices
- 2 green bell peppers, cut into ¾-inch-wide strips
- 1 onion, cut into ¼-inch slices
- 2 cloves garlic, minced
- 1 35-ounce can plum tomatoes, lightly drained and chopped (about 2½ cups)
- 3 tablespoons chopped fresh parsley

1. In a shallow bowl, toss together the flour, ½ teaspoon of the salt, and ¼ teaspoon of the black pepper. Dredge the chicken in the seasoned flour, shaking off the excess.

2. Heat 2 tablespoons of the oil in a large pot or Dutch oven over moderately high heat. Put the chicken breasts and wings in the pot, skin-side down, and cook, turning once, until well browned, about 8 minutes. Transfer the pieces to a plate and repeat with the thighs and drumsticks. Pour off most of the fat from the pot.

3. Add the mushrooms to the pot and cook, stirring constantly, over moderately high heat until they begin to release their juices, about 2 minutes. Add the remaining 1 tablespoon oil and the bell peppers, onion, and garlic. Cook, stirring, until just barely tender, about 5 minutes. Stir in the tomatoes, parsley, and the remaining ¼ teaspoon salt and ¼ teaspoon black pepper. Bring to a simmer over moderately high heat and return the chicken to the pot.

4. Cover and cook at a slow simmer, turning the chicken pieces occasionally, until the chicken is cooked through, about 30 minutes. If the sauce seems too thin, remove the lid for the last 10 minutes.

—DIANE DARROW AND TOM MARESCA

CHICKEN COLOMBO

When indentured servants were brought from India to Guadeloupe in the nineteenth century, they brought with them a curried dish called *colombo*. Since then, colombo has taken a bit from the French and a bit from the African to become truly Creole. Serve it over boiled or steamed white rice.

WINE RECOMMENDATION This exuberant Caribbean-inspired dish will really sing with a big, spicy red wine without too much tannin. How about a smooth and fruity California zinfandel?

SERVES 4

1½ teaspoons coriander seeds

1½ teaspoons allspice berries

1½ teaspoons cumin seeds

1 teaspoon peppercorns

¼ teaspoon turmeric

1 chicken (3 to 3½ pounds), cut into 8 pieces

2½ tablepoons lime juice (from about 2 limes)

Salt and fresh-ground black pepper

3 tablespoons butter

2 tablespoons olive oil

1 onion, chopped coarse

2 scallions including green tops, minced

1 shallot, minced

1 clove garlic, minced

2 tablespoons minced flat-leaf parsley

2 sprigs fresh thyme

2 tomatoes, peeled, seeded, and chopped coarse

1 chayote, peeled and cut into 1-inch chunks

1 small eggplant (about 1 pound), peeled and cut into 1-inch chunks

1 Scotch bonnet chile, pricked with a fork

1. In a small skillet, toast the coriander, allspice, cumin, and peppercorns over moderately high heat, shaking the pan, until fragrant, about 30 seconds. Remove from the pan to cool. Grind in a mortar with a pestle or in a spice grinder. Add the turmeric.

2. In a large bowl, toss the chicken with 1½ tablespoons of the lime juice. Season with salt and pepper.

3. In a large pot or Dutch oven, melt the butter with the oil over moderately high heat. Add the chicken and cook until browned on one side, about 4 minutes. Turn the chicken and add the onion, scallions, and shallot. Reduce the heat to moderate and cook until the chicken is browned on the other side, about 4 minutes. Add the ground spices and the garlic, parsley, and thyme. Cook, stirring, until the garlic is fragrant, about 2 minutes. Add the remaining 1 tablespoon of the lime juice and enough water to just cover the chicken

(about 2 cups). Simmer over very low heat for 30 minutes.

4. Add the tomatoes, chayote, egg-plant, and chile and season with salt and pepper. Cover and simmer until the vegetables are tender and the chicken is cooked through, about 30 minutes. Transfer the chicken to a plate.

5. Boil the stew over moderately high heat until the liquid is slightly reduced, about 4 minutes. Discard the thyme and the chile. Return the chicken to the pot, season with salt and pepper, and heat through.

—JESSICA B. HARRIS

CHICKEN WITH
HUNGARIAN PAPRIKA SAUCE

A puree of vegetables thickens the smooth-textured sauce in this zesty dish.
For truly authentic flavor, be sure to use imported Hungarian paprika.

WINE RECOMMENDATION
According to legend, the residents of the Hungarian town of Eger fought so fiercely that the invading Turks were sure their opponents were drinking bulls' blood. In Hungarian, that's *egri bikavér*, and the wine of that name is actually a soft, medium-bodied, spicy red. It will marry well with the paprika here.

SERVES 4

1 chicken (3 to 3½ pounds), cut into 8 pieces, neck, back, gizzard, and heart reserved

Table salt and fresh-ground black pepper

5 tablespoons butter

2 tablespoons cooking oil

¾ pound mushrooms

2 onions, chopped coarse

2 cloves garlic, chopped

1 carrot, chopped coarse

1 rib celery, chopped coarse

½ green bell pepper, diced

¼ cup sweet or hot Hungarian paprika

2 tomatoes, peeled, seeded, and chopped coarse

3 cups Chicken Stock, page 61, or canned low-sodium chicken broth, more if needed

1 teaspoon coarse salt

1 cup sour cream

2 teaspoons minced fresh parsley

1. Sprinkle the chicken lightly with table salt and black pepper. In a large frying pan, melt 2 tablespoons of the butter with the oil over moderately high heat. Add the chicken, including the neck, back, and giblets, in batches if necessary, and brown well on both sides, about 8 minutes. Transfer the chicken to a plate.

2. Meanwhile, chop enough of the mushrooms to make ½ cup and then slice the rest. Heat the fat in the frying pan over moderately high heat and add the onions, garlic, carrot, celery, bell pepper, and the chopped mushrooms. Cook, stirring, until the vegetables just begin to soften, about 3 minutes.

3. Add the paprika, stir to coat the vegetables, and cook for about 3 minutes. Add the tomatoes and cook over high heat, stirring, until most of the moisture has evaporated, about 2 to 3 minutes. Remove the pan from the heat.

4. In a large pot or Dutch oven, bring the stock to a simmer. Add the vegetable mixture and the coarse salt and bring to a boil.

5. Add the chicken giblets, back, and neck to the saucepan. Put the drumsticks and thighs on top of them in one layer, and then put the breast pieces on top of the drumsticks and thighs (putting the breasts on top keeps them from overcooking). Reduce the heat, cover, and simmer until the chicken is cooked through, about 20 minutes.

6. Meanwhile, in a medium frying pan, heat the remaining 3 tablespoons butter over moderately high heat. Add the sliced mushrooms; cook until softened and lightly browned, about 5 minutes.

7. Transfer the chicken to a plate. Cover loosely with aluminum foil and put in a warm spot. Skim the excess fat from the broth. Strain the broth into a saucepan. Discard the giblets, back, and neck. Puree the vegetables in a blender or food processor until completely smooth, adding a little of the broth if necessary. Press the puree through a fine sieve into the broth.

8. Whisk ½ cup of the sour cream into the sauce until smooth. Season with table salt and black pepper. Reheat the sauce over low heat; do not let it boil. If it is too thick, add a little stock. Add more table salt and black pepper if necessary.

9. Put the chicken on four plates and top with the sliced mushrooms. Spoon the sauce over the chicken and top with a dollop of the remaining ½ cup sour cream. Sprinkle with the parsley.

ANA'S CIORBA

A cross between a soup and a stew, *ciorba* is a Romanian dish that is very easy to prepare and can be cooked through step 2 a day in advance. A last-minute addition of sour cream and egg yolk thickens the sauce.

WINE RECOMMENDATION
This stew needs a white wine that is herbal rather than fruity and full enough to match the richness of eggs and sour-cream. Go for a northern Rhône white made from marsanne and roussanne, such as Hermitage. Its sheer power will make a dramatic statement.

SERVES 4

- 1 chicken (3 to 3½ pounds), cut into 8 pieces
- 2 carrots, grated coarse
- 1 green bell pepper, cut into thin 1½-inch-long strips
- 1 red bell pepper, cut into ¼-inch dice
- 8 scallions including green tops, chopped
- 2 tomatoes, chopped
- ¼ pound very thin green beans, cut into 2-inch lengths
- 1 cup small cauliflower florets
- 3 cups water
- 2 cups Chicken Stock, page 61, or canned low-sodium chicken broth
  Salt and white pepper
- ½ cup chopped fresh dill
- ½ cup chopped fresh parsley
- 4 ounces vermicelli
- 2 egg yolks
- ⅔ cup sour cream
- ¼ cup lemon juice

1. In a large pot or Dutch oven, combine the chicken, carrots, bell peppers, scallions, tomatoes, beans, and cauliflower. Add the water, stock, 1 teaspoon salt, and ½ teaspoon white pepper. Bring to a boil over moderate heat. Reduce the heat to low and simmer, partially covered, occasionally skimming the foam from the surface, until the chicken is cooked through, about 1 hour.

2. Add the dill, parsley, and vermicelli. Cook until the noodles are tender, about 5 minutes. Remove from the heat, let stand for 5 minutes, and then skim off any fat that has risen to the surface.

3. Beat the egg yolks and sour cream in a small bowl until blended. Gradually whisk in 2 tablespoons of the broth. Stir the mixture into the stew. Stir in the lemon juice and season with salt and white pepper.

—ANA COTAESCU

CHICKEN STEW WITH CORNMEAL DUMPLINGS

Dumplings are a traditional accompaniment for chicken stew, and here they're made with cornmeal for extra flavor. Our warming wintertime version is packed with vegetables—celery, carrots, onions, and kale.

WINE RECOMMENDATION
This rustic dish needs a fruity, low-tannin red for a lively contrast. Try a Fleurie, one of the ten crus of Beaujolais. Grown on granite hills in the very north of the region, the crus represent the best, richest, and most individual wines. Fleurie, as its name implies, has intoxicating scents of violets and other blooms.

SERVES 4

- 1 chicken (3 to 3½ pounds), cut into 8 pieces
- 4 cups Chicken Stock, page 61, or canned low-sodium chicken broth
- 1 bay leaf
- 2 ribs celery, cut into thin slices
- 4 carrots, cut into thin slices
- 6 small white onions, peeled and halved lengthwise
- 4 sprigs fresh thyme
- 2 small bunches kale, stems trimmed, leaves washed well and chopped (2 packed cups)
   Salt and fresh-ground black pepper
- 1 cup flour
- ½ cup cornmeal
- 2 teaspoons baking powder
- 2 tablespoons cold butter, cut into pieces
- ⅔ cup milk

1. Remove the skin from all the chicken pieces except the wings. Put the chicken, stock, and bay leaf in a large pot or Dutch oven. Bring to a boil over high heat. Reduce the heat, turn the chicken, cover, and simmer for 15 minutes.

2. Skim any fat from the surface of the broth. Stir in the celery, carrots, onions, and thyme. Simmer, partially covered, until the carrots and onions are just tender, about 15 minutes. Stir in the kale and season with salt and pepper.

3. Meanwhile, toss the flour with the cornmeal, baking powder, and ½ teaspoon of salt in a bowl. Using your fingertips, work the butter into the flour until crumbly. Stir in the milk with a fork until blended.

4. Drop tablespoons of the dumpling batter onto the stew. Reduce the heat, cover, and simmer until the dumplings are cooked through, about 10 minutes. Discard the bay leaf and thyme sprigs.

—SUSAN SHAPIRO JASLOVE

Coq au Riesling

Mushrooms flambéed in cognac are served over the chicken here rather than cooked with it. When you ignite the brandy, stand back from the pan. The flames will flare and then die down quickly.

WINE RECOMMENDATION
What else with this traditional Alsatian dish but a heady riesling from Alsace itself? Try one of the fuller versions typical of such producers as Zind-Humbrecht, Weinbach, or Schoffit.

SERVES 4

¼ pound lean slab bacon, cut into 1-by-¼-inch matchstick strips

4 tablespoons butter, at room temperature

1 chicken (3 to 3½ pounds), quartered

1 onion, chopped coarse

1 clove garlic, chopped coarse

1 carrot, chopped coarse

1½ cups dry riesling

½ cup Chicken Stock, page 61, or canned low-sodium chicken broth

1 pound mushrooms, quartered

2 tablespoons cognac or other brandy

¼ teaspoon lemon juice

Salt and fresh-ground black pepper

1 tablespoon flour

2 teaspoons minced fresh parsley

1. In a large pot or Dutch oven, cook the bacon over moderate heat, stirring occasionally, until golden, about 3 minutes. Using a slotted spoon, remove the bacon from the pot; drain on paper towels. Reserve 1 tablespoon of the bacon fat.

2. In the pot, melt 2 tablespoons of the butter with 1½ teaspoons of the bacon fat over moderately high heat. Add the chicken and brown on both sides, about 8 minutes in all. Transfer the chicken to a plate.

3. Add the onion, garlic, and carrot to the pot and cook over moderate heat until the carrot is soft, 10 to 15 minutes. Add the wine and stock and bring to a boil, scraping the bottom of the pot to dislodge any brown bits.

4. Heat the oven to 250°. Return the chicken to the pot, reduce the heat, cover, and simmer until the breasts are cooked through, about 15 minutes. Put the breast quarters on a platter and put in the oven to keep warm. Continue to cook the leg quarters until the juices run clear when the thigh is pierced, about 10 minutes. Transfer the leg quarters to the platter. Cover the pot and simmer the sauce for 5 minutes.

5. Meanwhile, in a large frying pan, melt 1 tablespoon of the butter with the remaining 1½ teaspoons bacon fat over

moderately high heat. Add the mushrooms and cook until they are soft and have absorbed all of the liquid, about 5 minutes.

6. Add the cognac and carefully ignite it with a match; shake the pan until the flames subside. Add the lemon juice and season with salt and pepper. Spoon the mushrooms over the chicken and pour the juices on top.

7. Blend the remaining 1 tablespoon butter with the flour to form a Beurre Manié (see box, page 211). Bit by bit, whisk in enough of the Beurre Manié so that the sauce lightly coats a spoon. Simmer for 3 minutes.

8. Sprinkle the bacon around the edge of the platter. Pour the sauce over the chicken and sprinkle with the parsley.

—ANNE DISRUDE

GIBELOTTE OF CHICKEN WITH LARDONS AND RUTABAGA

Gibelotte comes from the Old French word *gibecier*, which means hunting. Today the word is used synonymously with *fricassee*, but most often refers to one made of game or domestic rabbit rather than chicken. This version is inspired by my memories of similar dishes as well as a recipe from Marin, a famous eighteenth-century French cook.

WINE RECOMMENDATION

A white-wine stew like this will be well served by pinot gris. Like gewürztraminer, pinot gris is full-flavored and spicy; unlike gewürztraminer, it is better balanced by vibrant acidity and has a nutty, honeyed taste of fruit.

SERVES 4

- 1 chicken (3 to 3½ pounds), quartered
- ½ onion, grated
- 1½ teaspoons flour
- ½ cup dry white wine
- ½ cup water
- ¼ teaspoon fresh thyme leaves, or ⅛ teaspoon dried thyme
- ½ teaspoon salt
- ¼ teaspoon fresh-ground black pepper
- 1 ¼-pound piece lean salt pork, cut into lardons (1-by-¼-inch strips)
- 1 rutabaga (about 1¾ pounds)
- 2 tablespoons capers
- 1½ teaspoons lemon juice
- 2 anchovy fillets, mashed to a paste
- 1 tablespoon chopped fresh chervil or parsley

1. Heat a large pot or Dutch oven over moderately high heat. Add the chicken, skin-side down, and cook until the skin is nicely browned and most of the fat has been rendered, about 15 minutes. Turn the pieces over and brown on the other side, 3 to 5 minutes. Transfer the chicken to a plate and pour the fat into a bowl.

2. In the pan, heat 1½ teaspoons of the chicken fat over moderate heat. Add the onion and cook until golden brown, about 3 minutes. Add the flour and cook, stirring, for 1 minute. Whisk in the wine, water, thyme, salt, and pepper. Bring to a boil, whisking until smooth. Reduce the heat and simmer for 3 minutes.

3. Add the chicken and return to a boil. Reduce the heat, cover, and simmer for 20 minutes. Remove from the heat and transfer the breast quarters to a plate; let cool. Remove the bones from the breasts and return the meat to the sauce.

4. Meanwhile, put the salt-pork lardons in a saucepan, cover them with water, and bring the water to a boil. Drain the lardons,

rinse them with cold water, and then drain them again.

5. Heat 1½ teaspoons of the chicken fat in a small frying pan over moderate heat. Add the lardons and cook, partially covered, until well browned, 6 to 8 minutes. Drain the lardons on paper towels.

6. Cut the rutabaga into 1½-inch cubes. Round the edges of each piece with a knife. Put the rutabaga pieces in a large saucepan and add cold water to cover. Bring to a boil and cook for 5 minutes. Drain.

7. Heat 1½ tablespoons of the chicken fat in another large frying pan over moderate heat. Add the rutabaga and cook, stirring occasionally, until browned, 8 to 10 minutes.

8. Add the rutabaga and the lardons to the sauce and bring to a boil. Reduce the heat, cover, and simmer for 10 minutes. Add the capers, lemon juice, and anchovies. Bring to a boil. Transfer the chicken and vegetables to a platter and top with the sauce and chervil.

—JACQUES PÉPIN

MAKE IT AHEAD

Prepare the recipe, through step 3, up to one day in advance; cover and refrigerate. The lardons and rutabaga can be prepared up to four hours ahead and set aside at room temperature.

CHICKEN AND SAUSAGE STEW WITH PARSLEY AND LEMON

Like many stews, this one is even more flavorful when prepared in advance and then reheated. Pass around a loaf of crusty semolina bread for mopping up the plentiful sauce.

WINE RECOMMENDATION
The potpourri of herbs and savory sausage suggests a full-flavored, somewhat herbal red wine. Northern Rhône wines have just these qualities. A good St-Joseph or Crozes-Hermitage will be terrific here.

SERVES 4

5½ tablespoons olive oil

10 ounces mild Italian sausage, pricked with a fork

1 chicken (3 to 3½ pounds), cut into 8 pieces, giblets reserved

Salt and fresh-ground black pepper

1 large onion, chopped fine

2 ribs celery with tops, cut into 1-inch diagonal pieces

3 cloves garlic, minced

1 teaspoon dried oregano

¾ teaspoon dried thyme

1 bay leaf

2 tablespoons flour

⅔ cup dry white wine

1⅓ cups Chicken Stock, page 61, or canned low-sodium chicken broth

2⅓ cups canned plum tomatoes with their juice (from a 28-ounce can), chopped

10 ounces small mushrooms, stems removed

⅔ cup black olives, such as Niçoise or Kalamata, pitted

⅓ cup chopped flat-leaf parsley

2 teaspoons fine julienne lemon zest

1. In a large pot or Dutch oven, heat 1½ tablespoons of the oil over moderate heat. Add the sausage and the chicken giblets and cook, turning occasionally, until well browned, about 10 minutes. Transfer the sausage to a bowl.

2. Add the chicken pieces, skin-side down, to the giblets in the pan. Season with ¼ teaspoon salt and ⅛ teaspoon pepper. Cook until golden brown, about 4 minutes. Turn, season with another ¼ teaspoon salt and ⅛ teaspoon pepper, and brown on the other side, about 4 minutes longer. Transfer the chicken pieces to the bowl with the sausage. Discard the giblets and pour off the fat from the pan.

3. Put the pan over moderate heat and add another 2 tablespoons of the oil, the onion, celery, garlic, oregano, thyme, and bay leaf. Reduce the heat to moderately low. Cover and cook, stirring occasionally, until

the onion is soft and golden, about 15 minutes. Uncover and sprinkle the flour over the vegetables. Cook over very low heat, stirring, for 5 minutes. Do not allow the flour to color.

4. Gradually whisk in the wine. Add the stock and the tomatoes with their juice. Bring to a boil over moderately high heat, stirring. Reduce the heat, partially cover, and simmer until the sauce is slightly thickened, about 20 minutes.

5. Cut the sausage into 1-inch diagonal pieces. Return the sausage and the chicken to the pan and cook, uncovered, until the chicken is very tender, about 30 minutes.

6. Meanwhile, heat the remaining 2 tablespoons oil in a medium frying pan over moderately high heat. Add the mushrooms and cook until they begin to yield their juices, about 5 minutes. Season with salt and pepper and remove from the heat.

7. Using a slotted spoon or tongs, transfer the chicken to a serving bowl; cover and put in a warm spot. Add the mushrooms with their juices and the olives to the sauce. Simmer for 5 minutes.

8. Skim off the fat from the surface of the sauce. Stir in the parsley and pour the sauce over the chicken. Sprinkle the lemon zest on top.

—MICHAEL MCLAUGHLIN

MAKE IT AHEAD

Prepare the stew, through step 7, one day in advance. Pour the sauce over the chicken and let it cool to room temperature. Then cover and refrigerate. Reheat the stew over low heat, stirring occasionally, and then stir in the parsley.

SPICY CHICKEN STEW
IN A CRISP PLANTAIN CRUST

An unusual combination of sweet and savory, this recipe comes from Quebradillas, on the northwest coast of Puerto Rico. If your supermarket doesn't carry plantains, try a Latin American market.

WINE RECOMMENDATION
The sweet plantains, salty feta, tangy tomato, and spicy chile in this robust stew will simply steamroll a delicate wine, so turn instead to a lusty, grenache-based red, such as Châteauneuf-du-Pape. Châteauneuf has power and flavor to spare.

SERVES 4

- 1 chicken (3 to 3½ pounds)
- 1 cup plus 2 tablespoons cooking oil
  Salt and fresh-ground black pepper
- ½ cup water
- 1 onion, chopped coarse
- 1 red bell pepper, chopped coarse
- 2 cloves garlic, minced
- 2 scallions including green tops, sliced
- 2 tomatoes, chopped coarse
- ½ teaspoon fresh thyme leaves
- 2 teaspoons hot or mild pure chile powder
- 2 very ripe plantains, cut into 1-inch-thick diagonal slices
- 3 ounces feta cheese, crumbled

1. Heat the oven to 400°. Put the chicken in a roasting pan and rub it with 1 tablespoon of the oil. Season with salt and black pepper. Roast, basting often with the pan juices, until golden and cooked through, about 1½ hours.

2. Put the chicken on a plate and pour off the fat from the pan. Put the pan over moderate heat, add the water, and simmer for 2 minutes, scraping the bottom of the pan to dislodge the brown bits. Pour the juices into a bowl. Remove the chicken meat from the bones and discard the bones. Cut the chicken into 1-inch pieces and put on the plate.

3. In a large frying pan, heat another 1 tablespoon of the oil over moderately low heat. Add the onion and bell pepper and cook, stirring, until softened, about 8 minutes. Add the garlic and scallions and cook, stirring, until fragrant, about 3 minutes. Add the tomatoes and simmer over moderate heat until the liquid evaporates, about 5 minutes. Stir in the thyme and chile powder and cook, stirring, for 3 minutes. Add the chicken and any accumulated juices and simmer for 2 minutes. Season with salt and black pepper and transfer to a bowl.

4. Wipe out the skillet and heat the remaining 1 cup oil over moderately high

heat until shimmering. Add a single layer of plantains and fry, turning once, until well browned and cooked through, about 4 minutes per side; lower the heat if necessary so the plantains cook through without burning. Put them on a plate and repeat with the remaining plantains.

5. Heat the oven to 400°. Put the plantains between layers of plastic wrap and, using a mallet or rolling pin, gently flatten them to a ⅓-inch thickness. Press the plantains, slightly overlapping, over the bottom and up the sides of a 9-inch glass pie plate.

6. Spoon the stew into the pie plate and sprinkle the feta over the top. Bake until the filling is heated through and the plantains on the bottom of the pie are sizzling, about 45 minutes. Cut into wedges and serve.

—MARCIA KIESEL

chapter 11

CURRIES &
OTHER BRAISED DISHES

Mediterranean Chicken with Lemons and Olives, page 307

BAKED ACORN SQUASH STUFFED WITH CURRIED CHICKEN

Though acorn squash gets top billing, it takes two types of squash to make this tasty curry—butternut inside and acorn to hold the finished product.

WINE RECOMMENDATION
The sweet squash and curry will be nicely contrasted by a full-bodied wine that is somewhat earthy or nutty. Try a big Australian sémillon from the Hunter Valley. When aged, sémillon develops intense nut-like flavors that evoke new oak. Its opulence of texture will also suit this dish.

SERVES 4

4 tablespoons clarified butter (see box, next page)

1⅓ pound boneless, skinless chicken breasts (about 4), cut into 1½-by-¼-inch strips

1 large Spanish onion, chopped coarse

1 red bell pepper, cut into ¼-inch-wide strips

1 clove garlic, minced

½ teaspoon turmeric

¼ teaspoon cinnamon

¼ teaspoon ground cardamom

¼ teaspoon ground cumin

¼ teaspoon ground coriander

¼ teaspoon dried red-pepper flakes

Pinch ground cloves

½ cup Chicken Stock, page 61, or canned low-sodium chicken broth

½ cup apple juice or cider

1 tablespoon tomato paste

2 acorn squash

1 small butternut squash (about 1 pound), seeded

½ cup heavy cream

½ teaspoon salt

Fresh-ground black pepper

1. Heat the oven to 350°. In a large heavy frying pan, heat 2 tablespoons of the clarified butter over high heat. Add the chicken strips; stir-fry until golden brown, 3 to 5 minutes. Transfer the chicken to a plate.

2. Add another 1 tablespoon of the clarified butter to the pan and reduce the heat to moderate. Add the onion, bell pepper, and garlic and cook, stirring, until the onion is translucent, about 5 minutes.

3. Stir in the turmeric, cinnamon, cardamom, cumin, coriander, red-pepper flakes, and cloves and cook, stirring, until the mixture is fragrant, about 2 minutes. Stir in the stock, apple juice, and tomato paste. Return the chicken to the pan, cover, and simmer gently for 45 minutes.

4. Meanwhile, pierce each of the squash in a few places with a paring knife. Put them

287

in a baking pan and bake for 20 minutes. Turn and cook until the squash are fairly soft to the touch, 20 to 25 minutes longer. Remove the pan from the oven, but don't turn the oven off. Let the squash cool slightly.

5. Peel the butternut squash and cut the flesh into ¾-inch cubes. Add the butternut squash and the cream to the curried chicken. Season with the salt and black pepper to taste.

6. Cut each acorn squash in half and scoop out the seeds and strings. Melt the remaining 1 tablespoon clarified butter and brush the cut surfaces of the acorn squash with it. Put the acorn-squash halves cut-side up in a baking pan and mound the chicken mixture in the hollows. Cover loosely with aluminum foil and bake until the acorn squash is tender, about 30 minutes.

—JEAN ANDERSON

CLARIFIED BUTTER

Clarified butter is butter with the milk solids removed; it can be heated to a higher temperature than regular butter without burning, and keeps longer in the refrigerator, too. A pound of butter makes about one-and-a-half cups of clarified butter. Melt the butter in a small pot over moderately low heat, and then remove from the heat and let sit for five minutes. Skim off the foam and pour the yellow clarified butter into a container, leaving the milk solids in the bottom of the pot. Store the butter, well-wrapped, in the refrigerator until ready to use.

STUFFED CHICKEN LEGS WITH CURRY SAUCE

In a twist on the usual curry, the garnishes—coconut, mango chutney, peanuts, and raisins—are stuffed into the chicken, which is then cooked in the sauce.

WINE RECOMMENDATION
The exotic flavors and full body of gewürztraminer will work deliciously with the chutney, raisins, and coconut. Go for an off-dry one from California or Long Island.

SERVES 4

- 4 whole chicken legs
- 6 tablespoons grated fresh coconut
- ¼ cup mango chutney
- ¼ cup chopped dry-roasted salted peanuts
- ¼ cup raisins
- 3 tablespoons clarified butter (see box, opposite page)
- 1 clove garlic, bruised
- ¼ cup fine-chopped green bell pepper
- ⅛ teaspoon dried red-pepper flakes
- ¼ teaspoon ground cumin
- ¼ teaspoon ground cardamom
- ¼ teaspoon mace
- ¼ teaspoon cinnamon
- ½ teaspoon ground ginger
- 1 teaspoon turmeric
- 1 teaspoon ground fenugreek
- 2 teaspoons poppy seeds, lightly crushed
- 1 cup Chicken Stock, page 61, or canned low-sodium chicken broth
- ⅓ cup plain yogurt, at room temperature

1. Bone the chicken legs (see box, page 221). In a bowl, combine the coconut, chutney, nuts, and raisins. Stuff into the cavities of the chicken legs, using about ¼ cup for each and dividing it evenly between the drumsticks and thighs. Close with toothpicks.

2. Heat the clarified butter in a large frying pan over moderate heat. Add the chicken and brown lightly on both sides, about 4 minutes in all. Remove from the pan.

3. Add the garlic and bell pepper to the pan; cook for 1 minute. Add the red-pepper flakes, cumin, cardamom, mace, cinnamon, ginger, turmeric, fenugreek, and poppy seeds. Cook, stirring, until fragrant, about 1 minute longer. Discard the garlic.

4. Return the chicken to the pan, add the stock, and bring to a boil. Reduce the heat, cover, and simmer, turning once, until tender, 20 to 25 minutes. Transfer the chicken to a platter; keep warm. Raise the heat to high. Cook until the sauce is reduced to ¾ cup, 3 to 4 minutes.

5. Put the yogurt in a small bowl. Gradually stir about ¼ cup of the sauce into it. Stir the mixture into the pan and pour the sauce over the chicken.

SWEET-AND-SOUR CHICKEN WITH CARROTS

Called a dry curry because it has very little sauce, this sweet-and-sour chicken has its origins in Calcutta's Jewish community. The chicken is skinned, resulting in an almost fat-free dish. If you prefer to leave the skin on, remove the grease from the sauce just before serving it.

WINE RECOMMENDATION

High in ripe, fruity acid yet delicately balanced with natural sugars, the off-dry rieslings of Germany's Mosel region are piquant and refreshing. A kabinett will be perfect here: Its subtle sweetness will taste dry with the chicken, while its citrus tang will cleanse the palate.

SERVES 4

2 tablespoons corn or peanut oil

2 carrots, shredded fine

1 onion, cut into thin slices

2 cloves garlic, minced

2¼ teaspoons minced fresh ginger

⅓ teaspoon turmeric

¾ teaspoon salt

1 chicken (3 to 3½ pounds), cut into 8 pieces and skin removed

¾ cup water

2 small bay leaves

3 cardamom pods, lightly cracked

2½ tablespoons lemon juice, more to taste

1 tablespoon light brown sugar, more to taste

1. Heat 1 tablespoon of the oil in a frying pan over moderately low heat. Add the carrots and cook until softened, about 3 minutes.

2. Heat the remaining 1 tablespoon oil in a Dutch oven over moderate heat. Add the onion, garlic, ginger, turmeric, and salt and cook, stirring occasionally, until the onion is soft and translucent, about 3 minutes. Add the chicken; cook, turning once, until it is white all over, 8 to 10 minutes.

3. Add the water, bay leaves, and cardamom. Cover and cook, turning the chicken occasionally, for 15 minutes. Add the carrots and cook for 10 minutes longer. Add the lemon juice and brown sugar. Stir well and cook, partially covered, over moderately low heat until the chicken meat is almost falling off the bone, about 10 minutes.

4. Uncover and boil over moderately high heat until the liquid is almost evaporated, 5 to 10 minutes. Season with more lemon juice and sugar if desired. Remove the bay leaves and the cardamom pods.

—COPELAND MARKS

290

CHICKEN CURRY CALCUTTA-STYLE

Here's a curry that can be completely cooked, then refrigerated and reheated when you're ready to serve it. All you'll have to do to get dinner ready is steam some rice to go alongside.

WINE RECOMMENDATION
Beer, unlike wine, is made in just about every country in the world. For this curry, with its sweet and hot flavors, select a lean, crisp lager from among the many good examples available from India. You may have to locate a store that specializes in a wide selection of foreign beers.

SERVES 4

1 tablespoon corn or peanut oil

½ onion, chopped coarse

2 cloves garlic, minced

1 teaspoon minced fresh ginger

2 teaspoons curry powder

½ teaspoon dried red-pepper flakes

1 chicken (3 to 3½ pounds), cut into 8 pieces

¾ cup water

1 tablespoon cider vinegar

½ cup coarse-chopped fresh or canned tomato

1 red potato, peeled and cut into ½-inch cubes

2 teaspoons dark brown sugar

½ teaspoon salt

1. In a large deep frying pan or flame-proof casserole, heat the oil over moderately low heat. Add the onion, garlic, and ginger and cook, stirring occasionally, until the onion is translucent, about 5 minutes.

2. Add the curry powder and red-pepper flakes and stir until fragrant, just a few seconds. Add the chicken and cook, turning once, until golden, about 4 minutes on each side.

3. Add the water, vinegar, tomato, potato, sugar, and salt. Simmer, turning the chicken occasionally, until cooked through, 30 to 35 minutes.

—COPELAND MARKS

CHICKEN BREASTS WITH ORANGE SAUCE AND TOASTED ALMONDS

For this ideal summertime dish, chicken breasts are braised, cooled, sliced, surrounded by green and yellow squash, and topped with an orange mustard sauce and a sprinkling of almonds.

 WINE RECOMMENDATION
The combinination of citrus, squash, and nuts opens a range of intriguing possibilities for wine. Try one made from Müller-Thurgau. Light-bodied and floral, delicious Müller-Thurgaus are made in Italy's Alto Adige and Germany's Franken region.

SERVES 4

⅓   cup slivered almonds

6   boneless, skinless chicken breasts (about 2 pounds), at room temperature

2   large oranges

1   egg yolk

1   tablespoon plus 1 teaspoon white-wine vinegar

½   teaspoon Dijon mustard

Pinch sugar

Salt and white pepper

1¼   cups safflower oil

2   small zucchini, cut into ¼-inch rounds

2   small yellow summer squash, cut into ¼-inch rounds

2   tablespoons minced fresh parsley

1. In a small frying pan, toast the almonds over moderately low heat, stirring frequently, until golden brown, about 5 minutes. Or toast them in a 350° oven for about 8 minutes. When the nuts are cool enough to handle, chop them.

2. Using a mallet, flat meat pounder, or rolling pin, lightly pound the thicker end of each chicken breast so it is an even thickness. In a large frying pan, bring ¼ inch of water to a simmer over moderately high heat. Add the chicken breasts, cover, and reduce the heat. Simmer, turning once, until the chicken is just cooked through, 10 to 12 minutes. Remove the chicken breasts and let cool.

3. Grate the zest from the two oranges (there will be about 1½ tablespoons) and squeeze ¼ cup of juice. In a bowl, whisk together the egg yolk, 1 tablespoon of the orange zest, the orange juice, vinegar, mustard, sugar, ½ teaspoon salt, and a pinch of pepper. Add the oil slowly, whisking. Cover and refrigerate.

4. In a medium saucepan of boiling water, cook the zucchini for 30 seconds. Remove with a slotted spoon and rinse with cold water. Cook the summer squash in the boiling water for 30 seconds. Drain and rinse with cold water. ➤

5. Cut each chicken breast on the diagonal into seven or eight slices. Fan them out on a platter or individual plates and sprinkle lightly with salt.

6. In separate small bowls, combine the zucchini and squash with 1 to 2 tablespoons each of the orange sauce and toss to coat. Season with salt and pepper. Arrange the squash in rows around the chicken, alternating the zucchini and summer squash slices.

7. Spoon some orange sauce over each chicken breast. Toss together the almonds, parsley, and the remaining orange zest. Sprinkle this mixture over the chicken and serve the remaining sauce on the side.

MAKE IT AHEAD

The chicken breasts can be poached up to one day in advance. Cool, cover, and refrigerate. The sauce can be prepared up to a day ahead as well.

CHICKEN BREASTS WITH ANCHOVY AND CELERY SAUCE

There's no cooking, heating, or reducing required for this unusual sauce. Just mix it up in a bowl, let it stand for an hour, and spoon it over sliced chicken breasts.

WINE RECOMMENDATION

Green chile, celery, and anchovies make a fresh, herbal white come to mind, but one with some power as well. Look to the southern Italian island of Sardinia, where the vermentino grape is used to produce most of the wine. While herbal, vermentinos can also be surprisingly full-bodied and stunningly aromatic.

SERVES 4

4   boneless, skinless chicken breasts (about 1⅓ pounds), at room temperature

3   large anchovy fillets, rinsed and chopped fine

⅓   cup minced celery

⅓   cup minced green bell pepper

2   teaspoons minced hot green chile pepper

1   small clove garlic, minced

3   tablespoons olive oil

3   tablespoons white-wine vinegar

⅛   teaspoon fresh-ground black pepper

1   tablespoon minced fresh parsley
    Salt

3   plum tomatoes, cut into thin slices

1. Using a mallet, flat meat pounder, or rolling pin, lightly pound the thicker end of each chicken breast so it is an even thickness. In a large frying pan, bring ¼ inch of water to a simmer over moderately high heat. Add the chicken, cover, reduce the heat, and simmer, turning once, until just cooked through, 10 to 12 minutes. Remove the chicken and let cool.

2. In a small bowl, combine the anchovies, celery, bell pepper, chile, garlic, oil, vinegar, and black pepper. Let stand for 1 hour. Just before serving, stir in the parsley and season the sauce with salt.

3. Cut each chicken breast on the diagonal into five or six slices. Fan them out on a platter or individual plates and sprinkle lightly with salt. Spoon the sauce over the chicken and garnish with the tomatoes.

MAKE IT AHEAD

The chicken breasts can be cooked up to one day ahead. Cool, cover, and refrigerate. The sauce can be prepared a day ahead as well; cover and refrigerate. Let the chicken and the sauce come to room temperature before serving.

THAI CHICKEN AND FRESH BASIL

Shredded raw cabbage serves as the bed for this version of a popular Thai dish. The chicken cooks in only ten minutes, so if you want to serve rice alongside, start steaming it before you begin the recipe.

WINE RECOMMENDATION
This hot and spicy dish is best served with a cool Thai beer, as its chile peppers and other piquant flavors will be too much for most wines. If you want to be adventurous, however, try a German auslese riesling from the Rheinhessen or the Pfalz. Either should have enough acidity and residual sweetness to hold its own.

SERVES 4

4   teaspoons peanut oil

5 to 8 small red or green chile peppers, seeded and minced

4   teaspoons chopped dried lemongrass,* wrapped in a cheesecloth bag, or 1 teaspoon grated lemon zest

½   cup canned unsweetened coconut milk*

1⅓ pounds boneless, skinless chicken breasts (about 4), cut crosswise into ½-inch strips

2   tablespoons Asian fish sauce (nam pla or nuoc mam)*

1   tablespoon minced fresh basil or cilantro

1½ cups shredded green cabbage

*Available at Asian markets, specialty-food stores, and some supermarkets

1. In a large frying pan, heat the oil over moderate heat until shimmering. Add the chiles and cook, stirring, for 3 minutes. Add the lemongrass and coconut milk. Raise the heat to high and boil until the sauce is slightly thickened, about 2 minutes.

2. Reduce the heat to moderate. Add the chicken and cook, stirring occasionally, until cooked through, about 5 minutes. Stir in the fish sauce and basil. Discard the lemongrass.

3. Put the cabbage on a large platter and spoon the chicken and sauce on top.

—KEO SANANIKONE

CHICKEN AND DUMPLINGS

Everybody loves dumplings—they evoke feelings of nostalgia even for those of us who didn't grow up having chicken and dumplings for Sunday dinner. You'll see here that they're not at all difficult to make.

WINE RECOMMENDATION
The Languedoc-Roussillon region of southern France is a vast and fertile swath of vineyards once known only for oceans of cheap and undrinkable wine. Since 1979, however, increased investment and government incentives have made it one of France's most exciting wine areas. Enjoy one of the many good-value chardonnays labeled Vin de Pays d'Oc.

SERVES 4

- 1 chicken (3 to 3½ pounds), cut into 8 pieces, with giblets
- 2 teaspoons salt
- ½ teaspoon fresh-ground black pepper
- 2 carrots, cut into thin slices
- 2 onions, cut into thin slices
- 2 ribs celery, cut into thin slices
- 3 cloves garlic, minced
- 2 cups sifted flour
- 1 tablespoon baking powder
- 2 eggs, lightly beaten
- ⅔ cup milk
- ½ cup chopped fresh parsley

1. Put the chicken pieces and giblets in a Dutch oven. Season with 1 teaspoon of salt and the pepper. Add the carrots, onions, celery, two thirds of the garlic, and enough water to cover. Bring to a boil over high heat. Reduce the heat to moderately low and simmer until the chicken is very tender, about 1 hour. Using a slotted spoon, transfer the chicken to a platter, cover loosely with aluminum foil, and put in a warm spot. Discard the giblets.

2. Meanwhile, combine the flour, baking powder, and the remaining 1 teaspoon salt in a medium bowl. Add the eggs, milk, parsley, and the remaining garlic. Stir with a fork until blended.

3. Bring the cooking liquid to a boil. Drop in rounded teaspoons of the dumpling batter, cover, and simmer until the dumplings are cooked through, about 15 minutes.

4. Remove the dumplings with a slotted spoon and place them around the chicken on the platter. Spoon the vegetables and some of the broth over the chicken.

—JOHN ROBERT MASSIE

CHICKEN WITH PIQUANT SAUCE

Although the recipe serves four, there's so much flavorful sauce here that it can be stretched to accommodate unexpected guests; just throw in a few more pieces of chicken.

WINE RECOMMENDATION
Syrah has a smoky, briny aroma that will effectively echo the olives here. The wine is robust enough for this hearty dish, and also has the acidity necessary to balance the tomatoes.

SERVES 4

2½ tablespoons safflower or corn oil

4 bone-in chicken breasts (about 2¼ pounds in all)

4 chicken thighs

1 onion, chopped coarse

2 ribs celery, chopped coarse

½ green bell pepper, chopped coarse

2½ tablespoons flour

1¾ cups canned crushed tomatoes in thick puree

2 cups Chicken Stock, page 61, or canned low-sodium chicken broth

¼ cup water

2 tablespoons tomato paste

1 bay leaf

1 clove garlic, minced

1½ teaspoons lemon juice

½ teaspoon hot-pepper sauce

½ teaspoon salt

¼ teaspoon fresh-ground black pepper

2 tablespoons chopped scallion greens

1 tablespoon minced fresh parsley

6 pimiento-stuffed olives, sliced

1. Heat the oil in a Dutch oven over moderately high heat. Add the chicken breasts and thighs and brown on both sides, about 8 minutes in all. Transfer the chicken to a large plate

2. Add the onion, celery, and bell pepper to the pot and cook over moderate heat, stirring, until softened, 5 to 8 minutes. Using a slotted spoon, transfer the vegetables to the plate.

3. Add the flour to the pot and cook, whisking, for 1 minute. Then cook, scraping the bottom of the pan to dislodge any brown bits, until the roux turns a rich brown, about 10 minutes.

4. Stir in the tomatoes, stock, water, tomato paste, bay leaf, garlic, lemon juice, hot-pepper sauce, salt, and pepper. Bring to a boil. Add the chicken and cooked vegetables and simmer, stirring and skimming the fat from the surface occasionally, until the chicken is tender and the sauce is thickened, about 1 hour. Stir in the scallion greens, parsley, and olives. Remove the bay leaf.

—LEE BAILEY

CHICKEN-AND-SAUSAGE GUMBO

If you have Thanksgiving leftovers, make this gumbo with turkey and canned stock instead of the chicken. Just start with step 4. However you make it, you'll want to serve the dish over hot steamed rice.

 **WINE RECOMMENDATION**
Sinfully rich and savory, this gumbo can partner a big red wine with ease. Go for a spicy, fruity, full-bodied zinfandel from Sonoma's Dry Creek or Russian River valleys. In these areas, some of the vines are over eighty years old, yielding incredibly concentrated fruit with jammy, almost exotic blackberry flavors.

SERVES 4

1 teaspoon butter

1 chicken (3 to 3½ pounds), cut into 8 pieces, backbone, wing tips, neck, and giblets reserved

2 onions, 1 quartered, 1 chopped fine

1 carrot, quartered

2 ribs celery, 1 quartered, 1 chopped fine

4 cups water, more as needed

1 sprig parsley, plus chopped fresh parsley for serving

⅔ cup flour

Salt

¼ teaspoon cayenne

Fresh-ground black pepper

Pinch white pepper

¼ cup plus 4 teaspoons corn oil

1 green bell pepper, chopped fine

10 ounces smoked pork sausage, sliced

Louisiana hot sauce

Chopped scallion greens, for serving

1. In a large pot or Dutch oven, melt the butter over moderately high heat. Add the chicken backbone, wing tips, neck, and giblets and the quartered onion, carrot, and celery. Cook, stirring, until browned, about 5 minutes. Add the water and the parsley sprig and bring to a boil. Reduce the heat and simmer for 1 hour. Strain the broth, pressing on the bones and vegetables to get all the liquid.

2. Combine ⅓ cup of the flour, ½ teaspoon salt, the cayenne, ⅛ teaspoon black pepper, and the white pepper in a large paper or plastic bag. Add the chicken breasts, wings, thighs, and drumsticks and shake to coat. Shake off the excess. Reserve any remaining seasoned flour.

3. Heat the 4 teaspoons oil in a large heavy frying pan over high heat. Add the chicken and brown on both sides, about 8 minutes in all. Remove the chicken.

4. Add the remaining ¼ cup oil to the pan and scrape the bottom to dislodge any brown bits. When the oil begins to smoke, gradually whisk in the remaining ⅓ cup

flour and any remaining seasoned flour. Reduce the heat to moderate and cook, whisking until the roux is a dark red-brown, 3 to 4 minutes. Remove the pan from the heat and stir in half of the chopped onion, celery, and bell pepper. Stir until the roux cools slightly, 3 to 5 minutes.

5. Add enough water to the broth to make 5⅓ cups and pour into the pot. Add the remaining chopped onion, celery, and bell pepper and bring to a boil over high heat. Whisk in the roux, a spoonful at a time. Reduce the heat and simmer for 45 minutes.

6. Add the chicken and sausage to the pot and cook until the chicken is very tender, about 45 minutes longer. If the gumbo becomes too thick, add a little water. Remove from the heat and let stand for 20 minutes.

7. Skim off all the fat from the surface of the broth. Season the gumbo with salt, black pepper, and hot sauce to taste. Sprinkle the scallion greens and chopped parsley over the gumbo.

—ALEX PATOUT

CHICKEN THIGHS WITH TARRAGON WINE VINEGAR

Buttered noodles with lots of black pepper would be an ideal partner for this tangy sauce. Don't worry about using a whole head of garlic; long cooking mellows it so much that it won't overwhelm the other flavors.

WINE RECOMMENDATION
The tomatoes and vinegar call for a high-acid red with both spiciness and fruitiness. Sounds like Chianti Classico, and a good one will work beautifully. Look for wines from the northerly commune of Greve.

SERVES 4

2 tablespoons flour

½ teaspoon celery seeds

1 teaspoon salt

½ teaspoon fresh-ground black pepper

8 chicken thighs

2 tablespoons olive oil

1 head garlic, cloves separated and peeled

1 cup tarragon wine vinegar

1¾ cups canned crushed tomatoes in thick puree

1¼ cups Chicken Stock, page 61, or canned low-sodium chicken broth

1 tablespoon tomato paste

1½ teaspoons dried tarragon

¼ cup chopped fresh parsley

1. In a medium bowl, combine the flour, celery seeds, salt, and pepper. Dredge the chicken in the mixture. Shake off the excess.

2. In a large pot or Dutch oven, heat the oil over moderately high heat. Add the chicken and brown on both sides, about 8 minutes in all.

3. Reduce the heat to low and add the garlic. Cover and cook, turning the chicken once, until the garlic is tender, about 15 minutes.

4. Spoon off the fat from the pot. Add the vinegar to the pot and cook over high heat until reduced by half, 5 to 7 minutes. Add the tomatoes, stock, tomato paste, and tarragon and bring to a boil. Reduce the heat and simmer, turning the chicken once, until it is cooked through, about 15 minutes.

5. Transfer the chicken to a platter, cover loosely with foil, and put in a warm spot. Press the sauce through a sieve, or puree in a food processor or blender. Stir the parsley into the sauce and pour it over the chicken.

—BOB CHAMBERS

BRAISED CHICKEN WITH LEEKS

Madeira and leeks combine deliciously with chicken in this straightforward dish. Serve the sauce as is, or add the optional crème fraîche to enrich it.

 WINE RECOMMENDATION
Often we think in terms of "white-wine foods" and "red-wine foods." When a dish such as this one seems to fall right in the middle, reach for a pinot noir, whose medium body and light tannin bridges the gap. If you use the enriched sauce, stay with pinot noir; just select a big, full one.

SERVES 4

½ cup flour

2 teaspoons coarse salt

Fresh-ground black pepper

1 chicken (3 to 3½ pounds), quartered

3 tablespoons butter

1 tablespoon cooking oil

8 leeks, white and light-green parts only, split lengthwise, cut into 1-inch pieces, and washed well, or 12 scallions including green tops, cut into 1-inch pieces

1 clove garlic, minced (optional)

Pinch dried thyme

Table salt and white pepper

12 baby carrots, or 1 cup 2-inch carrot pieces

⅔ cup Madeira, more if needed

¾ to 1 cup Rich Chicken Stock, next page, or canned low-sodium chicken broth

¼ cup crème fraîche (see box, page 148) or heavy cream (optional)

Lemon juice (optional)

1 tablespoon minced fresh parsley

1. In a medium bowl, combine the flour, coarse salt, and black pepper to taste. Dredge the chicken lightly in the mixture, shaking off the excess.

2. In a Dutch oven, heat 1 tablespoon of the butter with the oil over moderately high heat. Add the chicken; brown on both sides, about 8 minutes in all. Remove the chicken.

3. Heat the oven to 375°. Wipe out the pot and melt the remaining 2 tablespoons butter over moderately low heat. Add the leeks and stir to coat. Add the garlic, if using, and the thyme and sprinkle with salt and white pepper. Cook over low heat until the leeks begin to wilt, about 4 minutes. Add the carrots, raise the heat to moderate, and cook for 2 minutes. Stir in the Madeira, scraping the bottom of the pot to dislodge any brown bits.

4. Put the leg quarters in the pot, burying them in the vegetables. Put the breast quarters on top and spoon a layer of vegetables over them. Add stock to come halfway up the chicken. Cover the pot with aluminum foil or parchment paper and then with the lid. Bring to a boil. Put the pot in

the oven and bake until the chicken is cooked through, 35 to 40 minutes.

5. Put the chicken pieces on a platter and, using a slotted spoon, place the vegetables around them. Put the pot over moderately high heat and bring to a boil, skimming the fat from the surface of the sauce. Cook the sauce until slightly reduced and thickened, 10 to 15 minutes. If you like, add the crème fraîche and reduce the sauce further.

6. Season the sauce with table salt, white pepper, and a few drops of lemon juice or more Madeira. Pour the sauce over the chicken and vegetables and sprinkle with the parsley.

RICH CHICKEN STOCK

Although this wonderfully rich stock calls for two whole chickens, it's really not wasteful. The birds are removed as soon as they are cooked, so you can use the meat for other dishes or for sandwiches.

MAKES ABOUT 3 QUARTS

4 pounds chicken carcasses, backs, necks, and/or wings

2 chickens (3 to 3½ pounds each)

6 quarts water

3 large carrots, sliced

2 large onions, sliced

4 leeks, white and light-green parts only, split lengthwise, sliced, and washed well, or 1 additional onion, sliced

2 ribs celery with leaves, sliced

Bouquet garni: 8 sprigs parsley, 1 teaspoon dried thyme, 1 bay leaf, ½ teaspoon peppercorns, and 3 cloves

1. Put the chicken parts in a large pot; put the whole chickens on top. Add the water and bring to a simmer over very low heat and continue simmering for 1 hour. Occasionally skim the foam and fat from the surface.

2. Add the carrots, onions, leeks, celery, and bouquet garni to the pot. Simmer, partially covered, until the chicken is cooked, about 45 minutes. Remove the whole chicken and separate the meat from the skin and bones. Save the meat for another use, discard the skin, and return the bones to the pot. Continue to simmer the stock, skimming occasionally, for about 4 hours.

3. Strain the stock, pressing firmly on the bones and vegetables to get all the liquid. If using the stock immediately, skim the fat from the surface. If not, refrigerate the stock for up to a week or freeze; scrape off the fat before using.

BRAISED CHICKEN WITH CIDER CREAM GRAVY

No apple juice here—the cider called for is hard (that is, alcoholic), not sweet.
A good imported French cider will have the proper crispness and intense flavor.

WINE RECOMMENDATION
Foods this rich require full-flavored wines, but the combination works best when the wine has sufficient acidity to leave your palate refreshed. Try a Corton-Charlemagne, the steely structure and strong contrasting minerality of which fit perfectly. Though pricey, Corton-Charlemagnes are the least expensive of the white Burgundy grand crus.

SERVES 4

- 2 tablespoons butter
- 1 chicken (3 to 3½ pounds), cut into 8 pieces
- 3 shallots, minced
- 10 ounces small mushrooms
- ⅓ cup Calvados
- ⅓ cup hard cider
- ⅔ cup heavy cream
- ½ teaspoon salt
- Pinch fresh-ground black pepper
- 2 tablespoons minced fresh parsley

1. In a large stainless-steel frying pan, melt 1½ tablespoons of the butter over moderately high heat. Add the chicken pieces and brown well on both sides, about 8 minutes in all. Remove the chicken from the pan.

2. Melt the remaining ½ tablespoon butter in the pan. Add the shallots and mushrooms and cook, stirring, until lightly browned, 2 to 3 minutes. Reduce the heat to low, cover, and cook until the shallots are soft, about 10 minutes.

3. Return the chicken to the pan and spoon the mushroom mixture on top. Pour the Calvados over the chicken. Warm it briefly and then carefully ignite it with a match. When the flames subside, add the cider. Cover and simmer over very low heat until the chicken breasts are cooked through, about 15 minutes. Transfer the chicken breasts and mushrooms to a plate, cover with aluminum foil, and put in a warm spot. Cook the drumsticks and thighs until cooked through, about 10 minutes longer; add to the breasts.

4. Boil the liquid in the pan until it is reduced to a thin glaze, 8 to 10 minutes. Add the cream and boil until slightly thickened, 4 to 5 minutes. Add the salt and pepper and 1 tablespoon of the parsley.

5. Spoon the sauce over the chicken and mushrooms. Sprinkle with the remaining 1 tablespoon parsley.

—JEAN ANDERSON

MEDITERRANEAN CHICKEN WITH LEMONS AND OLIVES

Today many supermarkets carry an array of imported olives, bottled or in bulk. If you like, remove the pits before adding the olives to the chicken. To continue the Mediterranean theme, serve orzo alongside.

 WINE RECOMMENDATION
Greek wines have not been thought of highly, with some justification, but recent improvements in quality have produced some excellent bottlings. See if you can find a Robola of Cephalonia, a rich, earthy wine made from Greece's best white grape.

SERVES 4

1 pound Greek or Italian green olives

2 cups boiling water

1½ lemons, 1 cut into thin slices, ½ squeezed to make 2 tablespoons juice

2 teaspoons salt

½ cup flour

1 teaspoon fresh-ground black pepper

1 chicken (3 to 3½ pounds), cut into 8 pieces

3 tablespoons olive oil

2 onions, chopped fine

2 cloves garlic, chopped

1 tablespoon coriander seeds, crushed

½ cup chopped fresh parsley

¼ teaspoon ground saffron

1½ cups Chicken Stock, page 61, or canned low-sodium chicken broth

1. Put the olives in a bowl, pour 1½ cups of the boiling water over them, and let stand for 20 minutes. Drain.

2. Put the lemon slices in a small bowl, sprinkle with ½ teaspoon of the salt, and pour the remaining ½ cup boiling water over them. Let stand for 2 to 3 minutes, then drain and cover.

3. In a paper or plastic bag, combine the flour, ½ teaspoon of the salt, and ½ teaspoon of the pepper. Add the chicken pieces and shake to coat. Shake off the excess. Heat the oil in a large stainless-steel frying pan over moderate heat. Add the chicken, in batches, and brown on both sides, about 8 minutes in all. Remove with a slotted spoon.

4. Add the onions, garlic, coriander, parsley, saffron, and the remaining 1 teaspoon salt and ½ teaspoon pepper to the pan. Cook, stirring, over low heat for 4 to 5 minutes. Return the chicken to the pan, add the stock, and bring to a boil over moderately high heat. Lower the heat, cover, and simmer until the chicken is just cooked through, 15 to 20 minutes. Remove the pan from the heat and stir in the lemon slices, olives, and lemon juice.

CHICKEN IN BEER WITH LEEKS

Cooking the chicken in beer gives it rich depth of flavor. The finishing touch is a classic sauce made from stock, crème fraîche, and sliced leeks.

WINE RECOMMENDATION
Have this chicken with a full-bodied California chardonnay. The wine's butter, nut, and tropical-fruit flavors will blend well with the sweet maltiness of the dark beer and the creaminess of the sauce. Go for a lightly oaked example from the Santa Cruz Mountains.

SERVES 4

1½ tablespoons butter

1 chicken (3 to 3½ pounds), quartered, giblets chopped coarse

3 shallots, chopped

1 12-ounce bottle dark beer

¼ teaspoon dried thyme

1 bay leaf

1 teaspoon salt

½ teaspoon fresh-ground black pepper

4 large leeks, white part only, split lengthwise, cut into 1-inch pieces, and washed well

¼ cup Chicken Stock, page 61, or canned low-sodium chicken broth

1 cup crème fraîche (see box, page 148) or heavy cream

1 tablespoon chopped fresh chives

1. Melt the butter in a large frying pan over moderately high heat. Add the giblets and shallots and cook, stirring, for 3 minutes.

2. Add the chicken quarters and brown on both sides, about 8 minutes in all. Add the beer, thyme, bay leaf, ½ teaspoon of the salt, and ¼ teaspoon of the pepper. Cover and cook over low heat until cooked through, about 12 minutes for the breast quarters, 20 minutes for the leg quarters.

3. Meanwhile, in a large saucepan of boiling, salted water, cook the leeks until tender, about 12 minutes. Drain well.

4. In a medium saucepan, combine the leeks, stock, ½ cup of the crème fraîche, and the remaining ½ teaspoon salt and ¼ teaspoon pepper. Bring to a boil over moderately high heat and cook for 4 minutes. Keep warm over low heat.

5. Skin the chicken and return it to the frying pan. Add the remaining ½ cup crème fraîche and cook over high heat until the chicken is hot and the sauce is slightly thickened, about 5 minutes. Discard the bay leaf.

6. Transfer the chicken to a platter. Spoon the leeks and their sauce around the chicken. Pour the sauce from the frying pan over the chicken. Sprinkle with the chives.

—DOMINIQUE NAHMIAS

CHICKEN IN CHAMPAGNE SAUCE

Chicken basks in Champagne and crème fraîche for a simply elegant entree. If you like, add some sautéed mushrooms: Cut half a pound of mushrooms into quarters, sauté them in two tablespoons butter, and add them to the sauce at the end along with the chicken.

WINE RECOMMENDATION
Now that you've opened the bottle, you're not going to let the rest go to waste, are you? Not just an aperitif, Champagne can accompany main dishes, too. Pick a full-bodied one such as Veuve Cliquot or Bollinger; a more delicate wine will be overpowered.

SERVES 4

1 chicken (3 to 3½ pounds), cut into 8 pieces

Salt and fresh-ground black pepper

10 tablespoons butter

2 tablespoons olive oil

3 shallots, minced

1¼ cups brut Champagne

1 cup Chicken Stock, page 61, or canned low-sodium chicken broth

1 cup crème fraîche (see box, page 148), or heavy cream

1. Heat the oven to 375°. Season the chicken with ½ teaspoon salt and ½ teaspoon pepper. In a large ovenproof frying pan, melt 4 tablespoons of the butter with the oil over moderate heat. Add the chicken and brown on both sides, about 8 minutes in all. Remove the chicken from the pan.

2. Add the shallots to the pan, reduce the heat to moderately low, and cook, stirring, until just softened, about 1 minute. Return the chicken to the pan and turn to coat with the butter. Pour the chicken, shallots, and butter into a colander and let drain for 2 to 3 minutes. Return to the pan.

3. Add the Champagne and bring to a boil over moderate heat. Cook for 2 minutes. Turn the chicken and partially cover the pan. Boil until the liquid is reduced by half, about 5 minutes.

4. Add the stock, bring to a boil, and cover tightly. Put the pan in the oven and bake until the chicken is cooked through, about 10 minutes. Remove the chicken, cover loosely with foil, and put in a warm spot. Add the crème fraîche and boil over moderate heat until the sauce lightly coats a spoon, about 15 minutes.

5. Reduce the heat to low. Gradually add in the remaining 6 tablespoons butter, 1 or 2 tablespoons at a time, whisking until the sauce is smooth and thickened. Season with salt and pepper. Add the chicken.

—GÉRARD BOYER

INDEX

Page numbers in **boldface** indicate photographs.

CONTRIBUTORS

Jeffrey Alford and Naomi Duguid are the authors of *Flatbreads and Flavors: A Baker's Atlas* (William Morrow).

Jean Anderson, a cookbook author and editor, is currently working on *The American Century Cookbook*.

Elizabeth Andoh is the author of *An Ocean of Flavor: The Japanese Way with Fish and Seafood* (William Morrow).

Colman Andrews is a food writer and an editor at *Saveur* whose latest book is *Flavors of the Riviera* (Bantam).

Lee Bailey, a cookbook author, has most recently completed *Lee Bailey's The Way I Cook* (Clarkson Potter).

Gérard Boyer is chef at Les Crayéres in Reims, France.

James W. Brown is a cookbook editor.

Linda Burum is a food writer and author of *The Guide to Ethnic Food in Los Angeles*.

Jane Butel is a cooking teacher and writer currently working on *Fiestas for Four Seasons* (Clear Light Publishing).

Hugh Carpenter is a chef and cooking teacher whose books include *Pacific Flavors* and *Fusion Food Cookbook*.

Penelope Casas is a writer and cooking teacher. Her latest book is *¡Delicioso! The Regional Cooking of Spain* (Knopf).

Bob Chambers is executive chef at Lâncome-L'Oréal in New York City.

Julia Child's most recent project is the *Baking With Julia* television series and book (with Dorie Greenspan; published by William Morrow).

Bruce Cost is a cooking teacher, food writer, and the author of *Bruce Cost's Asian Ingredients* (William Morrow).

Diane Darrow and Tom Maresca are the authors of *La Tavola Italiana* (William Morrow).

Robert Del Grande is the chef/owner of Cafe Annie in Houston, Texas.

Julia Della Croce is a cookbook author whose most recent work is *Classic Italian Cooking* (DK Publishing).

Anne Disrude is a New York-based food stylist.

Chata DuBose is a cooking teacher in Houston, Texas.

Jeannette Ferrary and Louise Fiszer are food writers and the authors of *A Good Day for Soup* (Chronicle Books).

Jim Fobel is a cookbook author whose most recent book is *Jim Fobel's Casseroles* (Clarkson Potter).

Joyce Goldstein is a chef, cooking teacher, and the author of *Kitchen Conversations* (William Morrow).

Dorie Greenspan is a cookbook author and food writer. Her latest book is *Baking With Julia* (William Morrow).

Paul Grimes is a freelance chef, teacher, and food writer.

Jessica B. Harris is a cookbook author whose books include *Sky Juice and Flying Fish* (Fireside).

Madhur Jaffrey is a food writer whose latest book is *Madhur Jaffrey's Quick & Easy Indian Kitchen* (Chronicle).

Susan Shapiro Jaslove is a food writer and a recipe developer and tester.

Marcia Kiesel is the associate director of FOOD & WINE magazine's test kitchen.

Peter Kump was the founder of Peter Kump's New York Cooking School.

Karen Lee and Alexandra Branyon, caterers and cooking teachers, wrote *The Occasional Vegetarian* (Warner Books).

Eileen Yin-Fei Lo is the author of *The Chinese Way: Healthy Low-Fat Cooking From China's Regions* (Macmillan).

Copeland Marks is a cookbook author, food writer, and cooking teacher.

Lydie Marshall is a cooking teacher and food writer whose latest book is *Chez Nous* (HarperCollins).

John Robert Massie is a New York-based food stylist.

Michael McLaughlin is a cookbook author and food writer. His most recent book is *All on the Grill* (HarperCollins).

Perla Meyers is a cookbook author whose books include *The Art of Seasonal Cooking* (Simon & Schuster).

Steve Miller is a wine consultant, educator, and writer. He regularly contributes to *International Wine Center Notes*.

Dominique Nahmais is chef at L'Olympe in Paris, France.

Janice Okun is a food writer and restaurant reviewer.

Molly O'Neill is a cookbook author and writes a column for the *New York Times Magazine*.

Alex Patout is chef/owner of Patout's in New Orleans.

Jacques Pépin is a chef, cookbook author, and TV host of *Jacques Pépin's Kitchen: Cooking with Claudine* (KQED).

W. Peter Prestcott is Entertaining and Special Projects Editor at FOOD & WINE magazine.

Michael Roberts is a cookbook author, cooking teacher, food writer, chef, and culinary/restaurant consultant.

David Rosengarten is a food writer, teacher, wine columnist, and co-author of *Red Wine with Fish* (Simon & Schuster).

Phillip Stephen Schulz is a food writer and the author of *America the Beautiful Cookbook* (Collins).

Tracey Seaman is a cookbook author and the test-kitchen director for *Great American Home Cooking*.

Barbara Tropp is a cookbook author, cooking teacher, and restaurant and menu consultant.

Anne Willan is a cooking teacher whose most recent book is *In & Out of the Kitchen in 15 Minutes or Less* (Rizzoli).

Lance Dean Velasquez is the chef of Heritage House in Mendocino, California.

We would also like to thank the following individuals and restaurant for their contribution to this cookbook: **Ana Cotaescu; Monique Guillaume; Mary Lynn Mondich; Harry Reillo; Alain Sailhac; Keo Sananikone; Susan Wyler;** and **Yamato,** San Francisco.